The Great Absquatulator

The Great Absquatulator

Frank Mackey

Baraka
Books

Montréal

© Frank Mackey

ISBN 978-1-77186-273-8 pbk; 978-1-77186-286-8 epub; 978-1-77186-287-5 pdf

Cover by Maison 1608
Book Design by Folio infographie
Editing and proofreading: Robin Philpot, Blossom Thom

Legal Deposit, 2nd quarter 2022

Bibliothèque et Archives nationales du Québec
Library and Archives Canada

Published by Baraka Books of Montreal

Printed and bound in Quebec

TRADE DISTRIBUTION & RETURNS
Canada – UTP Distribution: UTPdistribution.com

UNITED STATES
Independent Publishers Group: IPGbook.com

We acknowledge the support from the Société de développement des entreprises culturelles (SODEC) and the Government of Quebec tax credit for book publishing administered by SODEC.

Financé par le gouvernement du Canada
Funded by the Government of Canada | Canadä

Société de développement des entreprises culturelles
Québec

For Patrick Dorais and Benjamin Haberman –
bright young stars that guide us.

CONTENTS

FOREWORD

Aly Ndiaye, alias Webster

I first got to know Frank Mackey through his seminal book, *Black Then: Blacks and Montreal 1780s-1880s*. The story of Alexander Grant, who could clearly be described as the first activist of African descent in Lower Canada, was so amazing that I wrote a rap song about him titled Alex Grant. While waiting for a lecture to begin at Montreal's Château Ramezay, I found myself sitting beside a man who struck up a conversation by introducing himself as—you guessed it—Frank Mackey. "THE Frank Mackey?!" I asked. *"Black Then* Frank Mackey?!" I was both impressed and honored to be able to chat with one of the country's most erudite researchers into Afro-Quebec history. A man who, while I was still working on my ABCs in elementary school, had committed body and soul to this very tough field of research.

Since then, we have maintained an extremely stimulating and edifying correspondence. He has led me into the dustiest corners of a past deeply buried in our collective memory. Thanks to him I was able to discover people and events who should be celebrated today as pillars of Afro-Quebec history. Whenever I think I've found something, I share it immediately with Frank who, unsurprisingly, adds details to what I presumed to be a discovery. Even today, I am amazed by his encyclopedic knowledge and feel privileged that he takes time on each occasion to answer me and share the results of his massive research work.

Frank Mackey has a knack of digging up and dusting off stories that, were it not for him, would very likely have been swallowed up by time. Or to put it more metaphorically, he has forced Time to cough up its children who have been buried for centuries. That's what he did with Alexander Grant, and now it's Alfred Thomas Wood's turn.

"Egocentric Revolt"

What can be said about Alfred Thomas Wood's destiny? As Frank Mackey has shown, such an ingenious man or woman could surely have become what he or she claimed to be, maybe even more. But that could only happen in the absence of the systemic obstacles and undying prejudice that have shaped the modern world. As I read about Wood, I cannot help thinking about Malcolm X's life a century later. The power racism has to douse the flames that only require a bit of oxygen to burst into wildfire is illustrated by a well-known anecdote. As a youngster in Michigan, the boy whose name was then Malcolm Little, was brilliant in school and liked by everybody. When his English teacher asked him what he had in mind for his future, young Malcolm Little mentioned that he wanted to be a lawyer. The teacher replied that he should be realistic and that studying law was not a goal for n*****s, that it would be better for him to think about becoming a carpenter. After that, Malcolm Little slowly turned to a life of crime, putting his sharp mind to work to generate small profits in the underworld, which could easily have cost him his life. It was only after a stint in jail that he converted to Islam and became the militant we all know.

Malcolm X and Alfred Thomas Wood are obviously very different people. Yet in both of their life stories, we can see that, even though many life choices were strictly reserved for White people, they were able to find a way to break out of the fenced-in grounds they were assigned to.

Though it's easy to see Wood as an impostor, which he obviously was, as Frank Mackey has shown, we cannot but be struck by his determination not to be crushed by a battery of laws and racial prejudice which, because of the color of his skin, confined him to a very specific and unchanging place in the social, political and spiritual order of the day.

Paying little heed to collective needs and aspirations, Wood conducted his own small personal revolution. It was a rebellion that took him to three continents, in the company of some of the most eminent mid-nineteenth-century figures. This sort of ego-centric revolt—if we can call it that—definitely has its limits, not the least of which is the necessity of being constantly on the look-out and disappearing as soon as cracks appear in the façade of the ongoing scam. And that does not take into account the many vic-tims he left in his trail, including his wives, his pastoral flocks, the donators he ripped off, the young Merrick/Myrick . . ..

He resisted for his own benefit. Did he really believe in the demands for enhanced racial justice? Maybe he was just a scam artist in the right place at the right time and with the required talent? Maybe he was all of that wrapped up in a single person?

Catch me if you Gump

Alfred Thomas Wood's life reads like a cross between the scams and impersonations (real or proven) of Frank Abagnale (author of *Catch me if you can*, made into a film by Steven Spielberg in 2002) and the tribulations of Forrest Gump (told in Winston Groom's novel made into a film in 1994). Wood played the roles of a carpenter, a pastor, a doctor of theology, a medical doctor, an architect, and more, just as Abagnale who, a century later, would claim to have been a pilot, a doctor, a lawyer and a teacher. Whereas Abagnale seems to have created these personae as a means of self-promotion (to bask in his own scam artistry), Wood had every interest in keeping his exploits shrouded in secrecy.

Just as the fictitious Forrest Gump witnesses milestones of the twentieth century, A.T. Wood is party to many momentous events in Afro-descendant and African history in the nineteenth. Along with famous abolitionists like Robert Morris, Samuel Ringgold Ward, Henry Bibb and William Lloyd Garrison, he challenges the adoption of the *Fugitive Slave Act* (1850). He could be seen at the First Independent Baptist Church in Boston. He is in Liberia just a few years after the country becomes independent and is appointed Chaplain of the Senate. He travels throughout England and Ireland in search of funding, as did some of the great anti-slavery leaders of the time. He speaks publicly in Montreal at a vigil in honor of John Brown in 1859. He crosses and recrosses the southern states during the tumult of Reconstruction and was chosen delegate to the national Republican Party Convention in 1868 for the county of Rutherford, Tennessee. Whereas Forrest Gump seemed to stumble innocently onto the stage at crucial moments in twentieth-century history, A. T. Wood is a player, either close at hand or at a distance, in many events that shape his times.

Unlike the stories told in those two Hollywood blockbusters that marked the turn of the century, Alfred Thomas Wood's story is entirely true. When I talked about this astonishing story with Frank Mackey, he said that if the exact same story were to appear in a novel, it would surely be shot down for being exaggerated and very dubious. And yet . . ..

The Anti-Wood

The destiny of this complex and multidimensional man reminds me of the equally incredible life of a contemporary of his, Muhammad Ali Said, alias Nicholas.[1] Born in the central African empire of Bornu in the 1830s, the teenaged Said was swept up in the Trans-Saharan slave trade. Sold as a slave in Tripoli, he accompanied his owner to Mecca where he was transferred to Istanbul and, shortly thereafter, to a Russian diplomat who took him to St. Petersburg, where he was freed. As a free man, he was employed by another Russian aristocrat who took him on a long tour of Europe, from Switzerland to Germany, France, Italy and England. A remarkable linguist, Muhammad Ali Said learned languages very quickly. He spoke Kanuri (his mother tongue), Arabic, Ottoman Turkish, Russian, German, Italian and French (to name just a few).[2]

---

1. Lovejoy, Paul. (2017). Mohammed Ali Nicholas Sa'id: from enslavement to American Civil War veteran. Millars: Espai i Història. 24. 219-232. 10.6035/ Millars.2017.42.9.

2. Said, Nicholas, *The Autobiography of Nicholas Said; a Native of Bornou, Eastern Soudan, Central Africa*, Memphis, Shotwell & Co., Publishers, 1873, p. vii.

After his trip through Western Europe, he desired to return home to Bornu. However, the call of adventure resounded once more, and he was hired by a Dutch couple with whom he crossed the Atlantic to visit the Caribbean, South America, the United States and the Canadas. When his employers abandoned him in the town of Aylmer in Canada-East (Quebec), he survived by getting work on a steamboat. Then he became a French teacher for young African Americans in Detroit, a sergeant in the 55th Massachusetts Infantry Regiment during the American Civil War, a public speaker and teacher in the South during Reconstruction. The final words of his autobiography published in 1873 in Memphis, Tennessee, could arguably be addressed to Alfred Thomas Wood, who had died five years earlier, also in Tennessee.

My honest and ardent desire is to render myself useful to my race wherever it may be. I have no aspirations for fame, nor anything of the sort. But I shall always prefer at all times to find myself in the midst of the most ignorant of my race, and endeavor to teach the rising generation the advantages of education.

Self-denial is now-a-days so rare, that it is thought only individuals of insane mind can speak of it. A person who tries to live only for others, and puts himself in the second place, is hooted at, and considered a fit inmate for the asylum.

The man who artfully extorts the earning of his fellow man, and who seems to have no feeling for his daily wants, is, by a strange perversion, deemed the wise.

To me, it is impossible to conceive how a human being can be happy through any other channel, than to do as much good as possible to his fellow-man in this world.[3]

Obviously, there's no indication that these words were addressed to A. T. Wood. Yet . . . "The man who artfully extorts the earning of his fellow man [...] is, by a strange perversion, deemed the wise[!]"

At a hip-hop concert, it would be tempting to shout: "Shots fired!"

---

3. Said, Nicholas, *Autobiography*, p. 212-13.

INTRODUCTION

The man you are about to meet was the subject of "Mr. Wood as a Matter of Fact," a story I wrote around the year 2000, based on the little I then knew of his activities, in Montreal and England. It was published in 2004 in a book called *Black Then*. I had stumbled on him while scouring old newspapers for clues about the lives of Black Montrealers of the mid-19th century. The Montreal *Pilot* of 25 December 1852 had carried this news brief from England:

> AN IMPUDENT IMPOSTOR. – One "Rev. Alfred Thomas Wood, D.D.," is in custody in Hull on the charge of obtaining money by false pretences. He levied contributions on the charitable for the alleged support of a church in Liberia. He told one of the witnesses against him, that George and Eliza Harris, mentioned in "Uncle Tom's Cabin," were "members of his church," and that Cassy died six weeks after her arrival in Liberia. "He attended her death-bed, and she died a very happy death."

The item had no direct bearing, as far as I knew, on the subject of Black Montrealers, but it had come bobbing along in a Christmas Day newspaper like a message in a bottle—who could resist such a gift? On the surface, the message was ludicrous. Still, you couldn't help but wonder, was this man trying to breathe real life into fictional characters, or did he consider that his own life needed creative enhancement? Imagine my surprise a day later, maybe two, when, plowing on through old papers at the Quebec provincial archives (today the Bibliothèque at Archives nationales du Québec), I came upon Wood in Montreal in 1859. He was promoting a lecture he was to give about West Africa. Yesterday he had been pastor of a church in Liberia, accused of fraudulent soliciting in England; today, he billed himself as a long-serving public official from Sierra Leone. And the purpose of his visit to Montreal? Was he still in touch with George and Eliza? What was his game?

Few answers were at my disposal when I wrote Wood's story. Intrigued by him, I later set off in pursuit, spending a decade at it. There was little relevant material online then; finding it required visiting various archives, libraries or other repositories, here and abroad, or securing copies of documents by mail. In early 2013, the manuscript was practically finished, but a research trip to Tennessee was needed. The trip had to be abandoned: Health problems, and the fact that the Internet age was upon us, had shaken my curiosity and my resolve. Problems in the composition of the manuscript, molehills in retrospect, appeared then to be mountains. The subject matter no longer seemed as compelling as it had been and, worse, the form had lost its appeal. I had lost faith in the value of books as a valid platform for communicating historical information in the age of websites and blogs. Nobody reads books anymore, do they?

The succeeding years blunted my disillusionment and softened some of my doubts, age made me forget them, and thanks to a nudge from Aly Ndiaye in 2020, my interest revived. It became clear that there are elements in A.T. Wood's life that needed airing. The decisive push came when Aly, a historian in his own right, of Senegalese-Canadian descent, who raps in French under the English stage name Webster, read the manuscript and urged me to publish it. I reconsidered my earlier decision, dusted it off, rewrote bits of it and now give it a try.

While the Internet unsettled me years ago, I admit now that it is a priceless tool in the mining of information. But for any enterprising researcher who wishes to explore Wood's life more fully, it is important not to attend only to the material that has been digitized and ignore the rest, the way, for example, some people used to consider that news didn't happen unless it appeared on TV. For example, the *Portland Pleasure Boat,* a quirky newspaper of Portland, Me., that proved crucial to the composition of the opening chapters of the book, is not online at the time of this writing, neither are some other Maine newspapers quoted here, or the *Liberia Herald, Montreal Pilot, Montreal Transcript*, etc. The fact that information is not available online does not mean it does not exist, only that it needs finding. For example, while it is almost certain that Wood stepped onto the world stage from Nova Scotia, that fact remains to be proven. Everything about his origins, his childhood and youth is still unknown.

If I was drawn to Wood, if he stood out, it was because he struck me as so different from the historical image of Black men I had formed from readings—poor, hopeless, menial creatures, prey to discrimination, husks with the dreams crushed out of them, under constant threat, frozen out of life's rewards big and small, searching for a real meaningful human emancipation.... If I and many others, I believe, formed such impressions, it was largely because this is the collective image conveyed by so much that has been written about a persecuted people. We tend to forget that there are "success" stories among Black men and women of the Victorian era as of other times. A very few "celebrities" among them draw all our admiration, and the suffering many draw all our sympathy. The lesser stars like A.T. Wood, far from admirable but just as far from helpless, get no consideration. Yet he was in his own way a success.

Wood was very much a creature of his time, a product of nonsensical, long-lasting racial divisions, yet exceptional in many ways and uncommonly knowledgeable. The dominant White world imposed its standards and codes, geared to promoting the advancement of Whites and the failure of Blacks. Wood seems to have resolved, in his youth or as a young man, that he would not be crushed. He would work around the rules, twist them to his advantage. He would exploit them and the hypocrisy behind them by outmatching the hypocrites, playing on such elements as White guilt, Black stereotypes, ignorance of the "Dark Continent," national divisions, sympathy for the underdog, etc. Where Uncle Tom was, in the eyes of Whites, a fictional creation embodying all that was good (submissive?) about a Black man, Rev. A.T. Wood was a Black man's humorless, unscrupulous send-up of the world as it was. He was a 19th-century creation, yet so very different from Black luminaries of the time as they are usually portrayed—

earnest and valiant heroes and/or martyrs of the struggle for respect and justice, tied to a particular locality, state or country, all reasonably virtuous or trying to be, principled, steadfast, recognized today as winners. Wood has no place in this posthumous winner's circle. He was anything but a garden-variety role model.

Over the years, as the pieces of the puzzle accumulated and I blurted out whatever I had learned to anyone who would listen, more than one acquaintance suggested that the details of Wood's life would make a good novel. But the facts of his life, set in a novel, would be viewed as forced and implausible. Who would believe them? The work would seem to consist of a thin, didactic narrative built around an improbable anti-hero. In his wanderings, this unlikely figure would bump into one too many African-American milestones—anti-miscegenation laws, the historic First Independent Baptist Church in Boston, the rise of Abolitionism, colonization and the invention of Liberia, *Uncle Tom's Cabin,* John Brown's raid, the U.S. Civil War, the Emancipation Proclamation, the repeal of Illinois's Black Laws, Abraham Lincoln's assassination, Reconstruction Era politics, etc. Enough with the disguised history lesson, readers would say, and rightly so.

While the book is not a work of fiction, it is a study in narrative form that does at times take on the air of an epistolary novel. The "plot" is carried by many transcriptions, brief or extensive, of letters, newspaper articles and notices, and other documents, some from the hand of Wood himself. The reader who has no time for 19th-century language may consider these passages boring. The prose may be overstuffed, by modern standards, but they are not really boring. It is to be hoped that those who take the time to read them will, besides savoring some of the vocabulary and phrasings, gain their own insights into Wood's character and the spirit of his times and follow the threads of the intrigue more easily than those who skip the prosy bits.

One other element that readers will readily notice: No photograph or sketch of Wood appears in these pages, not even a thorough physical description that would allow us to imagine what he looked like. That, I believe, is no accident. By the end of the book, if not well before, readers will understand why Wood would have had his reasons to avoid sitting for a photograph. He would not have done so out of fear that the photographer would steal his soul, but that he or she would capture his physical appearance, a hazard in his chameleonic line of business.

This account of his life is the fruit of an effort to puzzle out the character and motives of an uncommon Black figure of the 19th century. It is my reading of him. Is it an accurate portrayal? It is a fair one, I think, but I cannot be sure of having caught his exact likeness because many pieces of the puzzle remain missing and, just as importantly, in the 22-year span of his life sketched here, he was never himself. He is trapped in the pages of this book, locked in history's hard drive for all to see, but he escapes us. A mirror placed squarely in front of him—or a photograph, had one ever been taken—would not have reflected him as he was because the face he presented to the world was not his real face but a distraction.

Read on and see.

1. 'WOLF!' THEY CRIED IN MAINE

Never before had the people of back-country Maine taken their preaching from a Black man. So, A.T. Wood was a novelty, in more ways than one. He was not just any Black man, not a neighborhood fixture or a familiar type, not a New Englander, say, or a refugee from Southern slavery. He was an English chap from Liverpool, so he said, fresh off the boat. Out of the mist, he had appeared at tiny Amherst, east of Bangor, in the fall of 1846, and for the next two years he had made the rounds, edging ever north, to Greenfield and beyond—to Burlington, Lowell, Lee, etc.—doing God's work.

Or was it the Devil's? If the *Christian Mirror* was to be believed, he was up to no good. Beware of the "wolf in sheep's clothing" with the "tongue set on fire of Hell," an anonymous correspondent of that Portland paper warned in November 1848, painting a picture of the wandering Wood as an angel of darkness.

But could the writer himself be trusted? Rather than show himself, he had kept to the shadows and submitted his screed to the newspaper unsigned. That had troubled Rev. Asa Cummings, DD, the owner-editor of the *Mirror*—for a second or two. In the end, Cummings, a Harvard-educated Congregationalist minister with more than 20 years' experience at the helm of his weekly paper, had chosen to publish the piece without verification, a grievous editorial sin which he sought to gloss over with a few words of high-sounding gibberish:

> The writer of the following should have appended his name, however undesirable the position. We, at first, had doubts whether we could properly publish it without a voucher. But if the tale be true, the security of the public from imposition requires that it should be spread abroad. If not true, it will be more easy to redress an individual, than

Rev. Asa Cummings, editor of the *Christian Mirror*.
(Find A Grave, Memorial ID 150787381)

it would be the public, if the whole is literal truth. The presumption is in favor of its correctness, as there are impostors, under all names, and of all ages, sexes and colors.

A WOLF IN SHEEP'S CLOTHING.

There shall arise false prophets and shall show great signs and wonders; in so much that if it were possible, they shall deceive the very elect.

Counterfeits are nothing rare in these days, but some kinds are rarer than others—*impostors* in *religion* are the last to be tolerated.

A man calling himself "Elder Alfred P. Wood" appeared in Amherst, Me., in the Autumn of '46. He was a colored man, and *professed* to be a Calvinist Baptist preacher, late from England, and in his passage thence to this country to have encountered shipwreck, losing a large sum of money and escaping only with what was about his person.

He *professed* to have very rich and much honored relatives in England and considerable amount of property. He professed to have been a Missionary and to have translated the Bible entire into several different languages. He wished employment as a preacher, and was retained as such during the winter of 1846-7, in Amherst and adjacent towns.

He possessed great power of language, was fluent and perhaps verbose, having much physical *nerve,* and withal a stentorian voice. He had considerable wit, shrewdness, out-cunning, a vivid and active imagination, unbounded self-esteem, but little wisdom. He often used amusing, and at times bold and striking figures, associating the sublime and the ludicrous, the grave and the vulgar, so as to render his performances sometimes amusing, and generally exciting. These traits, together with the novelty of his color, as a preacher, although he was not a negro but a mulatto, drew for a time a throng of hearers. The town hall, which he occupied, was crowded to overflowing. But some time before he left the place, his hearers began to leave him, so that he preached his last sermon to an audience of five or six. Not long had he been in the place, before the covering with which he had attempted to clothe himself would occasionally slide off, and discover to the surprise of the observing the wolf's head. His stories and conversations at different times, with the same individuals, were found to conflict; and his language in private and sometimes in public bordered on the profane—and he rarely spoke of religion save in the desk. He left, execrating with the most horrible curses those who would not sustain "Elder Alfred P. Wood." Soon he found his way to Greenfield and Lowell, where he continued to preach for a while on the Sabbath, and labor during the week as house carpenter. But not long could he conceal his true character there—it was soon seen that the wolf was somehow invested, but not always covered with the wool. At length he was obliged to abandon his post, and the same Elder Wood has recently been in Lee and vicinity preaching Universalism, saying that he belonged to the Union Baptists in England, and that they believe the same as the Universalists in this country. Such is the man who is in our State, ready with the weathercock to turn which ever way the wind blows. Once falling in with a Congregational minister, he called himself a Presbyterian. It is affirmed that he will lie, swear and cheat. It is probable that he never saw England, that the complexion of his heart is much blacker than that of his face, and that his tongue is set on fire of Hell!

Whence he came, or whither he will go, is not known to the writer, save that like another he goeth up and down the earth, now like an angel of light, and now like a roaring lion seeking those whom he may first deceive and then devour. "Beware of dogs, beware of evil-doers, beware of false prophets who come to you in sheep's clothing, but inwardly they are ravening wolves." Nov. 22, 1848.

"Impostors in *religion* are the last to be tolerated ..." Hmm. The writer himself sounded like a right preacher. Rev. X, as we might call him, should have stepped from behind the curtain and shown his face, at least to Cummings, who might have vouched for him and come up with a better justification for the verbal lynching of Elder Wood. *Mirror* subscribers who trusted Cummings' judgment may have been prepared to take Bro X at his word, but casual readers and others—skeptics, Quakers, free-thinkers, et al.—might have suspected that behind his outburst lay some religious hairsplitting or racial antagonism, or plain dislike of strangers. Could X have been envious of Wood's gifts, or upset at his devil-may-care juggling of denominational labels?

On the other hand, it was only natural that Wood's background story should meet with some skepticism. His "professed" English origin, wealthy relatives, and Bible translations were rather improbable credentials for a Black preacher in 1840s Maine. But to nail the case against him and prove the man a fraud, Bro X could have given some hint of how he knew Wood and how he had come by his information. He may have drawn his account from personal observation, but his accusations would have gained in credibility had he got Wood's name right. His reference to Alfred T. as Alfred P. hints that he was not so well acquainted with his target, and that maybe much of his tale was loose talk.

Besides withholding his own name and failing to indicate whether he drew his evidence from first-hand observation, X left out one other key element—motive. If Wood was a wolf from hell, why had he chosen to play the lamb in Maine, of all places? If he wasn't English, why pretend to be, in a state that felt no love for England? Bitterness lingered from the saber-rattling with Britain over the location of the Maine-New Brunswick border, a near-war brawl that had been settled by treaty four short years before Wood turned up. Was he an *agent provocateur*, out to renew hostilities? Bro X strongly hinted at a dark design on Wood's part. So, what was it that this black devil wanted—gold? timber rights? the souls of the pure-hearted? world domination? What!?

While likening Wood to a hellhound, X did note some of his earthly features. He was a "colored" man—"not a negro but a mulatto." He was not shunned for being colored; on the contrary, to his White hearers his color was a feature out of the ordinary that enhanced his appeal—for a while, at least. And when he wasn't on about God, he worked, like Jesus Christ, as a carpenter and joiner, a pretty down-to-earth business. His carpentry skills were not in dispute, but his credentials as a preacher were. Yet there was no denying that he had a gift in that department. He had at times drawn full houses with his strong, rich voice and an array of rhetorical punches, pious and profane, that had alternately tickled and thrilled his hearers.

Three weeks after the *Mirror* aired X's charges, they received wholesale endorsement, with added particulars, from a well-known Congregationalist minister. Rev. Marcus Keep, who made a point of signing his letter to Cummings and boasted of never pulling his punches, stated outright that the wolf was out to fleece the sheep. Money was Wood's object. Never mind his claim that his family in England was rich, in Maine he "preached his pond out," borrowed all that he could from the unsuspecting, then bolted.

But if money-grubbing was Wood's game, wouldn't it have struck him, two years on, that the pickings in the wooded heart of Maine were rather slim? The coastal city of Portland, with its 20,000-plus inhabitants, would have offered a fatter field than the scattered hamlets of the hinterland. And there were much bigger and wealthier cities farther afield, out of state, places like Boston, Baltimore, Philadelphia, New York ... There was also California, where the gold rush was drawing fortune hunters from every corner of the globe. Besides, there were quicker ways for the wicked to make a killing than by preaching to the pinecones and those who dwelt among them. Blackmail, counterfeiting, highway robbery,

THE **MAIN** QUESTION.

"The Main Question." British and U.S. forces are massing in the background
of this 1839 political cartoon showing Queen Victoria reluctantly being
dragged into battle with an equally reluctant President Martin Van Buren.
The dog represents the old warrior Duke of Wellington and the bull
is Maine governor John Fairfield, both spoiling for a fight.
(U.S. Library of Congress, Prints and Photographs
Division, LC-USZC4-6092)

kidnapping for ransom, murder-for-hire, smuggling and theft come
to mind. If Wood was as bent as they made him out to be, yet chose
to gain his ends by posing as God's Englishman in Maine rather
than by wielding pistol or knife in richer territory, he must have
been after something other than money, something more
elusive.

Keep prided himself on his bluntness, and his letter was itself
a blunt instrument. X had stated "nothing more than the facts,"
he said. How could he be so sure when, as he admitted, he had
never laid eyes on Wood? He even got his name wrong—Ward, he
called him:

An Impostor.

Mr. Cummings: I noticed in your paper of a late date, an account of "Elder Ward" a colored preacher in this vicinity. This Elder Ward I never saw, but having been for the last month or two upon the ground where he preached, last summer, I think, especially in Burlington, I would simply say that the report published in the Mirror is nothing more than the facts. I know not the author of that article but think he need not have feared to say what he did over his real name.

We are accused as a nation of being given to slander, and it may be true. But for my part I choose to say what I do about my neighbors, in the plainest terms possible. – From my earliest recollections I cannot recall a single instance when I complained of what any one chose to say, detrimental to my interests. But I have been sometimes tried with compliments and good wishes, which so carefully avoided evil speaking that it became the essence of slander. Such careful tongues with a look and a tone will communicate more than words can. It is a kind of refined christian slander which becomes a common or vulgar evil distilled. In whatever I communicate to the public, I choose to risk the charge of egotism rather than undertake to prove my knowledge of Latin, in giving my own signature rather than one from the Dictionary.

Elder Ward will probably go on imposing upon other communities. He despises "nigers" and is very anxious to get a white wife. He generally borrows all the money he can on the credit of his riches in England, or on the credit of his piety; he is not particular which. Those who have lent him on such security are rather still. After he has got what money he can, and preached his pond out, he goes to another place. But I would say in plainer terms still, there is probably something more to be dreaded from his influence than his dishonesty in money affairs, or hypocricy in religion—I mean moral baseness. Yours truly,

Marcus R. Keep.

Passadumkeag, Dec. 17, 1848.

Even as he contributed his mite to exposing "Ward" in the press, Keep showed little faith that doing so would stop the wolf in his tracks. He "will probably go on imposing upon other communities," he allowed. He then raised a startling alarm: Lock up your women, White sons of Maine, he seemed to say, this unholy black wolf "despises 'nigers' and is very anxious to get a white wife." Really? So, besides money, "Ward" wanted a wife, and a Black one would not do. Said who?

While Bro X had hinted at an evil purpose lurking in Wood's soul, Bro Keep warned in so many words that there was an element at the core of his being more sinister than a shadiness in matters of money and religion—"I mean moral baseness." As a punch line, that sounded rather muffled, coming from a man who claimed to speak plainly. "Moral baseness"—what the devil did that mean?

These cries of "Wolf!" did not carry as far and fast as some wished, so, in January 1849, the *Gospel Banner* in Augusta, the state capital, relayed them, reproducing Bro X's letter to the *Mirror*. Under the heading "An Impostor," the *Banner* gave the month-old piece a brief new preface, which does no more than add slightly to our knowledge of the territory that Wood covered, while reinforcing a suspicion that much of this sound and fury boiled down to a tempest in a sectarian teapot:

> We have heard of the man mentioned below before, but knew nothing of his character. In Topsfield, and perhaps some other town in the eastern section of the State, he deceived some of *our* friends for a short time, by pretending to be a Universalist,—though his prevailing pretensions have favored orthodoxy in some form. At any rate, it is time he was exposed and all honest people were put on their guard against him.

For a wolf with a big mouth and "great power of language," Wood remained remarkably silent. He never replied—not in print, at least—to these attacks. He did not growl or howl or whimper, did not sue or threaten to, did not bay at the moon or bite, either. The storm seemed to blow over, and he carried on as carpenter and preacher—until May, when he married a White woman, and all hell broke loose around Calais.

2. FORNICATION – IN BAILEYVILLE!

Rev. Keep may have been right after all, at least about Wood's matrimonial search. He had found his pearl, and she was White. Her name was Irene Stewart. She was in her early twenties, the daughter of innkeeper James Stewart of Baileyville, near Calais in Washington County, across the St. Croix River from St. Stephen in the British province of New Brunswick.

Two hurdles stood in the way of their union—her father and the law. Innkeeper Stewart could have had any number of reasons to oppose the marriage. It could be that he did not like the looks of his would-be son-in-law, or trust him. If he had got wind of those newspaper articles, or other like tales circulating about Wood, it could be that he was damned if he would see a child of his marry that English scamp, or damned if she would marry a colored man. On that last score, he would have had Maine law on his side. Few parents, with their children's best interests at heart, would approve of their embarking on married life by breaking the law, and Section 3 of the marriage law was as clear as any racist law could be: "No white person shall intermarry with any negro, indian or mulatto."

That should have been the end of it. Wood was a "mulatto," Irene Stewart was "white," and never the twain shall mate, said the law. But for determined twains of differing skin tones intercourting on the doorstep of New Brunswick, it was a simple matter to interskip over the threshold and go intermarry where no law forbade it. Alfred T. Wood and Irene A. Stewart crossed the line to be intermarried on 2 May 1849 by Rev. John Skiffington Thomson, the Anglican rector of Christ Church, at St. Stephen.

Couples who returned to Maine after skirting state law in this way were in for a rude honeymoon. In the eyes of the law, they were unintermarried as soon as they stepped back into the state.

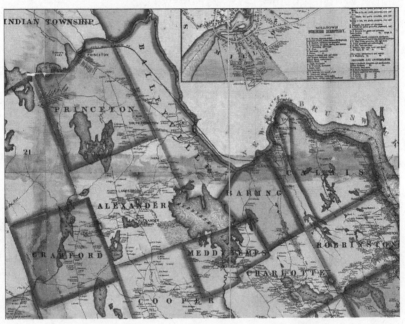

Marriage in the Parish of St. Stephens in the Year 1849 Alfred Thomas Wood Joiner and Irene A Stewart Spinster of Baileyville Co Washington State of Maine were married in this parish by licence this second day of May in the year of our lord one thousand eight hundred and forty nine By the Revd Sam Thomson L.L.D. Rector This Marriage was solemnized between us Alfred T. Wood in the presence of Wm Brown Irene A Stewart ...... Thomson

Alfred Thomas Wood was identified as a joiner when he married
Irene A. Stewart of Baileyville, Me., at St. Stephen, N.B., on 2 May 1849.
(Archives of New Brunswick, Marriage Registers,
Charlotte Co., vol. B, 1839-1854, p. 239)

Detail from an 1861 map of Washington County, Me.,
showing the proximity of Calais, Baileyville and Princeton to each
other and to the New Brunswick border.
(Library of Congress, Topographical map of Washington Co., Maine, by
Lee and Marsh, New York, 1861. https://www.loc.gov/item/2012592371/)

Section 5 of Maine's marriage act was as pointed as Section 3, if more wordy:

> When any persons, resident in this state, shall undertake to contract a marriage, contrary to the preceding provisions of this chapter, and shall, in order to evade those provisions, and with an intention of returning to reside in this state, go into another state or country, and there have their marriage solemnized, and shall afterwards return, and reside here, such marriage shall be deemed and held void, in this state.

There was no shorter distance between marriage and its dissolution. And if the offending couple persisted in interliving together, there was a word and a law for that: "If any unmarried man shall commit fornication with any unmarried woman, each of them shall be punished by imprisonment in the county jail, not more than sixty days, and by fine, not exceeding one hundred dollars."

Wood and his bride returned to Maine to face the wrath of Dad and the rigors of the law. Intermarried on a Wednesday, Wood was on the lam by Friday. The Calais *Frontier Journal* of 9 May carried this account:

GREAT EXCITEMENT.

> There has been a great excitement in town for the last three or four days, occasioned by the marriage of a negro itinerent [sic] preacher named Wood, and a white girl of a very respectable family in Baileyville.
>
> The Sheriff went from here on Friday to arrest said Wood for violating the law of the State, but did not succeed, said Wood threatening to shoot any person who undertook to lay hands on him. The Sheriff and a *posse* went after him again on Saturday morning, and met with the same luck, Sambo making his escape into the adjoining Province. On Monday morning another crew started from here, went to the house where he was stopping, about three miles from St. Stephen, put the 'huge paw' upon him, and brought him to Calais. We doubt their right to do so.
>
> This is the same dark complexioned imposter spoken of in the Christian Mirror, Gospel Banner, and other papers. He is said to be a man of considerable talent, and well educated, but possessing a heart blacker than his skin.

It is common report that he has one or two wives living, but as
the evidence will be difficult to be got at to prove him a bigamist, he
will probably get clear, and *clear* out of the county with his young
white wife.

Thus is a respectable family rendered miserable by the cunning
and artifice of a wolf in sheep's clothing, and we are sorry to say that
men of families in Calais, uphold him in his course. Let these individuals remember, that if such things are sanctioned, their own
households may be desolated by something similar, and if such a
thing should take place, which God forbid, they must expect the same
sympathy meted out to them as they have meted out to the distressed
parents in the present case.

P.S. Since the above was in type, he has been tried before S.P.
Briggs, Esq., on complaint of the girl's father, on an action for forni-
cation, and required to give bonds for his appearance at September
Court, and for want thereof was committed to jail.

A wolf in sheep's clothing, a heart blacker than his skin, blah
blah. We have heard all that before, although the "dark complexioned imposter" has now grown darker: The *Journal* makes him
a "negro," where Bro X had specifically told readers of the *Christian
Mirror* that he was "not a negro but a mulatto." Feeling vindicated,
the *Mirror* of 24 May reported Wood's arrest, copying an item
from the *Bath Times*:

Committed for Trial.—A negro intinerant [*sic*] preacher named
Wood, as we learn from the Frontier Journal, has been committed
for trial at Calais on the charge of fornication, growing out of his
marriage with a white girl in Baileyville. The girl is said to belong to
a respectable family and the complaint was lodged against the ethiopian by her father.

Wood is the same dark complexioned impostor against whom
the Christian Mirror, Gospel Banner and other papers have cautioned the public.–*Bath Times*.

Not only had the small-*e* "ethiopian" transgressed by trying
to pass for a big-*U* Universalist when he really favored small-*o*
orthodoxy, he had dared to interwoo and intermarry a White girl,
which was the height of barefaced Exogamy. The charge of bigamy
was new; Bros X and Keep had said nothing about Wood having
"one or two wives living." But tongues did wag, and the name-

Calais, shown in the top part of this 1879 birds' eye view, and St. Stephens, on the bottom, stand on opposite sides of the St Croix River. (Map by J.J. Stoner, Madison, Wis., G3734.C2A3 1879.P3, Courtesy Norman B. Leventhal Map & Education Center, Boston Public Library)

calling *Journal* was only too ready to heap on "Sambo" whatever dirt came to hand. As for the one clear crime committed—the Maine mob's abduction of Wood from New Brunswick—"We doubt their right to do so," the paper boldly stated.

The *Calais Advertiser* took a very different tack. It did not cite Wood's name or raise the cry of race, or even so much as hint that he was "colored." Rather than point a loaded finger at the alleged "fornicator," it quite rightly took aim at the posse:

"Have ye heard of our hunting, o'er mountain and glen,
"Though cane-break and forest—the hunting of men?"

The old direction was "Let him that is without sin, throw the first stone." Our community has been throwing rocks with a vengeance for the last few days. Our neighbors are bright, moral and intelligent, and well versed in the scriptures. They can hear nothing in the least out of the way. Pure themselves, they *will* have purity in others. The rumor that a fornication had recently been committed in the neighboring town of Baileyville, has almost turned our town inside out. The young men all turned as red as rooster's [*sic*] combs with virtuous indignation. They effervesced and boiled over with the swelling morality within them. The idea that fornication had been committed in Baileyville was perfectly horrid to their pure souls! Fornication is an offence against the Statute, and against the moral law, and if not punished in this instance, what outrageous results might not follow? Who would answer for the future condition of our young chastity? To what temptations might not our virtuous youth be exposed!

Our young men set their fears like flint against fornication—in Baileyville. Nobody in *Baileyville* had any moral or legal right to commit fornication!

So the young men and the virtuous old men, men of great purity and high character, turned out *en masse,* all, it is supposed, at the expense of the State, to run down the fornicator, the damnably vile man who had committed fornication—in Baileyville. How many of these men would have followed on in the chase had there been any lewd girls in the bushes on the road side, can never be known. But no temptations offering to lure them from the virtuous pursuit they followed on with immense zeal and pertinacity, and chased the audacious fornicator from house to house, through morass and forest, pursuing him out of one town into another, until he was at last driven into the neighboring Province of New Brunswick.

Nor did the fornication zeal of our fellow citizens stop with the limits of our State. – Our enterprising fellow citizen, Mr. John Leddy, with some fifteen or twenty fit associates in the moral reform, rushed in hot haste over to the Little Ridge, and there with wonderful courage, they all succeeded in the accomplishment of the bold feat of capturing the fornicator! It is surprising that they could all, with pistols and guns, have mustered so much pluck as was required to arrest the man who had been guilty of fornication— in Baileyville! Their bold achievment [*sic*] should be sung by a

Homer, or told by a Macaulay. We confess ourself unequal to the task of chronicler.

The fornicator thus seized, was brought by force within our jurisdiction, and arraigned before Mr. Justice Briggs, by whom he was bound over to the District Court, which sets next September.

Beware then, young men and old men, saints and sinners, the moral sentiment of Calais is aroused, and will not tolerate fornication—in Baileyville! Our backs are up, our moral bristles all stand on end, we have discussed the matter thoroughly, and in all its aspects, in all the shops in town, and at the corners of all the streets in both villages, and it is now judicially decided in full town meeting, that fornication must not be committed—in Baileyville. Stick to Mrs. Gardner's and you are safe!

In other words, gentlemen of the mob, consider yourselves stoned. To poke such prickly fun at all "the young men and the virtuous old men, men of great purity and high character," and the Gardner madam, you would swear the writer was a woman.

The jail at Machias, Maine. Wood was held prisoner here
from mid-May to mid-September 1849.
(Library of Congress, Topographical map
of Washington Co., Maine, by Lee and Marsh, New York, 1861, detail.
https://www.loc.gov/item/2012592371/)

The barbs the *Advertiser* shot at the knights of chastity were pretty pointed but not half as painful as the treatment Wood received. Arrested on 7 May and held in Calais until he was committed to trial, he was transferred to the county jail at Machias on 9 May. He would spend the summer by the sea, behind bars.

• • •

Only now that he was locked up did he speak out and find someone to stand up for him. His advocate was not a lawyer but a maverick Quaker journalist named Jeremiah Hacker, self-appointed champion of the underdog, the all-in-one captain and crew of the *Portland Pleasure Boat*. No fan of interracial unions, Friend Hacker yet believed that governments had no business color-coordinating marriages. Wood begged for his help. Concerned that the Black preacher might be railroaded, Hacker appealed to his readers on 31 May:

CAPTIVES' HALL

Captives shall have a good Hall on board the Pleasure Boat, if they *are* assigned the "black hole" in other crafts; so step in, friends, and hear this captive's trials:

FRIEND JEREMIAH HACKER: – "Permit an unworthy servant of Christ, as I am—who have spent the morning of my days in the service of our divine master, not for money, nor for any worldly wealth or honor, but for the fulfilling of my commission and duty under God, as one of his creatures, and a friend to suffering humanity, to address you.

I was born in St. Mary's Parish, Great Britain. I received an education at Oxford: – experienced the love of God, and took leave of all that was near and dear, to preach the word to dying humanity. After being in the West India station some seven years, my health became impaired, on account of the warm climate, I was advised to leave and try a colder region. I returned to England, but it made no material change in my health. I left on the 28th of Feb. 1846, bound for North America. I was shipwrecked on the coast of Pictou, N.S. Lost all my money, clothes, books, &c.,—all but a few documents, I had about my person. Thus moneyless, friendless, and comfortless, I wandered into the State of Maine;

and have spent nearly three years in it, laboring under the slander and prejudice of its Priests and Jesuits. I have earned my living by working at the joiner business; and while situated at Princeton, doing pretty well, and having very good prospects, I became acquainted with Miss Irene A. Stewart, a young lady who became greatly attached to me, and finally it grew into inseparable, candid affection. Her father James Stewart, who is a publican, was greatly opposed to our union. He ordered his daughter out of doors. She came and threw herself on me for protection; – I went forthwith over on the English side, (knowing that the law of this State prohibited all officers from marrying a white person to a "darkey")— and procured a license from the Governor of New Brunswick, and was accordingly married to the girl. Recrossing the line again to settle up my business, that I might settle in the Provinces, Mr. Stewart, got out a warrant to arrest me, under the charge of fornication. I eluded their arrest for several days, and had repaired with my wife into the Province again, when the people of Calais raised a mob, came over seven miles from the territorial line, and took me and my wife, brought us to Calais, and there strove to make our marriage illegal, and under a mock form of justice, wrested my wife from my side by force! And now they have me confined in prison to await my trial as a fornicator! Oh! God of nature! Ye Angels! blush at this cruel, this Hellish treatment to one of God's creatures, and that too, in a land of Bibles and Meeting Houses. Surely this place has made an agreement with death and Hell. Did ever that God who gave nature its laws, order that wherever the affections of humanity met with reciprocity, those persons should be thus treated? Heaven would blush at the idea. 'Tis true I am a man of half black blood, but I have feelings as white as those of my prosecutor.

I wish you to give this a place in your Boat, and grant it a swift passage all over the world. Here I am in a helpless condition. Oh! that some kind friend to suffering humanity would aid me in this case. I am even without means to procure council [sic], at the time of trial. Dear Sir, is there any resource or assistance in your power! send it in God's name.

Any communication will be thankfully received by your humble servant, and injured servant

And friend to humanity,

ALFRED T. WOOD."

The above is a hard case, and the writer will find the people divided in their opinions. One class will sympathize with him, while the other will desire to see him punished to the full extent of the law, for presuming to marry a white. As for myself, I have never had a favorable opinion of the intermarriage of the white and colored people, yet believe they should be left to their own free choice. As one of my friends has observed, I see no better reason why law makers should say that a white shall not marry a colored person, than they have to say that one with a crooked nose shall not marry one with a straight nose. As to the intermeddling of friends and relations in such matters, it is a thing I despise; they have no right to resort to law, nor to utter a single word in objection to it, more than what they can utter in good will, with kind and tender feelings. I have seen too much of such meddling among men and women of all classes, to think favorably of it. Many who have been united by the most pure and holy principles and feelings of our nature, and who might have spent their lives in perfect harmony, have been torn asunder by meddlesome friends, and have lived and died feeling like lonely strangers in the midst of society. It appears that young woman married this colored man from choice. If she found his heart pure and good, it mattered not to her what color its covering was, and if her friends could not convince her in kindness, that she was in error, nor change her mind by truth kindly and affectionately expressed, they should have permitted her to exercise her own free will. Their conduct is certainly most outrageous, if the above letter contains facts. If they were married in the Province, and intended to settle there the authorities of Maine had no right to interfere. The sufferer has applied to the wrong source for aid. I have not funds nor influence to assist him, but will see if anything can be done with or by those in this State who profess to be friends to the colored race. Whether it is right or wrong for the white and the colored to intermarry—a point on which I will not now venture a more decided opinion than I have—the accused should, at least, be favored with a fair trial.

What say, ye Abolitionists of Maine, will you see that this brother has fair play? Think, act, be quick!

Hacker's anti-establishment views predisposed him to believe Wood's tale. Still, it sounded so outrageous. Prudence dictated that the skipper of the *Pleasure Boat* satisfy himself of the seaworthiness of Wood's account before venturing too far from land with it. He hailed Wood and asked him to send him proof. The *Pleasure Boat* of 21 June carried Wood's reply:

LETTER FROM A.T. WOOD – NO. 2.

Three or four weeks since, I published a letter from a mulatto, who is imprisoned at Machias, for marrying a white girl, in the Province of New Brunswick. I wrote to the prisoner inquiring into the particulars of the case, and the following is his reply:

MACHIAS JAIL, June 4th, 1849.

Dear Friend Hacker: –

I am happy to say I received yours of the 30th May, which gave me great comfort in my present situation.

You say that there are those who doubt the facts of the case, as stated in my letter. In order to substantiate the same, I am happy to announce to you, that I have a certificate of my marriage, now in my possession. I was married by the Rev. Skiffentin Thomson, L.L.D., Rector of St. Stephen's Parish, New Brunswick, on the second day of May, 1849, in presence of William Brown and Miss Abigail Bonney, of Princeton, Washington Co., Maine; these, with Mrs. Ann Thomson, (the Rector's lady,) are the witnesses who signed the certificate of marriage.

You may please write to any of the above named persons, if necessary, for any information required. As it regards the place, I was married in the Rev. Doctor Thomson's own house, in St. Stephens, New Brunswick.

In regard to my being taken on the English side, the constable himself, who took me, has told the jailer here, that it was all of nine miles from the State line where they took me. My best respects to Gen. Fessenden. I pray his attention to my case. The Court sits here at West Machias Court House, on the third Tuesday of September.

Tell all the friends they may place explicit confidence in my statements—they can all be proved.

Yours affectionately,

A.T. WOOD.

The Jailer at Machias has testified in the same letter, that he has seen the certificate above referred to, and there is no doubt in my mind that the prisoner has stated facts. Here then is a case that will sound the depth of the principles of the Abolitionists and Free Soil men of Maine. This man is a native of England, whose laws permit the white and colored races to intermarry. He married an American in the province of New Brunswick, under British laws, and by an officer qualified by said laws, to unite people in marriage. He then returned to Maine, as he says, to settle up his business, in order to settle in New Brunswick, when a warrant was got out to arrest him for *fornication*. He eluded the officers and returned to the Province and was there arrested by officers from Maine, who crossed the line for the purpose, in violation of law. The result is—he is now imprisoned at Machias, to be tried for *fornication!* How many slaves of the Southern States are treated worse! I hope for the credit of Northern abolitionists, that they will extend their kindness to this *slave* and victim of unjust laws at home, so far as to see that he has a fair trial, before they utter another word about Southern Slavery.

As I said in a former article, I have never thought very highly of the intermarriage of the two races, yet men have no right to enact laws to put them asunder. I close by calling on all friends of humanity, and especially those who call themselves the particular friends of the colored race, to see that this man has a fair trial, as he is entirely helpless in the hands of *their* law, not even having funds to employ counsel.

As many of our members of Congress think mulatto girls, and even those of the darkest hue quite good enough for *private* company, when at Washington, absent from their wives, I can see no very strong reason why there should be such a touse because a white girl has chosen a decent mulatto for her companion.

The jab at Congressmen was perhaps below the belt, but about the essentials, Hacker was on the right track. Wood deserved a fair trial; and how could men sitting in the state house sunder what the same men, sitting in church, held that no man could sunder? Hacker did have reservations about mixed marriages, and some of his readers needled him on this point. Some also objected to his putting Abolitionists on the spot when the case had nothing to do with slavery, their particular concern; it was about the enforcement of an unjust law and frontier justice run wild, which should have been a concern to all, regardless of skin color. Still, anti-slavery organs paid attention. The Abolitionist *Liberator* in Boston reproduced Wood's second letter in July, and in distant Ohio the *Anti-Slavery Bugle* sounded the alarm on 6 July: "The arrest of a man on British soil by the authorities of Maine, is an outrage upon the sovereignty of the English government, of which it will doubtless take proper notice. The law of Maine is disgraceful to the State, an outrage upon the inalienable rights of man; while the participants in this act of persecution deserve the scorn of all decent people."

However revealing it might be to probe Hacker's views on race, the subject at hand is A.T. Wood, the man, not J. Hacker, the social thinker. Wood—"decent mulatto" or "wolf in sheep's clothing"? That is the question.

All that we heard about Wood earlier came from the pens of his detractors, but he speaks for himself in the two letters published in the *Pleasure Boat*. He shows himself to be articulate, educated and talented, as even Bro X conceded. In an age of widespread illiteracy, the fact that he could write as he did was proof that he had made it well beyond basic carpentry in school. But his letters betray such a shiftiness. In his words, what should be meaty is fishy. He pretends to disclose information when, in fact, he withholds it. He is precise where precision does not matter, and vague where it would count. And he is careless in citing documents: He has his marriage certificate with him, he says, yet he misspells the given name of the officiating priest (it's Skiffington, not Skiffentin). His is the glib language of the fast talker, and it does not stand up on paper. It is probably just as well that he had not written a reply to the attacks on him in the press.

Take his first letter, beginning "Permit an unworthy servant of Christ..." Oozing sanctimony, its long opening sentence signals that, along with preaching and carpentry, he had studied the art of humbug. Rather than draw our sympathy, it makes us squirm. There follows a sketch of his life that is pure smoke, enough to set off multiple alarms.

— *Birthplace?* "St. Mary's Parish, Great Britain." Good luck finding that on a map. He might as well have said that he was born at home.

— *Age?* He will not say, but he will hint. The fact that he had passed the "morning of my years," and allegedly spent some seven years as a missionary "in the West India Station"—where precisely?—might lead a reader to infer that he must be in his thirties, born some time in the second decade of the century.

— *Religion?* Protestant, no particular denomination, anything but Roman Catholic. His labors had excited the "priests and Jesuits" against him. It was stout Protestants who had raised the cry against him, but never mind—in appealing to Friend Hacker, blaming "Papists" was a better card to play.

— *Education?* "At Oxford." Impressive! But weren't Oxford and Cambridge, England's sole universities, restricted to Anglicans? So was Wood a member of the Church of England? The truth is, the number of Black students or grads of Oxford in 1849 was zero.

— *Parents? Family?* Not a word about them. Rev. X had reported him as claiming to have "very rich and much honored relatives in England and considerable amount of property." Rev. Keep had also written of Wood's alleged "riches in England." But in dealing with Hacker, Wood could not well boast of rich relations while appealing for help as a poor man who couldn't afford a lawyer.

Our suspicions aroused, we come to the tale of how he reached Maine. He sailed from England on 28 February 1846, he says. The date is so startling in its exactness—and pointless in the context of his otherwise fuzzy letter. February 1846, or even 1846, would have done. But a precise date lends a touch of verisimilitude to a document that is suspiciously short of same. His stated destination? North America!—another seemingly hard but hugely vague fact. Where in North America? All we know is that he was not bound for Maine; his fetching up there was accidental, the result of a shipwreck off Pictou, N.S., from which he managed to save only his skin and his papers. He offers no details of this disaster—date, ship's name, master, casualties (there is no record of such a wreck off Pictou in 1846). But mind those papers, the only possessions of his that had not gone down with the ship. They were no doubt the documents he had used to land the preaching job at Amherst, where he surely had been asked for proof of his training and experience, letters of reference, something of the sort.

Pictou, across Northumberland Strait from Prince Edward Island, was not on any route to the U.S. from England. Had he perhaps been bound for some place in British North America? Then why had he not made his way there in the three years since his arrival? Instead, he had "wandered" as he said, "moneyless, friendless and comfortless," through Nova Scotia and New Brunswick into Maine, reaching Amherst, guided by God-knows what internal GPS. Finally, settled at Princeton, by Baileyville, he had been doing "pretty well," his prospects were "very good," the fair Irene had thrown herself at him ...

Hacker, oblivious to the published accounts of a "wolf in sheep's clothing," never probed Wood's past or his odyssey. He focused on the fornication business. On the basis of Wood's account of his interwedding, his intermarriage certificate, and the jailer's confirmation of his capture in New Brunswick, he was satisfied that "the prisoner has stated facts," i.e., Wood and Irene Stewart were properly intermarried and there was nothing fornicatious about their intercohabitation.

In publishing Wood's story in Wood's own words, Hacker had a scoop that gave him an opportunity to indulge his taste for challenging the powers that be and those whose deeds fell short of their blather. A week after printing Wood's second letter from prison, he rejoiced that the *Eastern Argus* had come on board, even as he groused that that mainstream Portland paper had cribbed its facts from the *Pleasure Boat* without so much as a by-your-leave. He quoted the *Argus* article of 23 June in full:

THE CASE OF A.T. WOOD.

If there be no fraud or imposture in this matter, the case of Wood is of the most extraordinary character. This man, who is a mulatto, is confined in Jail at Machias, under a charge of having intercourse with his own lawful wife. The secret is, she is a white woman. Wood was married to his wife the 2nd May last, in New Brunswick, by the Rector of St. Stephen's Parish. He has with him the regular certificate of his marriage. There is a law in force in this State, which declares such marriages here illegal; but, this, of course, relates only to marriages contracted in Maine. Every body knows, that the validity of a marriage depends, not upon the law of the place where the parties happen to be, but upon the law of the place where the marriage was contracted. Any other doctrine would lead to the most absurd and deplorable consequences. The whole proceeding against Wood, according to his account of it, is of so high-handed a character, that we cannot resist a suspicion of misrepresentation. No people in their senses would expose themselves to the consequences of so daring an outrage under our laws upon a fellow citizen. Still, if the facts, as stated by Wood, be substantially true, there will be a sorry day of reckoning for the mighty squeamish getters-up of the persecution. We hope, as our Legislature is now in session, they will wipe from the statute book this remnant of illiberal prejudice, which we have referred to. There is no danger in New England of such cases of intermarriage happening oftener than once in an age. Besides, the prohibition is directly in the face of the natural and equal rights of all classes of our citizens, as recognized by the Constitution. If any white woman wants a negro husband such weather as this is—why, let her have him.

In Hacker's view, the only "reckoning" needed was one free of all spirit of revenge, "that will liberate him [Wood], pay him fairly for his time and expenses, restore his wife to him and place them where the legal mob found them."

While the *Argus* could not shake off a "suspicion of misrepresentation" in Wood's tale, Hacker had no such qualms. Yet he did not return to the subject for the next two months, except to make passing reference to the preacher-prisoner in mid-July as "a stranger, and friendless and destitute of means." He published no further jailhouse letters from Wood, but at the end of August, about to close up shop till October, he made one last plea on his behalf:

What is to be done for A.T. Wood, the mulatto who is imprisoned in Machias Jail? Do any intend to see that he has a fair trial, or will the whole State look on in silence, and see their laws crush this friendless foreigner, for doing an act in his own country, and under the sanction of its laws! His offence is marrying a white girl in the province of New Brunswick, where the laws permit colored and white people to intermarry; but, because the girl was a yankee, he was taken by a mob in that province, and brought into Maine and imprisoned, to be tried for the crime of fornication. The court will set at Machias on the 3d Tuesday of September, before this paper is issued again—so that this is the last chance we shall have to mention his case before the trial. He is without means to procure aid. Now, what will be done? Shall he have a fair trial, or shall he be crushed by yankee law, for doing that in his own land which the laws of that land pronounce right and proper? Let all Maine answer this question if she would escape disgrace, and let the Abolitionists now prove their devotion to the interests of the colored race, and humanity in general, by their WORKS.

While Hacker rested from his labors, Wood stewed in jail, awaiting the opening of the District Court on 18 September. For Irene Stewart, ostracized, the summer cannot have passed any more pleasantly than it did for her husband. She was not prosecuted, even though the law provided that both parties to a fornication were liable to the same penalties. Her father had at least spared her that, filing a complaint against Wood alone.

No official record of the court proceedings survives, but the *Calais Advertiser* of 26 September gave a summary account of the outcome. While this sheet had seemed sympathetic to Wood and his bride in May, scoffing at the fornication uproar, it now took a cruel jab at both of them, branding him as worthless for being Black, her as worthless by association:

> We understand that Mr. Wood the colored man who has been in jail some three months awaiting his trial for the alleged crime of fornication has been acquitted by the grand jury without even the form of a trial. – No one appearing against him. – If the parents of the girl had shown as much sense in the first part of this affair as they have in the last, it would have saved them a good deal of unnecessary trouble and mortification. – For any white girl who thinks so little of herself and connections as to wed a black man is not worth looking after. – He has gone off to the westward with her.

In the end, then, the *Advertiser* consigned Irene Stewart to oblivion, urging her parents and everyone else to click on her and hit Delete—a bloodless honor killing. Wood, for his part, was freed on 20 September. The railroading Hacker had feared never took place. Perhaps the illogic of putting one-half of a "fornicating" pair on trial had hit home: No one had yet mastered the trick of fornicating alone. Or perhaps the circumstances of his kidnapping on foreign soil had cooled the ardor of his persecutors and led them to conclude that the wisest course would be to drop the matter. If they pressed the case in court, they risked a "sorry day of reckoning" and sparking a diplomatic row (though the New Brunswick authorities had remained stunningly silent about the border incursion). And they had nothing to gain. Irene Stewart was not about to leave her husband and slink back under her father's roof. As for Wood, hadn't he been punished enough? The law set a maximum jail term of 60 days for convicted fornicators, and, by the reckoning of jailer Abijah Crane, Wood—arrested illegally, never convicted—had already served 134, not counting the two he had spent in the clink at Calais.

Wood would later seek compensation from the U.S. government, "in consequence of his being arrested and detained by citizens of the State of Maine while resident in New Brunswick." His claim, one of several presented in London on 15 March 1854 to the "Mixed Commission on Private Claims, Established under the Convention Between Great Britain and the United States of America of the 8th February, 1853," was considered and rejected on 8 April.

Friend Hacker might have had something to say in conclusion, but after his holidays, the *Pleasure Boat* never revisited those troubled waters.

3. UNMASKED

Wood told Hacker that he and his wife had intended to make their home in New Brunswick, that they had returned to Maine after their wedding only to wind up his affairs. But on his release from jail, they skirted New Brunswick. As the *Calais Advertiser* reported, he and his bride headed west, away from the border. Out of sight of the *Advertiser,* they turned south, toward Boston, the cultural and intellectual hub of New England, home to 137,000 people, 2,000 of them Black (about 700 more than in the whole of Maine, according to the 1850 U.S. census).

A far cry from Baileyville, Boston was to some extent a hotbed of radical Abolitionism, its poets, writers, philosophers and activists seeking, in the face of widespread anti-Black feeling, to project an image of the city as keeper of the revolutionary flame of liberty, equality and the rights of all. It had been the home of Black tailor David Walker, who had published his inflammatory *Appeal to the Coloured Citizens of the World* in 1829. There too, in 1831, William Lloyd Garrison had launched the *Liberator,* the most provocative of Abolitionist newspapers. And in 1832, at the First African Baptist Church on Belknap St. (now Joy St.), Garrison, the White son of a New Brunswick sea dog, had presided over the founding of the New England Anti-Slavery Society, the first such group in the U.S. to demand an immediate end to slavery and the recognition of equal rights for Blacks.

This was also Massachusetts, in a sense the fount of the troubles Wood and his wife had seen. Maine had inherited its law against mixed marriages from Massachusetts, of which it had been a part until 1820. In that year, the District of Maine had separated from its parent state to become the twenty-third state of

The African Baptist Church in Smith Court, Belknap Street, Boston. In 1850,
Wood served briefly as pastor of this historic church. The building is now part
of the Museum of African American History.
(Massachusetts Historical Society. Photograph from Wendell Phillips Garrison,
William Lloyd Garrison, 1805-1879: The Story of His Life, extra illustrated
edition, New York, The Century Co., 1885, v. 1, Pt. 2, opposite p. 280)

the union; the twenty-fourth, admitted the following year, was
Missouri. The Missouri Compromise, as this political two-step is
known, featured one of several constitutional give-and-takes
aimed at quelling unrest North and South. The idea was to maintain the balance in the number of "free" and "slave" states. While
it broke free of Massachusetts, the new free state of Maine reen-
acted the old prohibition against intermarriage. But in 1843, six
years before the Woods reached Boston, Massachusetts had

repealed its objectionable law, something Maine would not do until 1883, long after the Woods had passed.

Wood and his wife reached Boston when Black residents were in the thick of a long-running battle against school segregation, a battle that would continue in different forms well into the twentieth century. An "entertainment for the benefit of the cause" took place on 16 January 1850. The speakers sharing the floor that evening were Garrison and leading lights of the Black community, among them, lawyer Robert Morris, journalist and historian William Cooper Nell, hairdresser John T. Hilton, a vice-president of the Massachusetts Anti-Slavery Society and general treasurer of the committee for equal school rights—and the Rev. A.T. Wood.

There is no record of the words Wood spoke, no telling how attuned he was to the concerns of his listeners, or how he was received. He had probably not been named pastor of the First African Baptist Church, also called the African Meeting House, and formally known since 1837 as the First Independent Baptist Church of People of Color, but he had made approaches. It so happened that the Rev. William B. Serrington, pastor since February 1848, had left for Providence, R.I., in October 1849. To the congregation, then, Wood's arrival on the scene at this moment might have seemed ... providential.

Through the 1830s and early 1840s, the church, now a National Historic Landmark and home of the Museum of African American History, had suffered from internal strife, leading 46 of its members to bolt in 1843. The cause of the trouble is unclear. Some have speculated that the friction stemmed from disagreements over the part the church and its pastor should play in promoting social reforms, notably the abolition of slavery. As historian George A. Levesque has written:

> From the mid-forties until the outbreak of the [Civil] war, the Church was ministered to by a succession of pastors and was intermittently without a settled shepherd. ... Much of the history of black Bostonians in the middle years was planned and plotted, debated and discussed in this very house. It is ironic, then, that the clerical heads of the Church at this time should have been so conspicuously uninvolved in the wars of the period. Were it not for the fact that the

names of the clerics who served from 1845 are preserved in the minutes of the Boston Baptist Association, such as Serrington's, Thompson's, Henson's, and others who had even briefer ministries, their existence would hardly be known to us.

After Serrington, William Thompson served as pastor in 1851-53. Between the two, researchers who have scoured the records have drawn a blank, concluding that the church had gone without a pastor for a year. Pastor Wood has vanished from the record, even though, in early 1850, he had been set to become a fixture there.

After the soirée for equal school rights in January, we glimpse him again on 27 March at a public meeting called at the church itself to denounce Massachusetts's hallowed Senator Daniel Webster for declaring that he would support the Fugitive Slave Bill sponsored by Senator James M. Mason of Virginia. This notorious bill, which was to become law that September, was part of another compromise designed to preserve the American union and ease the mounting tensions between free and slave states.

"The Chairman, on taking his seat, invited Rev. Alfred T. Wood to address the Throne of Grace." The *Liberator's* report on the anti-Webster meeting attributed no further role to Wood. His invocation went unrecorded, so we hear nothing of his sentiments on the Fugitive Slave Bill—or on African colonization, another topic on the agenda that made Abolitionists see red. Webster was a vice-president of the American Society for Colonizing the Free People of Color in the United States, better known as the American Colonization Society (ACS), the national body behind the effort to ship Black Americans to Liberia. John T. Hilton, William Cooper Nell, the celebrated slave-born orator and journalist Rev. Samuel Ringgold Ward of Syracuse, N.Y., and the ubiquitous Garrison were among the speakers who tore a strip off Webster that evening. A few nights later, on 2 April, Ward and ex-slave Henry Bibb addressed an anti-slavery meeting at Tremont Temple—and Rev. Wood was once more called on to say a prayer.

Presumably, he had taken up his post as pastor of the church in Belknap St. by then. He must have served at least a month, before May, when his tenure came to a dead end. A notice by the

NOTICE.

A special meeting was held by the First Independent Baptist Church, on Tuesday evening, the 14th instant, in their meeting-house, in relation to the unfavorable reports which are in circulation affecting the moral standing of the minister that has officiated for the Church and Society for some time past, who calls his name Rev. Alfred T. Wood, stating that he came from Liverpool, England. He also had documents, which he presented, which went to substantiate the same assertions. But there are persons in this city who state that his real name is George Andrew Smith, and that he came from Halifax, Nova Scotia, and that they are acquainted with his parents and relatives, and that the name of Wood is only assumed, for the better consummation of his own purposes.

In consequence of a person coming to this city and making these statements, he immediately left the church and city, without any formal notice, and did not make, nor wait for any investigation on the subject. In consequence of the above, the Deacons held a meeting, and presented a report to the Church, accompanied with the following resolution:—

Resolved, That the various unfavorable reports against the moral standing of Rev. Alfred T. Wood fully justify the Deacons in recommending to the Church the reconsideration of the vote by which he was constituted a member of this body, and likewise the one which called him to the pastoral charge of the same.

COFFIN PITTS,
JAMES SCOTT, } *Deacons.*
GEO. WASHINGTON,

The Report was accepted, adopted, and voted by the Church to be published in one or more papers, for the purpose of preventing any further imposition by him on the Church or the public.

By order and on behalf of the First Independent Baptist Church, Boston,

S. H. LEWIS, *Clerk.*

Boston, May 20, 1850.

At the end of May 1850, "unfavorable reports" concerning the Rev. Wood led to his dismissal as pastor of the African Baptist Church. (*The Liberator,* Boston, 24 May 1850, p. 3)

church, published in the *Liberator* of 24 May, sketched out how events had unfolded:

NOTICE.

A special meeting was held by the First Independent Baptist Church, on Tuesday evening, the 14th instant, in their meeting-house, in relation to the unfavorable reports which are in circulation affecting the moral standing of the minister that has officiated for the Church and Society for some time past, who calls his name Rev. Alfred T. Wood, stating that he came from Liverpool, England. He also had documents, which he presented, which went to substantiate the same assertions. But there are persons in this city who state that his real name is George Andrew Smith, and that he came from Halifax, Nova Scotia, and that they are acquainted with his parents and relatives, and that the name of Wood is only assumed, for the better consummation of his own purposes.

In consequence of a person coming to this city and making these statements, he immediately left the church and city, without any formal notice, and did not make, nor wait for any investigation on the subject. In consequence of the above, the Deacons held a meeting, and presented a report to the Church, accompanied with the following resolution: –

Resolved, That the various unfavorable reports against the moral standing of Rev. Alfred T. Wood fully justify the Deacons in recommending to the Church the reconsideration of the vote by which he was constituted a member of this body, and likewise the one which called him to the pastoral charge of the same.

> COFFIN PITTS,
> JAMES SCOTT,   *Deacons.*
> GEO. WASHINGTON,

The Report was accepted, adopted, and voted by the Church [...] for the purpose of preventing any further imposition by him on the Church or the public.

By order and on behalf of the First Independent Baptist Church, Boston,

> S.H. LEWIS, *Clerk.*

Boston, May 20, 1850.

Forget England and the moneyed kin. Forget the forlorn shipwreck survivor staggering to Maine with nothing but the shirt on his back, clutching his papers and spinning his cockeyed tale. Forget Alfred Thomas Wood of England, across the wide Atlantic, think George Andrew Smith of Nova Scotia, across the narrow Gulf of Maine. The facts of the case against him this time were more damning than any he had faced in Maine, if only because he confirmed them by running away. And he could not pretend that the "Priests and Jesuits" had had it in for him—his accusers were members of his own church. Rather than stand his ground, he had absquatulated, running for cover to New York City.

Other than that notice in the Boston papers, there seems to be only one other document attesting to his pastorate. It is buried in Homan's *Sketches of Boston, Past and Present,* a guidebook published in 1851. Under an engraving of the church building, a chronological list of its pastors included "A.T. Wood, inst. 1850, left 1850."

His church should have heeded the caution against impostors published years before by the Baptist Missionary Society of Massachusetts. Men of more piety than sense are easily conned, the society had warned: "A designing impostor will need nothing more to give him currency with such good men, than a false show of piety and humility [...] accompanied with unbounded assurances of being actuated by a holy zeal for God." Churches should never hire a stranger to preach "unless he brings a letter of introduction from some respectable character with whom they are acquainted."

Perhaps Smith/Wood and his credentials had appeared too impressive to be doubted; perhaps he was just too good at disarming people with his "holy zeal for God." However embarrassing the episode may have been, and whatever damage Smith had done, the church was wise to own up to its mistake rather than try to cover up the galling truth of his imposture. As an Asa Cummings might have said, "the security of the public from imposition requires that it should be spread abroad." Smith had presented his credentials as the Rev. A.T. Wood of Liverpool, probably the same documents he had used in neighboring Maine—who could have suspected that they were fake? He had not breathed a word about his days in Maine—he had clearly not produced any letters of reference from that quarter—and no one from the church seems to have heard the least whisper of his doings there. (Neither did Maine newspapers report his unmasking in Boston!)

In the history of the First Independent Baptist Church, whose building, erected in 1806, makes it the oldest Black church building still standing in the United States, Smith left hardly a trace, just a gap in the list of its pastors. Putting him back in that lineup might help explain a hiccup in the church's history. Historian Levesque attributed the sharp decline in its membership in 1850 to the workings of the Fugitive Slave Law, which came into force on 18 September that year. The church, he said,

> lost some thirty-five members as a result of the 1850 law. In 1852 the Boston South Baptist Association, the body with which the Independent Church was affiliated, adopted a resolution sympathizing with the "sufferings and trials" occasioned by the law "by which some of their leading members have been obliged to flee to Canada for protection." In this instance, the loss is reflected in membership totals; standing at 140 in 1849, the membership dropped to 104 in 1850 and numbered 110 in 1851.

Pastor A.T. Wood, "inst. 1850, left 1850," say the notes to this engraving
of the First Independent Baptist Church, aka the African Meeting House
or African Baptist Church, in an 1851 Boston guidebook.
(Isaac Smith Homans, *Sketches of Boston, Past and Present,
and of Some Few Places in Its Vicinity*, Boston, Phillips,
Samson, and Co.; Crosby and Nichols, 1851, p. 88)

It is not unreasonable to suppose that, before the Fugitive Slave Bill ever became law, Smith had contributed in some measure to the loss. In Maine, he had at first drawn a crowd, only to see the faithful defect as his true colors came to light. In Boston, no sooner had he entered on his ministry than "reports against the moral standing of Rev. Alfred T. Wood," aka Smith, drew the church's attention and, quite probably, led some of his flock to seek fellowship and counsel elsewhere.

When the curtain had fallen on the Maine dress rehearsal of Wood's career, a flint-hearted editor had urged everyone to blot out his wife. With his Boston performance at an end, the struggling African Meeting House photoshopped him out of the picture and moved on. History quickly loses sight of erased persons like Rev. and Mrs. Wood, but they remain forever lodged in history's hard drive.

• • •

George Andrew Smith is unknown in Nova Scotia. Not surprisingly, there is no monument to the Rev. A.T. Wood in the land of Evangeline and Sam Slick. You would not expect to find one, even if, in a non-literary sense, he ranks as one of that province's most remarkable fictional creations. You would not count on finding a statue to his memory or a plaque, but you might hope to find some trace of Smith, his creator. You might think that news of Smith's unmasking in Boston would have reached the bustling port city of Halifax and that a paper in Nova Scotia's capital would have picked up the story. But Boston newspapers had done no more than publish, without comment, the notice by church officials— and there was no account in the Halifax press, either, at least, not in any surviving newspaper issues.

A search for information about George Andrew Smith in Nova Scotia failed to turn up anything conclusive. Efforts to track him down through schools he might have attended proved unavailing. And if we do not know exactly what his life was like in Nova Scotia, we cannot be sure of why he left that life behind to go deceive the wide world. We cannot know, for instance, whether it was his choice to leave, or whether he was shown the door, by his family or others.

Besides the mystery of his origins, his education and how he had acquired his preaching skills, one of the many puzzling, if banal, questions about Smith is why he chose to go by a name not his own, and to cling to it through thick and thin. After burning his bridges in Maine as A.T. Wood, it would have made sense for him to drop that pseudonym and adopt a new one, to guard against the risk of seeing his troubling past follow him to Boston. As it turned out, no alias could have protected him in Boston; the person or persons there who knew him from Nova Scotia would have recognized him as Smith, no matter what identity he had adopted. But after he had been publicly exposed as the Nova Scotian Smith, his pose as the English Wood had become a liability. After Boston, a new name would have been in order, you think. Yet A.T. Wood he remained.

The fact is, he was trapped in his disguise. There were at least two reasons for this—his wife and his "documents." There is no reason to suppose that Irene Stewart had married him to play Bonnie to his Clyde. She was his dupe, one of the saddest of his many victims. She knew him as the Rev. Alfred Thomas Wood, a preacher from England. That is the man she had married, in defiance of her family, her community and the law. For him to admit that he had married her under a false identity would have blown everything, exploding his claim to be an honest-to-goodness minister of the gospel and raising grave doubts about the validity of their marriage. If, back in Maine, she had shut her ears against the nasty rumors and reports about him, she might now be inclined to open them wide and suspect the worst.

Wood could not tell her the truth unless he was prepared to make a clean breast of it, drop the clerical act, tear up his "documents," and go back to being George Andrew Smith, earning an honest living. He was not about to do that, nor was he about to leave her. The fact that, a year earlier, he had resisted the efforts of her father and the Calais posse to separate them, and had spent four months in jail for his pains, proved that he was attached to her, for better or worse. And clinging to her meant sticking to his story.

Chances are, Irene Stewart was not a faithful newspaper reader—there is reason to believe she was illiterate, as we shall

Black women selling flowers in the market at Halifax, N.S. This sketch
was published in 1872, but it depicts a scene that Wood would have
been familiar with as a young man.
(*Canadian Illustrated News,* 25 May 1872, p. 325)

see—and she had missed the notice about her husband in the
Liberator. Part of the explanation for their rushed retreat from
Boston perhaps lay in Wood's need to keep her in the dark, to
whisk her away before word of those "various unfavorable reports"
about him reached her ears. If she still had no inkling of her husband's duplicity, or the extent of it, she would have been puzzled
at the suddenness of their departure, and he would have had to
come up with a cover story, but he was an old hand at that.

In their marriage certificate, he was Alfred Thomas Wood, as
he was on those other papers that he had allegedly saved from
shipwreck and used to establish his standing as a preacher and
former missionary from Liverpool. If any of these documents were
printed ones (who would have printed them?), they might have
been difficult to alter or replace. If they were handwritten certificates, letters and testimonials that he had drawn up himself—
other than his marriage record and such other authentic papers
as may have come his way—he could have prepared another set
without much trouble, giving himself a new identity. But what was

the point? He could not be Rev. Wood to his wife and someone else to the world at large. Like it or not, George Andrew Smith was not really Alfred Thomas Wood, but he could be no one else.

So, forget Smith. Two months after his flight from Boston, it was as the Rev. A.T. Wood that he sailed for Liberia with the fair Irene. On the way, he picked up a doctorate of divinity.

4. LIBERIATION

The Fourth of July, flags were flying in Baltimore. It was a fitting day for the emigrants aboard the *Liberia Packet* to be sailing off to the continent of their ancestors and their wildest dreams, in search of their own Independence Day. The passenger list counted 55 of them—34 freeborn, 21 ex-slaves—all packed off by the American Colonization Society (ACS). All were U.S.-born except the Rev. A.T. Wood, 36, and his 24-year-old wife, Irene Stewart, from New York City. According to the list, both Wood and his wife had been born free, he in England, she at St. Andrew's, N.B. He was said to be a Presbyterian preacher, with a "liberal education," when the best that any of his fellow passengers could boast in terms of schooling was a bare ability to read and write. No such ability was noted for Irene Stewart, suggesting that she was illiterate. The list also gave no inkling that she was White—she was counted as one of the Black emigrants.

The details about Wood and his wife were those that Wood himself had communicated to the Rev. John Brooke Pinney, a former governor of Liberia, a life director of the ACS, and corresponding secretary of the New York State Colonization Society. It was Pinney who had booked their passage. "I shall send on A.T. Wood & wife to go in the Liberia Packet," he had written from New York to the Rev. William McLain, ACS corresponding secretary in Washington, a week before the ship's scheduled 1 July sailing. A few days later, he supplied McLain with a sliver of information about his protégés: "My Man Wood who goes, was Educated at Stepney Theological School England and is quite intelligent. His wife is very fair—a native of New Brunswick and I should not like to swear she has a drop of African Blood in her veins. I fear for her

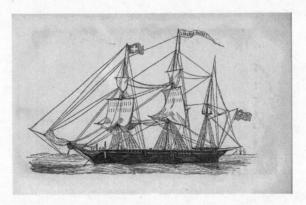

The barque *Liberia Packet*, on which the Woods sailed to Liberia in July 1850.
Above, a profile view of the ship. Below are top and cutaway views.
Wood and his wife were accommodated in the on-deck cabin, marked A.
(*Maryland Colonization Journal*, New Series, vol. 3, no. 16,
Oct. 1846, between pp. 248 and 249)

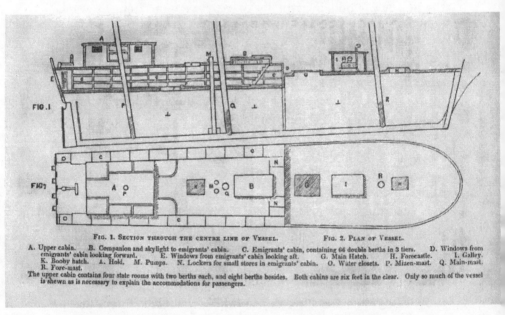

FIG. 1. SECTION THROUGH THE CENTRE LINE OF VESSEL.   FIG. 2. PLAN OF VESSEL.

A. Upper cabin.   B. Companion and skylight to emigrants' cabin.   C. Emigrants' cabin, containing 66 double berths in 3 tiers.   D. Windows from emigrants' cabin looking forward.   E. Windows from emigrants' cabin looking aft.   G. Main Hatch.   H. Forecastle.   I. Galley.   K. Booby hatch.   L. Hold.   M. Pumps.   N. Lockers for small stores in emigrants' cabin.   O. Water closets.   P. Mizen-mast.   Q. Main-mast.   R. Fore-mast.
The upper cabin contains four state rooms with two berths each, and eight berths besides. Both cabins are six feet in the clear. Only so much of the vessel is shewn as is necessary to explain the accommodations for passengers.

considerably and hope she & he will have as good accommodations
as the vessel will afford."

It is easy to picture who did the talking when Wood and his
wife met Pinney. Irene Stewart was no doubt well out of earshot
when the men got down to business. Honey-tongued Wood let the

Presbyterian Pinney believe that he, too, was Presbyterian, trained for the ministry not at Anglican Oxford but at essentially Baptist Stepney Academy at Stepney Green in East London; and he did not tell Pinney straight out that his wife was a White resident of Maine, but let him think that she was "nearly white," as noted in the margin of Pinney's letter, and a British subject from New Brunswick. Wood, of course, had reason to avoid mention of Maine; and as he sought to cadge a free ride from the ACS for his wife as well as for himself, it simplified matters to have her pass for not-quite-White, an eligible colored emigrant.

Back in Maine, Marcus Keep had alleged that Wood was eager to marry a White woman, as though this were a step calculated to help him fulfill some career ambition. The kind of benefit Wood could hope to draw from marrying White becomes clearer in his dealings with Pinney, even as he now appears to be toning down the whiteness of his prize bride. To him, it is worth an unquestionable free ticket to let Pinney go on thinking that she is a shade less White than she looks. At the same time, Pinney is struck by her pale complexion; her fair countenance stirs in him a concern for her welfare, a concern he clearly would not have felt had she looked "colored." He worries that this flower is too delicate to survive in tropical Africa. To smooth her passage there, he books a state room for her and her husband in the on-deck cabin at a cost of $100 each, rather than make them lie with the bulk of the $40 emigrants sardined in the three tiers of double bunks below. So, a free ride it is, and first-class, for the Woods.

Chalk up another success for the "ethiopian." When he had landed in Maine in 1846, he had been hired as a preacher. Hounded out of that state in September 1849, he had moved to Massachusetts and, within months, waltzed into a job as pastor of Boston's landmark Black Baptist church. Disgraced there in May 1850, he had decamped to New York City, and by early July, he and his wife were off to Africa at the ACS's expense. The man knew how to make his way in the world.

Tropical Africa would have been the worst destination Wood could have picked, had there been any truth to the yarn he had spun for Jeremiah Hacker about the climate of the West Indies having so impaired his health as to oblige him to abandon his mission work there some years before. In fact, the move to Liberia was inspired: He would put as much distance as possible between him and his recent misadventures, moving to a land whose equatorial setting he would find exotic but whose settler society would be familiar, with its American habits, language, and culture, minus the lethal prejudice against Blacks. Chances are the infant republic would welcome a man of his talents, and his past would be a thing of the past.

Colonization, the effort to resettle African Americans in Liberia, was the subject of a running propaganda war between the ACS and Abolitionists. The society operated on the premise that there was one thing the can-do U.S. could *not* do, and that was, accept the equality of Blacks and Whites. To those of its members who opposed slavery, this was regrettable but true; to those who favored slavery, it was a self-evident truth with nothing regrettable about it. The U.S. was seen as a White man's land whose critical problem was that, from its great pool of Black slaves, ever-growing numbers of free Blacks were emerging who were not wanted and never would be, and never could attain equal status with Whites. This view, coupled with the society's official hands-off policy on slavery, not to mention the support it needed and received from many slave-owners, made it anathema to die-hard anti-slavery activists and advocates of equal rights who believed that their country could and should be made to live up to its ideals of universal liberty, equality and justice. If Blacks were the victims of a poisoned legal, political and social system, the remedy was clear—get rid of the poison, not the victims.

In short, hard-line Abolitionists favored integration and deplored the emigration of Blacks as a move that sapped anti-slavery ranks at home. Colonizationists viewed integration as impossible and/or undesirable, and presented the assisted removal of the country's free Black population as a measure in the best interests of the Blacks themselves, the U.S. and Africa. Liberia, the colony founded by the ACS as a refuge for this unwanted population, "symbolized an alternative to racial integration in America," as historian Tom Schick has written. In other words, it was an expression of, and a testament to, American negrophobia.

In 1821, the ACS had begun acquiring lands on the west coast of Africa to serve as the new home of Black Americans. Would they go willingly? Slave or free, Blacks in the U.S. had absorbed the values and ideals of a Christian, Anglo-Saxon, republican America, and were attached to their homeland as much as Whites, however demeaned and abused they felt there. This had at least two significant impacts on the colonization movement. One was that it found relatively few willing Blacks, as can be seen from the fact that Wood and his fellow passengers brought to only 7,034 the total number of ACS emigrants sent to Liberia in 30 years. Of those, many had had little choice—they were slaves freed by their masters on condition that they accept a one-way ticket to Liberia. More Black Americans, slave and free, fled north to Canada, which was not ideal, but closer to home—you could get there and back on foot—and formally more *free* than home was. The other consequence was that, as those who emigrated to Liberia carried their values with them, most were, like Christian Whites, primed to look down on native Africans as "heathen savages." This attitude, mirroring the prevailing view in the Americas of Blacks as inferior, dovetailed with one of the ACS's main arguments in favor of colonization—that American Blacks, unwanted at home, could serve to civilize and Christianize Africa. Opponents of colonization had an easy time pointing out the hypocrisy of this view. A population that was considered a curse at home was supposed to constitute a blessing for Africa? Negroes who supposedly could not measure up as Americans in their native land were to be given the task of Americanizing Africa? As Richard Allen, founding bishop of the African Methodist Episcopal (AME) Church, put it in a letter to *Freedom's Journal,* the first African-American newspaper, in 1827: "We are an unlettered people, brought up in ignorance; not one in a hundred can read or write; not one in a thousand has a liberal education. Is there any fitness for such to be sent into a far country, among Heathens, to convert or civilize them; when they themselves are neither *civilized* nor *christianized?*"

Foreigners, not to mention many of the native Africans in the area, challenged the right of Liberia, a private venture and not a colony of the United States, to regulate and tax their trade and commerce on its shores. As a result, the private colony of Americo-Liberians, with the backing of the ACS, declared its independence in 1847 and quickly secured its recognition as a sovereign country by major powers England and France (racial realities in the U.S. meant that that country withheld official recognition until 1862). Liberia's ties with the ACS, on which it depended for support, remained close. And the new country's attitudes towards its population, as reflected in its Declaration of Independence and its constitution, remained essentially those of American colonizers practising a brand of exclusive democracy: "We, the people of the Republic of Liberia, were originally inhabitants of the United States of North America," the Declaration of Independence stated. The logic of independence dictated that "We, the people" exclude native Africans: Mistreated in their home country, these expatriate American democrats were not about to submit to rule by a majority made up of pagan natives or anyone else, hence the denial of voting rights to Africans. The same logic dictated the exclusion of Whites. The constitution was explicit on this point: "The great object of forming these colonies being to provide a home for the dispersed and oppressed children of Africa, and to regenerate and enlighten this benighted continent, none but persons of color shall be admitted to citizenship in this Republic."

• • •

Wood seems to have taken the Liberian plunge on the fly. He would undoubtedly have remained in Boston had his cover not been blown. Fleeing to New York and finding himself at loose ends, perhaps it was a meeting in a church there on 17 June 1850 that gave him the idea. At that "Meeting of Colored People to hear Statements about Liberia," two Americo-Liberian settlers had painted a heartening picture of their adopted country as a place that, while no bed of roses, offered Blacks the "greatest gift, a *free country*. Our own race are in *power* and *honor*. [...] We are a free and independent State, having a Constitution and Bill of Rights, like that of the

United States. We do our own voting, while you in most of this country do not." Perhaps Wood had also heard that Pinney's New York colonization society had just given the ACS $1,500 to cover the fare of 30 emigrants on the next sailing of the *Liberia Packet.* As it turned out, Wood and his wife were the only so-called residents of New York State to sail off on the ship that summer.

By the end of June, the *Liberia Packet's* 1 July departure had been postponed for two days because of delays in the delivery of cargo. Wood and his wife were instructed to leave New York for Baltimore on 1 July, a Monday. Late-arriving passengers further detained the ship. She sailed at last on Thursday, 4 July, but no sooner had she left Baltimore than a crew member came down with smallpox. Captain George L. Howe ordered his ship into Hampton Roads, Va., where the ailing seaman was put ashore, passengers were vaccinated and other necessary sanitary measures were taken to ensure that the crossing would be pox-free.

ACS secretary McLain had hurried to Virginia from Washington on 10 July to see to the sanitary arrangements and the welfare of the emigrants. As if the costly delays and smallpox were not enough of a headache, a new crisis cropped up on 17 July. "Dear Sir," captain Howe wrote to McLain, "I wish to have you Come onboard for Such work as there is here I cant have on this Ship as Wood got to beating his wife and he must go onshore or Stop fighting. I want you to come onboard anyhow."

All was evidently not well between Wood and his wife. We can easily imagine that he was keen to be off to Africa, his wife less so, perhaps not at all. But separating man and wife by putting one ashore could not be justified, although Howe's note shows that the possibility was raised. There was no point in removing Wood from the ship while keeping his wife aboard if she had little or no interest in going to Africa, and leaving her behind to fend for herself would not do, either. It was a ticklish problem, but somehow the crisis was resolved. No one was left behind. Rather than losing a passenger, the ship gained one, the delays making it possible for straggler Robert Wood, a carpenter from Antigua, to come aboard. On 24 July, the *Liberia Packet* and its now 56 passengers finally set off across the Atlantic.

McLain reported Wood's abusive treatment of his wife to Pinney. "I regret to hear of Wood's bad treatment of his white wife," the latter responded (now apparently clear that Irene Stewart was as White as she looked). "Had I anticipated such thing his case would have been very different. I hope you wrote to influential quarters as to his character & conduct."

Once more, Wood had burned his bridges. Pinney was the one person involved in the organization of the expedition who had formed a favorable opinion of him. McLain did not hold Wood in high esteem, nor did captain Howe. Dr. James Hall, business manager of the Maryland State Colonization Society, founder and first governor of the colony of Maryland in Liberia, and a life director of the ACS like Pinney and McLain, had been less than impressed when he met him at Baltimore. In writing to McLain about annoyances he had faced in getting the tardy Robert Wood from Baltimore to Hampton Roads, he observed: "His name is Wood & I begin to fear he is of the same character as Pinney's Wood." This was before "Pinney's Wood" had been caught abusing his wife. Something in his manner had clearly rubbed Hall and McLain the wrong way.

No further unpleasantness marred the voyage. The emigrants reached Monrovia, the Liberian capital, on 28 August. "Among the passengers are Rev. Mr. Wood & lady from New Brunswick," the *Liberia Herald* reported in announcing the ship's arrival. This

"View of Monrovia from the Anchorage." Print by an unknown artist based on a daguerreotype, now lost, by Augustus Washington. (*Twenty-Fourth Annual Report of the Board of Managers of the New-York State Colonization Society,* 1856, p. 30)

innocent salute displeased Wood, and the paper was duly apologetic in a later issue:

> *Correction.* – We correct with pleasure an error, to which our attention has been called in the list of passengers by the Liberia Packet, published in our last.
>
> Rev. Dr. Wood and Lady are from England, and not from New Brunswick, as we had stated. Dr. Wood was born in St. Mary's, London, and left Liverpool for the United States via New Brunswick in 1848, at which latter place he remained only a short time.

Few people would have thought such a slip in the press worth correcting; fewer still would have produced a correction that was such a fabrication.

For the first time, Wood styled himself "Dr.," pretending to hold a doctorate of divinity. This was brazen self-aggrandizement on the part of someone who believed himself a man of deep learning, or fit to pass for one. It was also a self-promotion calculated to awe: Which mere mortal could stand up to a godly man of such eminence? Yet by claiming to be "Rev. Wood, D.D.," Wood was also tempting fate. Blacks had trouble gaining access to basic schooling, let alone to institutions of higher learning—and he held a doctorate? Close questioning might have punctured that balloon.

His alleged trip out from England to North America was now quite a different story than it had been back in Maine. The stated year of his departure, 1848, was patently false. He himself had written from the jail at Machias the previous year that he had left England in February 1846. Even if we do not credit that claim, we do know that he had been at work in Maine since the fall of 1846. His revised account also makes no mention of a shipwreck off Nova Scotia. Now he says he had been bound for the United States via New Brunswick all along. And where precisely had he been headed in the United States? The "correction," of course, made not the slightest reference to Maine or Massachusetts, reducing the risk that someone—an Asa Cummings, say—might connect the dots between Liberian Wood and New England Wood. Cummings, the first newspaper editor to publish Wood's imposture, and still in charge of the *Christian Mirror* (he was to die in 1856), was a life member of the ACS. Had he spotted the name A.T.

Wood in one of the society's publications or in news reports from
Liberia, he might have raised a stink. But now, the smoke screen
thickened: Even Wood's Baileyville wife was said to be, like him,
a native of England. Reports reaching the U.S. of the *Liberia
Packet*'s safe arrival at Monrovia noted: "She carried out fifty-six
passengers, among whom were the Rev. Mr. Wood and lady, of
Liverpool."

Besides tending to his image, Wood moved quickly to find a
paying job. As the Rev. A.T. Wood, D.D., he was not about to seek
menial work and rely on his skills with hammer and saw, as he had
done in Maine. Yet, in the words of prominent Virginia-born
Liberian nationalist Hilary Teage, a Baptist preacher, politician,
writer and former editor of the *Liberia Herald,* that was precisely
what the new republic needed. "We need help in the shape of an
increased population," he advised McLain of the ACS. "You cannot give us too many *working* men—Men of the hoe, plane, axe,
&c." Wood did not fill the bill: "Send us modest men not boast-
ers—working men, not office seekers—Sensible men, not stupid
pedants. We have one Doctor of Divinity out here now in the person of A.T. Wood. He is enough for all Africa." Teage raised a
pointed question: "May I take the liberty to ask what it is in
Mr. Wood that Mr. Pinney should distinguish him with a Cabin
passage[?]" Pinney might have blushed to answer that.

Wood's arrival in Monrovia was as timely as his move to
Boston had been. The Providence Baptist Church, established in
1822 as Liberia's first Christian church, needed a pastor. A few
months earlier, the Foreign Mission Board of the fledgling
Southern Baptist Convention in the U.S., which in 1846 had
undertaken to evangelize Liberia, had noted of Monrovia in its
annual report: "The church at this place is highly respectable for
numbers and influence, and those [though?] supplied with preaching, was, when last heard from, without a pastor. The Board have
arranged to assist them in the support of a competent man, to be
chosen by themselves, who shall take the oversight of them; also
to aid in the establishment of a permanent school." Within a
month of his arrival, Wood was confirmed as pastor of this
church, housed since 1839 in its landmark stone building on Broad

Street. Writing to ACS secretary McLain, Henry M. Williams, a young teacher from Cincinnati who had sailed to Monrovia on the *Liberia Packet* with the Woods, reported: "I visited the different churches, on last Sabbath [29 Sept.], and found them doing very well indeed. We had a very interesting sermon in the afternoon at the Baptist church, delivered by the Rev. Mr. Wood, who came over with us."

Wood's appointment was cheering to some fellow Baptist missionaries stationed in Liberia. "I have the pleasure of informing you of the election of the Rev. Alfred T. Wood pastor of the Providence Baptist church, Monrovia," John H. Cheeseman wrote to the head of the Baptist Foreign Mission Board. "He is said to be a graduate of Cambridge College, England, and by birth an Englishman, but of African parents. I hope he will be useful." Robert E. Murray observed just as hopefully: "Dr. A.T. Wood, the pastor of the Providence Baptist church, will, I trust, be the instrument, in the hands of God, of building up this church."

Here then was Wood who, having had his passage to Africa paid by the ACS, now became a paid agent of the Southern Baptist Convention, that is, of the U.S. Baptist churches who, refusing to wholly renounce slavery, had parted ways in 1845 with their Northern colleagues. That is not to say that Wood was a traitor to his race, or pro-slavery. He was an impostor, always, even to his wife. His concern was not to express his beliefs or share confidences and opinions, but to invent and sustain as best he could a character called A.T. Wood. He cut his cloth to suit the changing stages on which he played. He was a weathercock and a cheat, and few could have approved of that, had they known, but no settlers in Liberia would have faulted him for his associations. Most of them had immigrated under ACS auspices, believing they would find in Liberia the status and fulfillment they despaired of finding in North America. One of them, North Carolina-born Rev. John Day, a drafter of Liberia's constitution and no friend to slavery, was superintendent of the country's Southern Baptist missions.

So, Wood's impersonation of a doctor of divinity paid off. As he had done in Boston, he found a conveniently vacant pastoral post to slip into. And there was this icing on his Liberian cake:

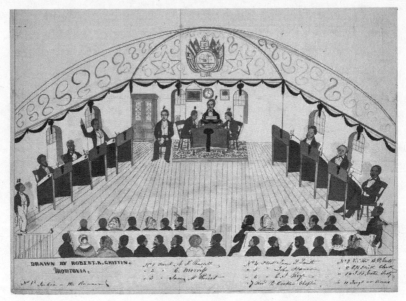

The Liberian senate in 1856. As chaplain of the senate in 1850-1851,
Wood would have occupied the seat of No. 7, to the right
of the vice-president, who acted as Speaker.
(Library of Congress, Prints and Photographs, LC-USZC4-4908)

When the legislature convened on 2 December, Dr. Wood was
appointed chaplain to the Senate.

He was fortunate not to be utterly undone by malaria, the
"acclimating fever" that beset almost all newcomers from temper-
ate zones on their arrival. Irene Stewart was not so lucky. "The
Rev. Dr. Wood ... has lost his wife," Dr. Henry J. Roberts of Monrovia
informed the ACS in a letter written at the end of December. The
precise date or cause of her death is not known; all we know is that
she died in Liberia about a year and a half after she had married
Wood. Word probably never got back to Baileyville.

5. HIRED AND FIRED SIGHT UNSEEN

Just before Christmas 1850, Wood fired off a peevish letter to Pinney, his erstwhile sponsor in New York. It was a childish, taunting, sticks-and-stones production. Sensing a threat in "rumors" he had heard about his mistreatment of his wife aboard the *Liberia Packet,* he lashed out, flashing his claws to show that if others could share damaging information about him, he was not above fighting back by spreading stories of his own, truth be damned:

> To day I heard rumors of a letter which you wrote to W.H. Ellis [i.e., H.W. Ellis] in relation to what McLain wrote you, which is all a downright Lie—there never was a word of dispute between myself & wife the whole voyage. McLain ought have wrote you of the cursed plot between himself & Capt How [*sic*], to rob me of my wife, and to carry her back to Norfolk Va. while laying in Hampton Roads. I frustrated their designs by taking a pair of new Pistols, loaded them in the presence of both McLain and Howe, and placed them in my pockets without saying a word. Their Hellish designs were made known to me through Mr. Smith mate—at a dead hour of the night.
>
> He also told I did not perform service on board, this is true, for this reason. I had a severe cough (you know) when I left and finding How wanted to take liberties with my wife I could as soon thought of preaching in Hell, as on board that Packet. Now Sir I am happy I had nothing to do with Mr. Ellis So you have not done me the injury you intended.
>
> A.T. Wood

Whatever Pinney, McLain, and Harrison W. Ellis, pastor of Monrovia's First Presbyterian Church, may have said about him in their letters, his outburst was inexcusable, as coarse in tone as it was undignified in content. He had heard that their exchange concerned his abuse of his late wife aboard the *Liberia Packet,* and here he was attempting to deflect blame by accusing others of worse behavior. His intimations that captain Howe had lusted after his wife, and that Howe and McLain had plotted to steal her from him, are the stuff of low melodrama. If Howe had had designs on Mrs. Wood, wouldn't he have preferred to keep her on board? If Howe and McLain had spoken of taking her off the ship, it was for her own protection, to get her away from her abusive husband. But Dr. Wood coated a kernel of fact with a gloss of impure fiction. This was his way with the truth.

He boasted of having put a stop to this sorry episode by pointedly loading two pistols in the presence of Howe and McLain, in a "Make my day!" show of bravado. As if Howe would have tolerated such threatening conduct from anyone on his ship! As if he and McLain would have brooked such an attempt at intimidation from a man Howe had been ready to toss overboard before Wood had made any threats. In writing as he did to Pinney, Wood had shot himself in the foot, although he would not feel the full effect of the shot for some time.

Not content with keeping his calumnies to his private correspondence, Wood spread the tale around Monrovia. "A.T. Wood has reported something here not very creditable to you," Hilary Teage informed McLain. "I have written it to Mr. Pinney. You have my authority to ask for the extract from my letter. Many here are inclined to believe him, because his wife was *White.*" Without lifting a finger, Irene Stewart served him well when she was alive, as she did from beyond the grave.

McLain and Pinney could have tried to check Wood's budding Liberian career then and there, but at what cost? He had shown that he was quite willing to go public and he had given them a taste of the mud he was prepared to sling. The outcome of an unseemly public scrap was foreseeable—sympathy for the recently bereaved pastor, a black eye for the ACS and its representatives, with the hoots of Abolitionists ringing in their ears. Under the circumstances, best to keep their mouths shut.

What was it that Rev. X had said about Wood in that Maine newspaper article—that he had plenty of guile and self-regard, but precious little wisdom? If that estimation of his character had been left largely unsubstantiated in 1848–1849, by 1851 Wood had done his best to confirm it, as well as Rev. Keep's reading of him as a latter-day Tartuffe exhibiting signs of "moral baseness."

As regards his church, the illusionist in him made it appear that his arrival on the scene had called forth a new dawn. "Many grievous things which have long retarded the prosperity of the church, are now removed and the spirit of love and labor have already begun to be seen," he wrote to the Southern Baptist mission board. "It is to be regretted that a school has not long since been established here, under the Baptist supervision. We hope ere long to commence one; if so, we shall need your cooperation."

If McLain and Pinney were unwilling to expose Wood publicly, many others who had crossed his path could have put a stop to his masquerade, if only they had scrutinized his "documents," made an effort to verify his pronouncements, or compared notes. It is dismaying to think, for instance, that Jeremiah Hacker, his champion back in Maine, seemed to have been unaware of the charges levelled at Wood in various newspapers there. In Boston, the *Liberator* had copied from the *Pleasure Boat* Wood's second letter from jail. His plight had been judged newsworthy, but no one at the *Liberator* recognized the name A.T. Wood when he turned up a few months later to be selected—and quickly deselected—as pastor of Boston's First African Baptist Church. Abolitionists, Colonizationists, churchmen and Black activists in general seem to have taken no serious note of the Boston episode, and of the announcement published in the *Liberator* of Wood's exposure and sacking. His reputation as a charlatan did not follow him. The impostor who had claimed in Maine to have received an Oxford education, and, in New York, to have studied at London's "Stepney Theological School," was able to present himself in Liberia not only as a graduate of "Cambridge College," but as a doctor of divinity. Fortunately for him, the newspapers that had pointed the finger at him generally had small circulations, the Abolitionist press spoke mainly to the converted, and any exchange of correspondence between officials of the ACS that impugned him went unpublished.

Still, any number of persons in Liberia could have tripped him up. A Hilary Teage, sniping at him from the first, might have caught him out had he looked beyond the D.D.'s self-important airs, and questioned the provenance of his improbable degree. Harrison Ellis, the Presbyterian pastor and former slave, might also have seen through Wood, given the chance. As a blacksmith in the Southern states, Ellis, the slave, had taught himself not only to read English and write it well, but also Latin, Greek, and the rudiments of Hebrew, all from a desire to plumb the Bible. On his arrival in Liberia in 1847, "the learned black blacksmith," as he was called, had set out to learn two African languages to help him in his ministry, when many other missionaries presumed to get by on English alone. A few minutes in Wood's company might have raised doubts in Ellis's mind as to the depths of the doctor's learning. But as Wood had written to Pinney, "I am happy I had nothing to do with Mr. Ellis." Happy was not the word; relieved was more like it.

Another who could have seen through the smoke that Wood blew was African-born British consul Augustus William Hanson. It is impossible to look at Hanson and not see in him the sophisticated character Wood aspired to play, the man he could have been had he focused his considerable talents and energies on being who he pretended to be.

Born at Accra, on the Gold Coast (Ghana), in July 1815, Hanson was the son of prominent British-African merchant John William Hanson, commandant at Accra from 1835 until his death in 1840, and his wife Margaret, a daughter of the Asante king Osei Kwame. Lured to the U.S. in 1837 by the promise of a job that did not work out, and strapped for funds in Salem, Mass., Hanson unburdened himself to William Lloyd Garrison in a long letter, a little too prim and prolix, from which we at least learn something of his background and of the culture shock he experienced on first reaching North America. Here is a taste:

> I am by birth an African, but of English descent—my father being a subject of Great Britain: my mother was a daughter of one of the petty sovereigns of the country. I was born in the British settlement of Accra, on the Western Coast of Africa. I was sent, at a very early

age, to England, where I received my education, in Reading, in the County of Berkshire. Since the completion of my education in 1827, I have resided with my father, transacting business with and for him: he carries on extensive commerce with the country [the African interior] and with England.

... [On reaching America] I was recognized immediately the vessel got to the wharf by a Mr. Sims, whom I had met several times on the coast of Africa, as super-cargo of a brig. I felt pleased, nay gratified by this circumstance; but judge Sir, *if possible,* of my feelings, when another person stepped to Mr. Sims, when I thought (I may have been deceived, but I thought) I heard him ask, 'What do you speak to that *nigger* for?' ... I was at that time totally ignorant—oh, how profoundly ignorant, of the existence of this groundless prejudice against people of our unfortunate color. ... [Once the realities of the color line were explained to him,] had a thunderbolt descended from the clouds, it could not have amazed me more. In England, I had enjoyed all the same privileges, without the least distinction, with others in the same station of society; and there I was taught to respect a man for his manners and moral character, and not his color.

In little time, the young man from Accra with the English accent, whose penmanship was "elegant" and whose business sense was, according to Garrison, "of the first order," found himself in New York City, hired by Black activist David Ruggles as agent for his new Abolitionist magazine, the *Mirror of Liberty,* and addressing antislavery meetings. In August 1838, he was appointed financial agent of the New York Vigilance Committee, dedicated to protecting Blacks from slave-catchers and their ilk. He also lectured on Africa, and took an active part in the temperance movement. By the spring of 1839, he had moved to Hartford, Conn., to study for the Episcopal (Anglican) priesthood. He played some small part in the *Amistad* case, being consulted on the language spoken by some of the Africans seized from that Cuban slave ship in 1839. Five of those Africans attended the missionary convention that Hanson was instrumental in organizing at Hartford in August 1841. At last, on 10 July 1842, he was ordained at Hartford's Christ Church.

Rev. A.W. Hanson then quit the U.S., returning to England, to be appointed in the spring of 1843 chaplain to Cape Coast Castle,

Monrovia's Providence Baptist Church, the oldest church in Liberia,
turned 200 years old in 2021, the year this protograph was posted
online. Wood was named pastor here in September 1850.
(ChristianAfrica.org. Illustration for article by Gerald C. Koynieneh
of *Front Page Africa* posted on 25 February 2021)

one of the old British forts and former slave-trading posts of the
Gold Coast. That same year, under the auspices of the British and
Foreign Bible Society, he published a translation of the gospels of
Matthew and John into the Ga language from ancient Greek.
Three years later, he was made chaplain of all "Her Majesty's Forts
and Settlements on the Gold Coast."

It was his next appointment that saw his path cross Wood's.
On 23 August 1850, he was named British consul at Monrovia, the
first diplomatic representative of any country posted to the new
republic and the first Black diplomat in Britain's service. He
turned heads at the Foreign Office in London when he called there
in October. The London *Times* reported:

A POLISHED GENTLEMAN OF COLOUR. – We understand that
Government have just appointed a gentleman of colour to the office
of British Consul at Liberia. This is, we believe, the first instance on
record in which a man of colour has received a similar appointment
from our Government. On the introduction of the new British

Consul, on Friday last [Oct. 18], at the Foreign Office, his personal appearance excited no inconsiderable interest. He is a man of superior intelligence and of highly polished exterior.

Rev. Consul Hanson, as he came to be known, reached Liberia in November. Americo-Liberians welcomed his appointment as not only a sure sign of their country's acceptance as a sovereign nation, but of the friendship of a powerful ally.

Fate placed Wood and Hanson in Monrovia at the same time. They were about the same age, both in their thirties (Hanson was born 25 July 1815), both outsiders who had spent a few years in the U.S. The one pretended to be an Englishman, the other was an Englishman by descent and nine years of schooling. One was a self-styled minister with a counterfeit degree, the other an ordained Anglican cleric. One apparently claimed to have translated the Bible into several languages, with no evidence to show for it; the other published a recognized translation of two books of the New Testament into his native African tongue. One who would not, or could not, be himself made deception his life's work; the other was who he was, less than perfect perhaps, but himself.

Apart from one known meeting between them in June 1851, it is impossible to say precisely what were the relations between Wood and Hanson in Monrovia, then a city of at most 1,500 inhabitants. They had at least official contacts. Hanson would later state that he had seen Wood often, perhaps even daily, that he knew him as Dr. Wood, pastor of the Baptist church and chaplain of the Liberian senate, and that he had signed his name "Alfred T. Wood, D.D., in my office, to public documents." There had never been any conflict between them—"on the contrary, he [Wood] knows that I have done him kindness."

The Foreign Mission Board of the Southern Baptist Convention announced Wood's appointment as its man in Monrovia in its annual report of May 1851. "This being the seat of government, and the largest town in Liberia, the Board have been for some time desirous of extending aid to enable the church to sustain an efficient pastor, who should be wholly devoted to the ministry. They have at length secured the services of Brother A.T. Wood, who is believed to be well qualified for this position." The board also disclosed that it had sent Wood funds to set up a school.

Perhaps as a result of the dissemination of this report, some persons finally did compare notes on Wood. At a meeting of the mission board in Richmond, Va., on 9 July, "Brother William Crane enclosed a copy of a letter of objectionable tone and spirit written by A.T. Wood, missionary of the Board at Monrovia, to Rev. Mr. Pinney." This was the petulant letter Wood had sent to Pinney the previous December. On looking into the matter, the board was advised by Rev. Spencer Houghton Cone of the First Baptist Church in New York City, who had been for many years head of the American and Foreign Bible Society, that Wood was not to be trusted. As a result, the board cut off its support of Wood that August.

Hired and fired sight unseen, Wood was unaware of what was passing at headquarters. The board was equally ignorant of what he was up to. Before the investigation of his conduct had even begun, he had left Liberia.

As recently as 6 May, he had written the board asking for a supply of hymn books, promising that "I will take charge of them, make the Sales, and remit you the proceeds." It would have taken months, perhaps a year or more, for his order to reach its destination, for the books to be shipped and for him to dispose of them, and collect and remit payments. Yet little more than a month after placing his order, he was knocking at Hanson's door, seeking letters of introduction to persons in England. And when the English barque *Clydeside,* J. White master, left Monrovia for Liverpool on 20 June, laden with palm oil, camwood and other African goods, it carried two passengers—"Rev. A.T. Wood and lady."

6. THERE WILL ALWAYS BE AN ENGLAND

Wood was to spend the next sixteen months begging, ostensibly for his church, and another eighteen months paying for it. He may have been inspired to go a-fundraising in England by the Rev. Elie Worthington Stokes, an itchy-footed American Episcopalian who had landed in Liberia in 1850, a few months ahead of him. They would have met in Monrovia, where Wood was chaplain to the Senate, and Stokes's newly organized St. Paul's Church met for worship in the Senate chamber until it could afford to erect its own building. It was to seek funds for this church project that Stokes set off for Ireland and Britain in the spring of 1851.

Stokes had hit up the British public before. In August 1847, as rector of Christ Church, a Black Episcopalian congregation in Providence, R.I., he had gone off on a year-and-a-half canvassing tour of the British Isles, seeking £500 ($2,000) to pay off the debt of his church. With the support of his own bishop and of the Anglican Church in Britain, from the Archbishop of Canterbury down, his canvassing trip had been a breeze. No wonder, then, that in 1851, once more in need of funds, he looked to Britain. The exact date of his departure is not known, but by late July he was preaching in Belfast. (He may have let his ambitions show—a Belfast paper referred to him as the "Bishop Elect of Liberia," when he was nothing of the sort.) With the Anglican hierarchy smoothing his path, he once again found donations pouring in. By the summer of 1852, he had collected the needed funds, and he returned to Liberia. Wood's progress would never be so smooth.

The *Clydeside* was bound for Liverpool, and this appears to be where Wood and his wife disembarked, at the end of August 1851. That would mean that it took the ship slightly more than two months to reach England. Hanson had made it from London to Monrovia in less than a month when he was appointed consul in 1850. Wood himself was later to claim that he had landed at Plymouth, on the south coast of England, and travelled to London by land before heading north to Liverpool. He was even to say that he had been arrested at both Plymouth and London, which hardly was to his credit, unless he meant it as evidence of persecution. The problem, of course, is that he cannot be trusted; his account may have been no more than a fiction cooked up to mask his enforced idleness in the fall of 1851. George Wright, a partner in the firm that owned the ship, later stated: "He [Wood] arrived at Liverpool in the autumn of 1851. He arrived in the barque 'Clyde-side,' Captain White. ... There was a person in his company said to be his wife. He called upon me and stated that he was the passenger in the 'Clyde-side'."

Wood wasted no time in wading into hot water. At the beginning of October, he was jailed for debt at Lancaster, a fact he later tried to conceal. How he had fallen afoul of the law so quickly is not known. (And he would have us believe that he had already spent time under arrest in Plymouth and London!) To the Court for Relief of Insolvent Debtors, then to the County Court of Lancashire, he was "Alfred Thomas Wood, formerly of Broad-street, in the city of Monrovia, Western Africa, Pastor of the Providence Independent Church, afterwards a lodger at No. 38, Watling-street, in the city of London, and late a lodger in Sussex-street, Liverpool, Lancashire, a Missionary from the said Church, and Agent." This would seem to confirm his account of the overland route he had followed in England, but the courts' identification of him is no sure guide because it clearly came from him, the giveaway being the name of his church in Monrovia, altered from Providence *Baptist* Church to Providence *Independent*. There was no Providence Independent Church in Monrovia. The name was one of Wood's fictions. In the United Kingdom, he tailored his religious affiliation to suit his purpose, as he had done in Maine. As he toured the country soliciting funds, introducing himself as the pastor of an "Independent," or simply "Protestant," church helped to broaden his appeal beyond Baptist circles, though he

LANCASTER CASTLE.

Lancaster Castle. Wood, just landed in England, was jailed
here for debt in October-November 1851.
(*Illustrated London News,* vol. 17, no. 445, 7 September 1850, p. 212)

may not have realized at first that in England, "Independent" sig-
nified Congregationalist. He would, in any case, present himself
"in different places as an episcopalian, an independent and a baptist, according to circumstances."

With her husband broke and imprisoned through October, this
second Mrs. Wood, a stepdaughter of Liberia's Collector of
Customs, James Cephas Minor, must have felt rather forlorn and
anxious, and her living accommodations cannot have been the
best. She frequently visited Wood in jail in Lancaster Castle.
Interned on 7 October, he was freed on 7 November. She died on
12 December, married less than a year. Poor woman. Hers was an
even shorter marriage than Irene Stewart's. Like Wood's first wife,
his second died far from home, a few months after he had whisked
her out of her element into an alien world.

LOCAL INTELLIGENCE.

The Rev. Mr. Baynes will address the working classes on Sunday evening next at the Concert-hall.

The public are cautioned against a man of colour, representing himself as a clergyman from Liberia, who is seeking subscriptions. He has obtained certificates from several clergymen under false representations.

This newspaper points the finger at Wood, though it does not name him. (*Liverpool Mercury,* 23 March 1852, p. 4)

A month in debtors' prison and the loss of his wife (never mind his other claimed incarcerations) made for a decidedly rocky start to Wood's conquest of England. More trouble lay around the corner. Rather than stick to his role of preacher, he sought to cast himself as also a commercial "agent." His agency activities led to his arrest in Liverpool early in the new year, on the complaint of Manchester merchant John Pender, of John Pender & Co. A detective escorted Wood back to Manchester to face the music. The *Guardian* newspaper reported:

At the Borough Court, on Monday [2 February], a man of colour named Alfred Wood, was charged with having obtained £15, the property of a mercantile house in Manchester, by means of false pretences. A gentleman stated that he was a partner in the firm, and that on Friday forenoon [30 January] the prisoner called at their office. He presented a letter of introduction, purporting to be signed by Mr. Roberts, the president of the republic of Liberia, which stated him to be a respectable man and worthy of credit; and asked witness to advance him a small sum of money to pay for some goods which he was sending to Liberia by a vessel which was about to sail in a short time. The letter of introduction was believed to be genuine, and £15 was advanced to the prisoner. The firm were afterwards applied to by a person in Manchester, to know whether they had any minute information respecting the prisoner. They in consequence wrote to Liverpool, and were informed by some friends there that Wood was an impostor. – Mr. Chief-superintendent [Richard] Beswick stated that, on Saturday, the last witness and Mr. [Thomas] Clegg called upon him, and stated that the prisoner had received from the firm £15, and had ordered from Mr. Clegg a large quantity of goods to go to Liberia, and that they had reason to believe that he was an impostor. Finding that the prisoner had gone to Liverpool, he (Mr. Beswick) sent Sub-inspector Neaves to apprehend him. – Sub-inspector Neaves stated that he apprehended the prisoner in Liverpool, and that after he was taken to the police office there, he found him endeavouring to tear up a letter, in consequence of which he (Neaves) took possession of all his papers. – Mr. Beswick stated that, when the prisoner was taken to the Manchester Town Hall, he said that he received the letter of introduction signed by Mr. Roberts while he was in Liverpool, but that he did not know from whom it had come. He also said that he had come from Liberia but a short time since, that he landed at Plymouth, and went from Plymouth to London, and thence to Liverpool. In Liverpool he had got goods to the value of £200. He had been in custody in Plymouth and London, and also at Lancaster. He was employed by a firm at Liberia called the Commercial Banking Co. which consisted of J.C. Minor, and Gill and Co.; and he expected them to send him some money to pay his accounts in a short time. He had shipped a quantity of goods in the Fire Fly and other vessels. He had been to many of the warehouses in Manchester. – The prisoner, in his defence, said that his tearing up of the paper at the Liverpool police-office was owing to his nervous system being affected in consequence of his having had the scarlet fever. – There being no evidence to prove that the document purporting to be a letter of introduction from President Roberts was not actually signed by him, the prisoner was dismissed. – When at the station-house, the prisoner stated that he was a minister connected with the independent Baptist church, and that he had preached in Hostley-street, London, and at Norwood Chapel, five miles from London. He also said that he had had other appointments to preach, but had been prevented by sickness from fulfilling them. In his possession was found a letter addressed to a Baptist minister in Manchester, and requesting that he would allow him (Woods) to preach in his chapel, as he wanted to raise £5 to take him back to Liberia. This letter was sealed, but had not been delivered. Wood's manner, while at the bar at the Borough Court, was such as to convey the impression that he has been used to speaking either as a native preacher, or in a similar capacity; as it closely resembled that of the coloured preachers who are frequently to be met with on our missionary platforms.

To any reasonable person, several of Wood's statements, as reported, would have sounded dubious, if not downright laughable, notably his feigned ignorance of how he had come by the letter of introduction from Liberian President John Jenkins Roberts, and his claim that in destroying evidence at the police station he

Virginia-born Joseph Jenkins Roberts, first president of the Republic of
Liberia 1848-1856. He visited England in the second half of 1852 while Wood
was canvassing there and in Ireland, but their paths did not cross.
(Library of Congress, Prints and Photographs, LC-DIG-pga-10949)

had acted under the effects of a nervous disorder brought on by
scarlet fever. But the *Guardian* report may not have been quite
accurate on these points. According to the *Manchester Courier* of
7 February, Wood claimed under questioning that he had received
the Roberts letter by mail in Plymouth; and if he had tried to tear
up his papers, including the letter from Roberts, at the Liverpool
police station, he had acted under the effects of "the shock his
nervous system had received through having recently lost his wife
by scarlet fever; he scarcely knew what he was doing." These
explanations, still highly dubious, were perhaps not as laughable
as those in the *Guardian* write-up.

Beyond that, the police and the court may have been stumped
in trying to untangle truth from falsehood in Wood's account,

especially as concerns his Liberian connections. Fortunately, we have a Monrovian witness of sorts to help us sort through the facts. Reproducing the *Guardian* article, the *Liberia Herald* of 6 April 1852 filled in some of the background and added choice comments of its own:

> The above slip from the "Manchester Guardian" was forwarded from England to a gentleman here, for the purpose, we presume, of enlightening the people of Liberia as to the character, and present employment, of the Alfred T. Wood formerly Pastor of the Providence Baptist Church in this place. The thanks of the community are due to the gentleman who so kindly forwarded this proof of Wood's fraudulent and criminal proceedings;– and it is our duty—we owe it to ourselves, as well as to the British public, to caution them against the fraudulent transactions of the said Wood. Wood came to this Country in 1850; he brought with him letters highly recommenda-tory; he said and so did his letters, that he was an Englishman, born in England,—that he was educated for the ministry and graduated at Cambridge.
>
> But that he felt it his duty to come to the "fatherland" & do what good he could by preaching the gospel. Very soon after his arrival here he was elected—yes! by the above named church. He had not associated with the church longer than nine months before he per-suaded it to let him go to England, where, he told them he could col-lect funds for its purpose. A majority of the members fell in with his views, and he left here in the bark "Clydeside" and safely arrived there, in Liverpool. We are positively assured that he obtained from here no letters of recommendation to persons, in England or else-where, unless, indeed, the authorization granted him by the Church, to receive donations for it, he construed as such. Nor had he any authority to draw for monies on any individual in Liberia, or on any church. Any monies or merchandize, that Wood may have received on documents purporting to be signed by any individual or individ-uals in Liberia are rank forgeries. Nor had Wood sent any merchan-dize to Liberia as stated by him before the "Borough Court"—nor has President Roberts written, or had written, or signed any letter recommending him or "stating him to be a respectable man and worthy of credit" nor is there in Liberia any such institution or firm as "Commercial Banking Co. consisting of J.C. Minor, and Gill and Co."—all such representations are false—and all documents pur-porting to sustain such declarations of Wood, are forgeries. Wood

left here, leaving unsettled several accounts—and owing several amounts of money, which he had obtained under promises faithfully made to reimburse. It is supposed, by many persons, that Wood obtained, while here, several sums of money under false pretences, but as he has written to a gentleman here, that he would pay all his accounts if bills are drawn on him for them, we say nothing about it. This may be some consolation to his creditors.

Had the prosecution produced an article of this tenor in the Manchester court before Wood's discharge, it still would not have constituted proof positive that the letter from President Roberts was a forgery. Outside of court, however, it stands as a pretty convincing refutation of the tale he told. By identifying him as "formerly" pastor of Providence Baptist Church, it seems to explode any claim that he was now legitimately soliciting funds for his church.

While Wood had presented himself in the U.S. and Liberia as an English-born graduate of a British institution of higher learning, he does not seem to have played this card in court. There was no mention of English roots or schooling, or of family connections in London, Liverpool or elsewhere, although the Belfast *Northern Whig,* copying the *Hull Advertiser,* later reported: "Though a man of colour, he [Wood] was born in London, within the sound of Bow-bells, and is really a British subject. His father was a West Indian." From the *Guardian* report, it appears that he claimed to be from Liberia, and there was said to be something of the "native preacher" about him. He appeared to be an alien, then, and he did not seek to establish his credibility by naming any rich relatives or acquaintances in England who could vouch for him, or by boasting of a diploma from an English institution. In fact, he seems to have dropped the honorific "Dr." and the "D.D." altogether at this stage.

There was no hint of social or educational pretensions, either, when he married again at Liverpool three days after his discharge by the court at Manchester. Wife No. 3, Frances Dales, was a farmer's daughter living in Sussex Street, the street where Wood was said to have lived before his imprisonment for debt the previous fall. Wood, identified in his marriage certificate as the son of farmer Theodore Wood, was now living in nearby Chester Street, an "Agent" by occupation, and a widower. He was no "agent" and no son of a Theodore Wood, but he was a widower: He had buried a wife less than two months before. He and Frances Dales married at the Anglican Church of St. James in the Parish of Walton-on-the-Hill (now St. James, Liverpool), a hop, skip and a jump from their respective homes.

Wood must have felt doubly relieved at his release by the court. Immediately, it meant that his wedding could proceed. In the long run, it also suggested that the authorities in England would find it difficult to bring him to book and prove that his Liberian papers were bogus. He was free again to go about his business. The thought must have struck him, however, that, for the first time, his "documents" had been challenged. The police and the business community in Lancashire had his number. The court had not convicted him, but this would not prevent others from ranking him among the "coloured impostors" who roamed the country at mid-century, pretending to be raising funds for some cause or other. There was a warning there to Wood to watch his step.

The coverage of the incident in the *Liberia Herald* helps clear up two questions. It indicates, for one thing, that however sudden Wood's departure from Monrovia had been, he had not simply absquatulated, deserting his post at the Providence Baptist Church, but had apparently secured the approval of his congregation for his canvassing tour of England. The second question concerns his reputation in Liberia. No one there had yet denounced him publicly as an impostor, as had happened in Maine and Massachusetts, and, after all, he had not been ousted as pastor while he lived in Monrovia. Had he pulled the wool over everyone's eyes? To those Americo-Liberians who had lent him money, Dr. Wood may have represented a bad credit risk, and perhaps there were some who suspected that, where money was concerned, he was not to be trusted. And surely the Baptist Foreign Mission Board would have advised his church in 1851 of its decision no longer to pay part of his salary, and of its reasons for doing so, which must have troubled at least some members of his congregation. But the publication of the *Herald* article gives us the first clear indication that Liberia's settlers were on to Wood. To the *Liberia Herald* and its readers, he was now a marked man, if he had not been so before. The paper would soon have further evidence of his nervy misrepresentations to lay before the public.

As a Liberian government official, his former father-in-law, James C. Minor, would have been none too pleased to learn that Wood had made him a partner in a non-existent banking company. As a parent, if Minor had not heard of his stepdaughter's death, he must have wondered what kind of rascal she had married. If he knew she had died, he must have wondered even more. In 1853, the *Hull Advertiser* went so far as to accuse Minor of having been an accomplice in Wood's counterfeiting of documents, but the charge seems to have been without foundation. A former Virginia slave who had trained as a printer before he was emancipated, Minor could conceivably have assisted Wood in forging documents, but Wood's forgeries were of a quality superior to anything that the printing facilities in Liberia could produce, an English court would later hear. In any case, Minor's reputation for probity was never questioned in Liberia. He later served as a judge of the Court of Quarter Sessions and Common Pleas.

Abandoning the idea of playing the commercial agent, Wood reverted to his more practised role of preacher. In that guise, he might reserve a hall and, with some legitimacy, advertise a public lecture on Liberia, a subject of which he had some limited personal knowledge. He would charge a modest admission fee and solicit donations. Or he might call on clergymen, asking for permission to lecture to their congregants and pass the hat. He was always prepared to flash his "documents" to prove his worthiness. If all went well at one church, he might come away with flattering report in the public prints confirming his genuineness or a letter of recommendation from the minister or from some other worthy to add to his mixed bag of genuine and spurious testimonials. This facilitated his approach to other churches in other towns, or to wealthy or prominent persons who might be called on privately for a contribution. The technique worked, and Wood might have gone on with his scheme indefinitely had it not been for his tendency to overreach himself. He had a way, in his lectures or conversations, of pandering to the prejudices of his audience, or so altering facts and humbly exaggerating his role in events that a knowledgeable person might have sprung up at any moment to expose him, or a persistently curious person, seeking to know more or to verify his assertions, could, without too much difficulty, have caught him out.

The editor of the *North Wales Chronicle* apparently came close to doing so in May 1852 on Wood's venture into the principality. Eight months later, he claimed that –

> we were grossly insulted on our own premises for intimating a doubt of the reality of the alleged mission of a black fellow, dressed like a clergyman, and calling himself the Rev. Alfred Thomas Wood, Baptist minister, who appealed to us for a contribution towards a fund, which he said he was raising for the extension of the gospel amongst the coloured population of the republic of Liberia, and for declining to accede to his solicitations, and give him money.

Wood's reported response to this rebuff appears to have been on a par with his reaction in Maine, when he allegedly subjected those who stood up to him to the "most horrible curses," or to the letter "of objectionable tone and spirit" he had written to Rev. Pinney from Monrovia, disputing accounts of his mistreatment of his wife. But the affronted Welsh editor, beyond refusing to make a donation, had not acted on his suspicions. He had not shared his doubts with his readers at the time, he said, fearing that publicly impugning the character of Rev. Wood might have been misinterpreted as an attack by a member of the established church on religious dissenters—an excuse that pointed to the rather raw state of religious feeling in Britain at mid-century.

Fortunately, we do know how Wood presented himself in these early days of his church canvassing, thanks to a somewhat fuller report in the *Carnarvon and Denbigh Herald* of a lecture he gave there on 17 May:

> THE REPUBLIC OF LIBERIA. – In accordance with announcement, a public meeting was held at Penrallt chapel, Carnarvon, on Monday evening last, to hear an appeal by the Rev. A.T. Wood, D.D., on behalf of the cause of Christianity in Liberia. This colony, of which the Rev. Mr. Wood is the accredited representative, is an independent republic

of liberated slaves, standing on the Western coast of Africa, and is inhabited by three and a half millions of population. During the rev. gentleman's eloquent discourse, he gave a sketch of the rise and progress of the settlement up to the present time. It was founded by America, in 1815, for the ostensible object of benefitting those negroes who might have obtained their liberties through servitude or purchase; but the real object being to carry on secretly and securely the detestable and degrading traffic of the slave trade among the healthy and rising generation. This being the case, after great suffering through such cruelty, the inhabitants in 1842 rose, and, shaking off the American yoke, declared their independence, and, to the no small chagrin of America, were immediately recognised by Great Britain and the rest of the European powers. In 1845 they elected a president and vice-president (who were both of Welsh blood), and since then they have been going on as prosperously as could be expected—with one exception, and that is the cause of Christianity. This is not in such a flourishing condition as could be desired. But Mr. Wood is now travelling for the purpose of advocating its cause with, and soliciting aid from, the Christian communities in this country. Although there is a population of nearly four millions, there are only six ministers and very imperfect places of worship to meet the urgent wants, which are continually presenting themselves, of the craving natives for a knowledge of Christianity. The speaker adverted to the field which now presented itself in that quarter, with the bright prospect of a rich harvest, for the missionary labours of those who were willing and zealous to serve in the cause of the gospel, and called in a most earnest and energetic manner upon the generous and mission-loving of all sects to assist to the utmost of their power in disseminating amongst his coloured brethren those principles which are ultimately to bring with them "Peace and good will to all men." This gentleman will, doubtless, meet with that support which his cause deserves; as, independent of his being a person of colour himself, his knowledge of the language, and long residence and labours in the country, give him a thorough knowledge of the characteristics of the people; and his sympathy being naturally with them, he with his coadjutors has been able to effect a great amount of good in his hitherto rather confined sphere; but, with a liberal assistance from the Christians of this country, he will be able to effect yet more. A collection amounting to upwards of 6*l.* was made.

Immediately following this report, the newspaper printed a letter from Wood, thanking his sympathetic hosts and audience for their ready willingness to believe him and for their generosity. They had swallowed his fiction whole:

To the leading officials and respective leading ministers of the town of Carnarvon.

GENTLEMEN AND FRIENDS, – I am called upon by the voice of duty on my part, and justice to your claims, to acknowledge your sympathy and generosity, both towards me as a *stranger,* and towards the country I represent, namely, Africa.

I rejoice that you have no affinity with slave-holding people, called Christians, nor any of those churches connected in fellowship with slave-holding parties. Neither have your religious principles been adulterated with that abominable *prejudice* to a man's colour, which so many professors betray, in their disdain to the Africans.

You have brought no suspicions in the one hand, nor vindictive malice in the other. You have placed no mis-constructions on reports; neither have you manifested an inclination to slander, or to favour that *abominable sin,* so common among religious societies in the world, who wish to crush all others, in order to their own prosperity [*sic*].

But, laying aside all such feelings, every minister as officer of your respective denominations has manifested that degree of true Christianity in recognizing myself, my object, and my case. Myself as identified with the down-trodden race of Africa; my object as one of deep importance as to call forth your aid and sympathy, in the spreading of the Word of God, and cause of Christ, in that dark and benighted part of the world; of my cause, as one upon which, not only my individual support (as a stranger in this country) depends, but the aid of a large Christian community in Africa, whose representative I am.

You have received their petition in the full bond of Christian affection, and have not strove against our claims as an imposition. You have acted for *God and his cause,* not for man and his notions. You (gentlemen), have imitated the example of the Blessed Saviour, not that of a worldly-minded and fault-finding Judas—or of a worldly hypocricy [*sic*].

Accept my sincere thanks and gratitude in behalf of the *Providence Independent Church,* in Monrovia, on whose behalf I left the shores of *Liberia,* to solicit the aid of God's dear people in Great Britain.

Desiring to return to my field of labour, there to spend my days, and to rest my bones upon the shores of my country,

I beg to subscribe myself, gentlemen,

Your very humble servant,

A.T. WOOD.

Carnarvon, May 20th, 1852.

From his pose as the "accredited" emissary of a non-existent Providence *Independent* Church, Wood slipped easily into roles as agent of the republic of Liberia and representative of all Africa, "that dark and benighted part of the world," as he termed it. He misdated the founding of Liberia by six years; he set its independence, and its recognition by European powers, five years before the fact. His reputed knowledge of the language—which one?—his long residence in the country—nine months!—and the idea that only six ministers of religion were active in Liberia, etc., were all nonsense. Throughout his letter ran an implicit message that whoever took him at his word was virtuous; whoever doubted him was prejudiced and sinful. A clipping of the wholly positive newspaper report and the letter would have made a wonderful marketing tool for presentation to marks far and wide, unlike the brief report on the same lecture in the *North Wales Chronicle* which consistently misidentified Liberia as ... Siberia:

> "Dr. Wood [...] gave a statement of the origin of Siberia, in 1815, and briefly touched upon its history up to the present time, and especially dwelling upon its religious condition, remarking that he was there [in Wales] as the representative of the Republic of Siberia, and of the cause of God in that place."

From Wales, it appears that Wood went on to canvass Ireland, another part of Britain's dominions racked by religious tensions, but the chronology of his travels at this time is unclear. The *Anglo-Celt* in Cavan reported him at Belfast in late April. We have seen that he spent much of the month of May in Wales. He was in Ireland again in June and July. Was that April jaunt to Ireland just a brief exploratory mission? Whatever the case, in late spring, he did cross the Irish Sea to hit up Ireland's Protestants, first stop Belfast, where, according to a subsequent report in the *Northern*

Whig, he presented himself as "Minister of an Independent Church in Liberia, and Secretary to the Cabinet."

> His visit to Great Britain and Ireland was represented to be for the purpose of urging various Missionary Societies to send out missionaries to the Colony. He preached in two of our Belfast pulpits with great effect, and by his plausible address received from a few friends of the African race about ten pounds, as his finances were exhausted, a bill which he exhibited not having been (as it should have been) duly honoured. He said he was in a hurry to return to Liberia by a steamer from Liverpool, and bid his friends farewell as he was to sail that night. – Instead of this, however, he went to Dublin [...]

In Dublin, he played the part of an Anglican, or a reasonable facsimile thereof, convincingly enough to hoodwink hardline Church of Ireland clerics grouped in the Reformed Romanist Priests' Protection Society. The society publicly blessed Wood's efforts in a notice published in June on the front page of the *Dublin Evening Mail:*

> We have heard the Rev. ALFRED WOOD'S statement respecting his missionary efforts to diffuse Christianity in the above named Republic, and we earnestly recommend our Christian brethren in Dublin, who are desirous to promote the conversion of the Heathen to vital Christianity, to attend a meeting of his to be held (D.V.) in the ROTUNDA, on TUESDAY, (to-morrow) the 29th of JUNE, 1852, at Twelve o'Clock, Noon, when he will give a fuller exposition of his missionary labours in Africa."

Wood does not seem to have realized that, from Ireland, his voice would carry as far as Liberia. Monitoring Irish or English papers, the *Liberia Herald* kept watch. It was far from tender in its assessment:

> *A.T. Wood.* – This wholesale imposter is still permitted to carry on his impositions in England. He was in Dublin in July, and we have before us a printed address of his, in which he styles himself a missionary Pastor in Liberia, and solicits money to complete a church in this city. In the address he says, that he has resided in Liberia ten years. He has collected several sums of money in the name of the church, but not a farthing of it, ever found its way here. Wood is a rank imposter, and we sincerely hope His Excellency President

"The Rotunda in Dublin."
(T. Percy S. Kirkpatrick and Henry Jellett, *The Book of the Rotunda Hospital*, London, Adlard & Son, Bartholomew Press, 1913)

Roberts, may find time to have him prosecuted for the many forgeries he has practised, and for collecting money under false pretences. The man never lived in Liberia one year in all his life.

At last, the "i" word was out: Liberia knew him for an impostor. But the *Liberia Herald* did better than sputter and expostulate. On 17 November it reported at length on Wood's Dublin lecture of 29 June, that readers might judge for themselves the nature of the man and the picture of Liberia he projected abroad.

True to form, Wood introduced himself by citing his "documents," including a licence allegedly signed by Liberian President J.J. Roberts authorizing him to collect funds for his church. We hear him adjusting his religion and the Liberian constitution to suit his audience, which included an ardent phalanx of ultra-Protestants and "reformed Romanists," i.e., Roman Catholic priests who had converted to Protestantism. His church, he says, while not connected with any in Britain, is practically Anglican, using the Anglican liturgy and rites. Likening the practices of the

Providence Baptist Church to Anglican services would have been a stretch; Wood gets away with it by masking the Baptist identity of his church and making it the "Independent Protestant Church." And he greatly exaggerates his connection with this church, claiming that he had lived 13 years in Liberia. He also professes to be well acquainted with the Liberian constitution of 1847, as he had taken part in its drafting! To the cheers of his listeners, he presents several anti-Catholic provisions that he claims formed part of the constitution—it contained nothing of the sort—while denying that it barred Whites from citizenship, which it did.

LIBERIA – WESTERN AFRICA.

[...]

The Rev. Mr. Wood [...] communicated to the meeting a resolution and letter of introduction, signed by members of the Independent Protestant Church of Monrovia, the capital of the Republic of Liberia, and accompanying license, bearing the signature J.J. Roberts, the president of that republic, and dated June, 1851, in which he was authorized to lay the case of their church before the Christian public of these countries, to solicit contributions for the purpose of completing a house of worship in Monrovia, and also to request that their missionary operation should be extended to the republic. [...] His thoughts returned to the field in which he laboured for thirteen years, where four and a half millions of human beings were distributed in little towns and villages, and of whom only about 1.225th part, who lived near the sea coast, enjoyed Christian privileges. [...] Dark, indeed, was the condition of the large proportion of inhabitants of the territory of Liberia [...] The country was beautiful enough to remind the traveller, on first arriving, of the description of the garden of Eden—such was its perpetual verdure—its never failing foliage [...] The Republic of Liberia was colonized in 1822, under the auspices of the American government [...] At that time it was given out that the object of the American Colonization Society, in connection with the colony, was to better the condition of the African; but while it continued under its auspices, the enlightened inhabitants had not the privilege even of erecting houses of worship or of establishing native schools. [...] The colony had, in fact, been established for the purpose of getting rid of the enfranchised African population of America, by whom the slave property there was kept under value, and at the same time of having a market for the supply of young and fresh slaves. They continued under that government until 1842, when the colony declared its independence. A constitution was then drawn up, and the inhabitants elected Joseph J. Roberts president of their republic. He was dispatched to Great Britain, and Queen Victoria was the first to acknowledge the independence of Liberia (applause); and that was not all, for her gracious Majesty also pledged the honor and power of the crown to defend it. [...] [...] They had now a flourishing population of fifteen thousand at Monrovia, according to the last census, connected with which were twenty-three schools [...]He begged to make a few remarks with reference to the climate of Africa. It had been generally termed the grave of the European. There was an impression that a contagious fever prevailed there, which was destructive to the lives of Europeans. He begged to remove that idea. He had the experience of thirteen years' residence, and he was able to say that the climate of Liberia was the most healthful on the coast of Africa. But in point of fact there was no such thing as contagious disease on the coast. Every foreigner going to Africa carried fever with him, it being nothing more nor less than the acclimatizing, or changing of the constitution to the temperature and the diet of the country. [...] By cautiously abstaining from fruit, native food, and especially spirituous liquors for five weeks after his arrival, the foreign resident would perfectly preserve his health. [...] A few words as to the church of Monrovia. In 1841 it contained not more than thirty members; but up to June 1851, he was happy to announce that there were 639 communicants [...] The church in Monrovia required 200*l.* for its completion. [...] It was true that their church was not connected with any one in this country; nevertheless, he did not confine his application to any particular church. The liturgy of the Church of England, its marriage and baptism services, and also the service for the dead, had been in use in the Church of Monrovia as long as he had been connected with it, so that it was actually part and parcel of the Protestant Church. From Sierra Leone down to the extremity of the coast of Liberia, at Cape Palmas, a range of 750 miles, there were but four[teen?] individuals who exercised the function of preaching the Word of God. He craved then their interest on behalf of the perishing sinners of Liberia. The laws of the republic were a perfect abstract of those of Great Britain, making allowance for some alterations which had been rendered necessary by circumstances. He had heard it said since he reached these shores that the constitution contained a clause prohibiting white men from becoming citizens of the republic. No such thing existed in it; and he knew the fact, for he wrote part of the constitution himself. But the 11th article, although it said nothing about colour, excluded certain persons from membership of the republic, under the following circumstances, viz.: – The inhabitants of Monrovia, [...] fearing lest the security of their church, as a Protestant people, might be interfered with, enacted in the 11th article, that "no persons professing to be of the Roman Catholic religion should become citizens or freeholders in the republic (applause).["] And there was also a clause that "all persons, citizens of the republic, who should at any time confess themselves to be converted to the Roman Catholic persuasion, should be allowed sixteen days to collect their effects and remove to some other place of residence [...] (applause). [...]

Meanwhile, back in Belfast, word had circulated that Wood had played his sympathizers there like fish, and instead of rushing off to Africa after leaving them, as he had told them he was bound to do, he had slipped down the coast to Dublin. Checks with contacts in Liverpool also uncovered the troubling truth that he was an insolvent debtor who had been imprisoned for debt in Lancaster the previous fall. The *Northern Whig* reported:

> "The Priests' Protection Society" was then written to through their Secretaries, Messrs. Scott and Rice, putting them on their guard against the wiley arts of their coloured friend, but their eyes could not be opened, and in reply to a letter from a Clergyman of the Established Church here [Belfast], they said that Mr. Wood courted inquiry, and demanded investigation, and that the clamour raised against him in Belfast proceeded from the Independents and other Dissenters who were jealous of this worthy Minister because he did not join some of them instead of the Church of England.

Such were Wood's powers that he had stout clerics of the established Church of England and Ireland in Dublin defending him as one of their own, refusing to believe, even as his hand slipped into their coats, that he was picking their pockets. His wife, Frances, may have been an unwitting accomplice here, playing a role similar to the one that Irene Stewart had filled earlier—the fair White spouse, like a statue, standing as a silent guarantor of Wood's reliability and good faith. "It seems he had a handsome woman in Dublin whom he represented as his wife," the *Northern*

Whig later reported. Wood had apparently left her behind when he had returned to England, the paper said. That smacks of salacious tittle-tattle. If, as seems likely, the woman was Frances, his wife of just a few months, he would not have dumped her in Dublin: It would have been too easy for her to make a fuss and wreck his game.

To Liberians, Wood's version of Liberian history and reality constituted a transparent fabrication. A flourishing population of 15,000 in Monrovia? The figure was ten times too high! Drawing the attention of its readers to the report of his lecture of 29 June 1852, the *Liberia Herald* of 17 November expressed surprise that no one had yet put a stop to the antics of this "most consummate of swindlers:"

> In our present number, our readers will find an address delivered by Alfred T. Wood, which, to say the least of, is a tissue of the most glaring falsehoods. We copied the address from an English paper. On former occasions, we pronounced this man an impostor, and not entitled to the least credit. We had no idea that he was still carrying on such a wholesale system of fraud among the good people in England. When we say that Wood is, and has been travelling through England under false colors, we wish it to be understood, that he is known here, as the most consummate of swindlers. We hope to hear by the next mail from England that he has been arrested, and severely punished.

7. HELP FROM UNCLE TOM'S CABIN

Any man juggling fact and fiction to fool the foolable is bound to fumble now and then, and fool himself. A.T. Wood did so in northeast England in the fall of 1852. He was once again styling himself "Dr." and posing as a member of the Liberian government, as he had done in Belfast. The slave-born Rev. Henry Highland Garnet, an African American who had been carrying the anti-slavery torch in Britain and Ireland for nearly three years, got wind of him. Was Wood's cause worthy of support? From Newcastle, Garnet wrote to John Scoble, secretary of the British and Foreign Anti-Slavery Society in London, on 10 August:

> ... I write to you in private to ascertain if you know any thing of the Rev. A.T. Wood DD of Monrovia one of the Cabinet of Prest. Roberts. I send you his circular. If he is right we will aid him. He is taking Collections now in Sunderland, and New Castle. Would the Secretary of the Aborigines Protection Society know something about the matter. Please write me by return of Post. Perhaps Mr. Bolton could give me the facts in the case.

Since Garnet was leaving the next day for Glasgow, on his way to Jamaica to take up an appointment as a Presbyterian missionary, he may not have received an answer in time. Otherwise, he would soon have had proof enough that Wood was far from "right."

The proof lay in the new wrinkle Wood added to the fundraising speeches he gave at Newcastle at summer's end. He preached at the Scotch Church in Blackett St. on the morning of Sunday, 29 August, and lectured there again on the evening of 31 August. On 15 September, he lectured on slavery at the Lecture Room on Nelson St. Large audiences turned out for each of these events and perhaps for a few others. "Additional interest was excited from

Henry Highland Garnet, born a slave in Maryland, was a leading abolitionist
who travelled and spoke widely against slavery in England and Scotland.
(James U. Stead, c. 1881, National Portrait Gallery,
Smithsonian Institution, Washington, D.C.)

the lecturer stating that he was acquainted with the heroes of
'Uncle Tom's Cabin'." He was not broadcasting that he was familiar with the blockbuster novel by Harriet Beecher Stowe, published first as a newspaper serial in 1851–52, and in book form in
March 1852; he was claiming that he knew its fictional characters
in person. For the next few weeks, in private exchanges as well as
in his lectures, he would occasionally claim that George and Eliza
Harris, two of the novel's main characters, were members of his
church in Monrovia, and that he had ministered there to Eliza's
mother Cassy on her deathbed.

The fact is that, at the close of the novel, George, Eliza and
Cassy, reunited by chance at Montreal, after escaping separately
from slavery in the American South, decide that emigration to
Liberia offers them the best chance at a decent life, free of racial
persecution. On that hopeful note, their story ends. But Wood
stretches out the plot and, in a patent effort to capitalize on the
novel's renown, counts these storybook stars among his acquaintances in real-life Liberia. This gambit was even more farfetched
than awarding himself a doctorate, rejigging the Liberian constitution to please Irish Protestants, or appointing himself to the

Uncle Tom's Cabin was all the rage on both sides of the Atlantic
in 1852. A theatrical production was playing at London's Olympic Theatre
that year as Wood was telling English audiences that characters from
the novel were members of his congregation in Liberia.
(Credit: *Illustrated London News*, 2 October 1852, p. 284.)

Liberian cabinet. The wonder is that he was not laughed out of the
house as soon as he uttered his claim.

From Newcastle, he headed south toward Hull in Yorkshire. At
the beginning of the week of 7 November, he blanketed the town
with circulars announcing that he would lecture at the Mechanics'
Institute on Tuesday, 9 November. His topic: *Uncle Tom's Cabin*.
Proceeds were to go to liquidate the debt of his church in Monrovia.
On the morning of his lecture, he called on the Congregationalist
divine, Rev. Christopher Newman Hall, and used the Uncle Tom
line on him in seeking to enlist his support. Newman Hall later
gave an account of that visit to the authorities:

> I am minister of the Independent Congregation in Hull. On the 9th
> November last, about Noon, the prisoner called at my House. He
> brought a letter of Introduction from a Deacon of an Independent
> Chapel at Malton. I believe he took that letter away as I have not seen
> it since. That letter stated that prisoner was collecting Money for a
> Church in Liberia. He then Shewed me two public Documents—
> those now produced & marked A & B, upon which I have put my
> initials. I read those Documents—the purport of his statement was

that he was the Minister of the Independent Congregation of Monrovia, that it consisted of about 2000 persons, that he came to collect £200 to liquidate the debt upon the New Church that they had created. I expressed my surprise that so large a church would be willing to lose their Minister for so long a time as is necessary for his coming to England, and that they should send him so far to collect so small a sum. He stated that most transactions in Liberia were conducted on the principles of Barter, that the Congregation there could furnish the principal expense but that this £200 was wanted in Cash and that Cash being scarce in Liberia, he was obliged to come to England for it, which accounted for his coming for so small a Sum. He stated that George and Eliza Harris, mentioned in the Book called Uncle Tom's Cabin, were members of his Congregation—that Cassy, mentioned in that Book, had died in Liberia and he had visited her on her Death Bed. I asked him how he had obtained his Diploma of D.D. He said he had obtained it by passing thro' a University in the United States—I forget the Name of the University. He said he obtained it in the usual Way. In the Course of the Conversation, he said the Government of Liberia had no Connection with any religious Sect. I promised to assist him, believing his Representations. I had some Conversation with him. He said his Congregation wore valuable Jewells, which increased my Surprise at their sending him so far for so Small a Sum. I was positive he said he was pastor or minister of the Independent Church. He did not produce any Book of Subscriptions. He complained of the Sectarianism existing in the Country, especially that the Baptists would not assist him because he was an Independent. I recommended him to give a Lecture on Liberia and to collect afterwards. I sent him with a Letter of Introduction to the Mayor. I gave him some names of Gentlemen. I wondered that he had been in England so long and had not got his Money. I told him so. He replied that he had been taken ill when he landed & had been detained in Liverpool & not been able to go about collecting until last June. I received an order from the Mayor for him in Answer to my letter, in case I should be satisfied with his statements. He was at my House near an hour—and he returned & dined with me. I then believed his Statements & particularly relied upon [one word illegible] of the two Documents produced. He left and went off to Malton. I said I would endeavor to make arrangements that he should preach a Sunday afternoon in my Church and have a Collection after. After he left me, I made Enquiries and declined to allow him to use my pulpit. He called again on the following Friday.

I then had obtained some information which made me doubt the Correctness of his Statements. I asked him if he had ever been in Lancaster. He at first appeared either not to know or not to recollect the place. He then told me he had passed thro' Lancaster on his Way to Carlisle but had only remained there a few minutes. He then went away. I went to Mr. Longs to make arrangements to assist him in the first instance.

On Cross examination: He did not ask me for money in so many words. He did not say, "Mr. Hall, will you give me a Subscription?" I did not give him a Subscription. He did not get a Dinner from me by false representations. I asked him in common hospitality, believing him to be an honest man. He got from me a Letter of Introduction to the Mayor. I made a conditional promise of my pulpit. If I had continued satisfied, he would have had my pulpit. I sent some Letter to the Mayor with my opinion ...

Newman Hall raised pertinent questions—about Wood's doctorate, which he now claimed to have obtained from an American university; about the fact that in more than a year he had not managed to collect the relatively modest sum of £200; about his congregation's willingness to dispense with his services for so long, etc. Wood seemed to have a ready answer to every query. It says something about his address and powers of persuasion that Newman Hall, for all his questions and dismay at several of Wood's assertions, still offered assistance, even after hearing him speak of his acquaintance with characters from *Uncle Tom's Cabin*. He later changed his tune, after checking with sources in various cities around the U.K.

Wesleyan minister Joseph Hargreaves was sceptical from the first. Wood approached him on the evening of Saturday, 13 November. "I first suspected him because he said that George and Eliza Harris, two fictitious characters, were members of his Congregation," he said. To hear the leery Hargreaves tell it, it took little more than a few innocent questions and simple logic to poke hole after hole in Wood's fundraising spiel:

... He brought a Note. I had previously received a Bill announcing a Lecture, and a Note requesting that I would announce the Lecture from my pulpit. He called with a Note from Mr. Cussons stating that Dr. Wood was a respectable Coloured Clergyman and wishing me to assist him. When he called, on a Saturday Evening preceding the day when the Lecture was to be delivered, he produced two public Documents, those marked A & B and, I think, also the Document marked D. I glanced over the Documents. He then gave me another Document. He said these are my Credentials and Testimonials. I don't recollect which Term he used. He produced another paper Signed by Clergymen recommending him. He took that paper back again. It had a list of Subscriptions and Collections printed on it. The Note he brought with him requested my Influence and assistance. He gave me the list of Subscriptions, which I understood a request for a Subscription. I had Conversation with him & after some time told him my Opinion. He said he had been in Dublin in April last and had assisted there at a public meeting. I knew this to be correct. I then enquired if he had been in Belfast. He said he had not. I then put the question again & looked at him with surprise. He then said: Oh Belfast in Ireland you mean? I said, of course. He then said: oh yes, I have been at Belfast. I had been at Belfast at the time; I then remarked that there was no Account of Monies collected in Ireland in the list which he said was a correct List. He said he had collected Small Sums in each place. He had been in Cork also but obtained nothing there. I said: what will the friends of Ireland think when they find their names omitted from the printed List of Contributions. His reply was: I made that up into one Sum and gave it to our President who has been over from Liberia and he has taken that [2 words illegible]. He distinctly said that the money collected in Ireland had been given to the president. I then enquired if the printed list contained all the Subscriptions except those collected in Ireland. He said it did. I then said, "I see no Reference to Liverpool—you were in Liverpool?" He said "I received nothing there." I said that is very remarkable Such a town as Liverpool—Do you tell me you obtained nothing in Liverpool? His reply was: I did receive a little in Liverpool but it was not for Liberia. It was for myself and therefore it was not entered in the list. I then said: I can have nothing whatever to do with you I am not satisfied. He said: Oh then I'll Shew you a Book, I am Sorry you are not satisfied. He then shewed me the Book produced, marked C. I there read these subscriptions at Cork & as he had said he collected Nothing at Cork, I declined to have any thing more to do with him.

On Cross Examination: I received a placard announcing the Lecture & a Note from prisoner. I don't remember the Terms of the placard. He was urgent to have the placard back and I gave it back.

The Note requested I would announce his Lecture. He called with a Note to request my general assistance. He said he was collecting for a Church in Liberia. He did not ask me in express words for money. He did not say "Will you subscribe?" I first suspected him because he said that George and Eliza Harris, two fictitious characters, were members of his Congregation. I could not understand his application otherwise than for a pecuniary subscription.

The day after he called on Hargreaves, Wood was arrested on suspicion of soliciting funds under false pretenses. The Hull Guardian Society, dedicated to protecting local businesses against bad credit risks and frauds, undertook to prosecute him. On his first appearance in police court on Monday, 15 November, he was remanded in custody for a week to allow the prosecution to study the many documents found in his possession. Mayor Henry Blundell, the presiding magistrate, later acknowledged that, "from what little he had seen of him," he had made up his mind then and there that Wood was a fraud who ought to be jailed.

The Guardian Society had collected a substantial file on Wood. Some of this material found its way into the "Caution" printed in the *British Banner* of 24 November in London:

A well-dressed negro, about thirty years of age, pastor of an Independent church in Liberia, visited Hull last week to collect money to aid in liquidating the debt on his church. As he said he had been seven months in Liverpool, the absence of certificates from [esteemed Congregational ministers] Dr. Raffles and Mr. Kelley excited suspicion. From letters received from various persons, there was strong reason to believe him to be an impostor. A merchant at Liverpool, at whose house President Roberts, of Liberia, was recently staying, wrote to say, that the certificates, signed professedly by the President, were *forgeries!* The Governor of Lancaster gaol wrote to say that a person answering to his description was in custody there last autumn for debt, and while there was visited by a black woman, who passed for his wife. He has a certificate of the death of a wife at Liverpool, dated October 12, and he was committed October 7. He states he has recently married at Malton, and has also admitted he buried a wife in Africa. He was apprehended on suspicion, and brought before the magistrates last Monday, and remanded for a week, till further evidence could be obtained, letters not being legal testimony.

Wood was back in court the following Monday, 22 November. "Communications had been received from Sunderland, Newcastle, Malton, and the Earl of Carlisle," the *Hull Advertiser* reported. "The subject matter of these communications was not made public, but we understand it was of a favourable character to the prisoner." Once more, the prosecution asked that he be remanded, pleading that his papers required further investigation. The Guardian Society's representative explained that he had been handed the collection only two days before, and had not yet had the opportunity to examine all of it. He had, however, found strong prima facie evidence of forgery in two certificates signed by a James Powell, acknowledging the receipt of £12 10s from Wood for the account of the Liberian Church Fund. One certificate was dated Dublin, 26 September 1852, the other was dated the same day at Malton, England—and the signature of James Powell was different on the two documents. The case was postponed to Friday, 26 November, Wood being released on his own recognizance of £50. Sensing hostility from Mayor Blundell, he complained that the magistrate was prejudiced against him. Blundell then announced that he would withdraw from the case.

That Friday, no matter how strong the suspicions, how incriminating the documents, how determined Mayor Blundell was to see Wood locked up, the prosecution had to be dropped. As the lawyer for the Guardian Society advised the court, "there were sufficient grounds for suspecting the prisoner's honesty, but as witnesses would have to be brought from Malton, Liverpool, Newcastle, and other places, even beyond the seas, he was instructed not to press the charge, as the funds of the society would not meet the expenses which would have to be incurred." For the second time that year, Wood escaped prosecution, notwithstanding the fact that his claimed acquaintance with the fictional George, Eliza and Cassy, was a falsehood so outlandish that it had newspaper readers chortling on both sides of the Atlantic.

Having once more outwitted the law, Wood was emboldened to go on the offensive. His lawyer spoke of suing Wood's detractors. Wood himself set up camp at Malton, about 70 kilometres northwest of Hull. From there on 6 December, he penned an indignant letter to the *York Herald,* complaining of the mistreatment he had suffered in his own motherland. This is one of the rare known instances during his stay in England when he publicly declared himself a native son; but he was ambivalent, appealing to Britons for sympathy as both a fellow countryman and a stranger.

THE CASE OF DR. WOOD, OF LIBERIA.

To the EDITOR *of the* YORK HERALD.

SIR, – I cannot forbear taking the liberty of writing on the cruel proceedings against an unoffending stranger in the town of Hull, some short time since. It was against one identified with the *African race,* although born under the flag, and on the shores of Britain.

Is it possible that the inhabitants of England can reflect on such transactions, and not feel that the national *honour* and *piety* of the country is too often sacrificed by those in authority? Yet, *God be thanked,* there are a few exceptions. What grounds I have to complain, being a stranger, far from my friends and adopted country, having sacrificed the comforts of a home, a living, as well as a peaceful congregation and a united community, for the purpose of seeking aid in England, to complete a place of worship for the poor *converted heathen,* to worship that God, who, the professing people of this country say they love! Having buffeted the waves of the proud *Atlantic* some thousands of miles, enduring many hardships and privations, arriving in England from *Western Africa,* I suffered (and still do suffer) the severity of *change of climate;* also, having met the severe and painful loss of the dear *wife* and *companion,* who accompanied me to this *strange land.* This took place shortly after my arrival at Liverpool!! But, besides all this, a host of praying *Ministers and people* array themselves in opposition to my object. Why? Because I refuse to bow and subscribe to their dear party *isms* and *jisms,* which (to all intent and purpose) is the modern idolatry of the land, at this present day. Therefore, A.'s society *don't know him;* B.'s *can't receive him;* C.'s *will not support him;* and D.'s *don't want him.* They combine to raise the *lightning* of slander, and the *thunder* of falsehood. No one sympathises. All are fierce to gaze through the telescope of *suspicion.* Why? "He is a stranger," says one; "he is black," says another; "his hair is woolly," says a third; &c., &c., &c. All this, sir, I have heard and observed, in the town of Hull; yes, where the tall column bears the majestic *memento* of Africa's great benefactor, one of Briton's noblest sons, WILBERFORCE. In that town, sir, the African Missionary has been basely slandered, and cruelly imprisoned falsely. I am imprisoned and degraded to satiate prejudice, heaven bear witness!!! Men in authority aid in this cruel action. I am treated as bad, nay, worse, than a slave! After canvassing the whole island, in order to receive aid in concocting a plan to destroy me, all fails. Oh! how disappointed, many sigh, having fully made up their minds to deal with a *rank impostor,* instead of an innocent and injured stranger. Large *placards* invite the public attention to the *newsmongers* to read the news of the alleged *clerical impostor.* But this repast is short; the day of trial arrives; no further proof or distinct charge can be proved. "Now he will be discharged." But can we not do something to crush him? Yes, insinuate. Rob him of his name and character, he is but a Negro; who cares for him. Turn him out in disgrace, like a *skinned hog* or a *shorn donkey.* Let him *die in the ditch.* Now, I ask, Mr. Editor, in God's name, is this religion? Is it the precept of Jesus Christ? Is it "doing to others as ye would they should do unto you?" Holy God of Justice! my heart bleeds for such a degraded state of religion in my mother country!! It is I, Sir, who have suffered all these things in the town of Kingston-upon-Hull.

Where is that professed zeal for the conversion of the heathen to the true and living God? Alas! it is too truly wedded with sinister motives, to support *sectarianism* and *bigotry.*

This act of persecution should be transmitted down to distant posterity, lest the people of another century conclude that malicious persecution by those professing to be *ministers of Christ* had ceased in this present far-famed religious country and period. The fact is, Sir, this is putting the *theory* of "Uncle Tom's Cabin" of America into real *English practice.* No *heathen Aborigine* could surpass this act of iniquity against an enemy, much less an unoffending stranger of another clime. I now claim the sympathy of the excepted characters—the generous, the humane, the truly religious. Tell me no more of the cruelty of Popery, or of cruelty to animals. There is a remedy for both these; but there is no society—no friend—no justice—no preventative of slander and cruelty to the poor unoffending missionary from Western Africa.

I am, Sir, yours respectfully,

A. T. Wood

In Britain and Ireland, Wood undoubtedly ran into antipathy based on race, but his suggestion that British racism was at the root of his legal problems is impossible to take seriously, when one of the voices calling most earnestly for his prosecution was Liberian, i.e., the *Liberia Herald.* In a more aggressive vein, he wrote to the editor of the *Hull News,* which published his letter on 18 December:

> Mr. Editor,—As you have inserted documents so unfavourable to a persecuted stranger, some short time since, while I was maliciously arrested and imprisoned in the town and gaol of Hull—in order that neither friends or enemies may be mistaken or deceived, my only redress is a Court of Queen's Bench, where, as a British subject, I shall move my claim to British protection; and, as an injured and victimized man, I shall seek no further retribution than what a jury of twelve men will agree to. The action will be entered. I have the evidence at hand to prove malicious arrest and false imprisonment; with taking from and detaining my personal property; also, libel and slander against the accomplices at other places. My evidence will be living witnesses, both from Africa and of this country. It is not my place to vindicate what the parties have failed to prove; all I have to do is to prove my charge, of which I have no difficulty. I have obtained the copies of the London papers, containing the bold and daring assertions from the hand of Hull orthers (*sic in M.S.*), impudent impostor, &c.
>
> As I have been so cruelly victimised by the parties in Hull, you cannot blame me for seeking redress. The evidence of those parties in Hull shall then be brought to its real bearing and intent; so that they may save themselves and those brought into the daring action with them, or take the result of justice themselves. Yours, the victimised
>
> Malton, Dec. 15.   A. T. WOOD

He also turned his guns on the editor of the *British Banner,* demanding a retraction from this London paper that had warned the public against him. His letter was not published until 5 January 1853:

> Sir, – As you have taken so conspicuous a part in publishing libel and slander against me (without just grounds to do so), in an article headed "Caution," relating to the diabolical attack made on me by

parties at Hull, I hereby notice you, that as I have entered action against the parties, and have grounds and evidence to prove your assertions libellous and unwarranted, I shall enter action against you as an accomplice, unless due satisfaction be made me in the space of twelve days. You assert in the document, that the papers purporting to be signed by the President of Liberia are forgeries. Now, Sir, I have living evidence of their being in his own handwriting, by the party who saw him affix his name thereunto. You say that I stated I was married at Malton. This is a positive falsehood, which I will make you prove or abide the result. In relation to my having buried a wife in Africa, I can prove it. In relation to my marriage in Africa to a second wife after the death of the first, I can prove also. In relation to my burying the second wife in Liverpool, I can prove she died on the 12th of Dec., and not in October, as you assert; there may have been a mistake in the paper alluded to, it being but a copy of certificate; I hold the original. In regard to my marriage since her death at Liverpool, I can prove; but you shall prove that I was married in Malton, or that I said so.

I await your reply the time specified herein, and no longer. You have laid me before the public as an impostor; this you shall prove. – Yours, the slandered

A.T. WOOD.

This was bluster, with much vaporing about details that were beside the point. He would have been well advised to withdraw from Yorkshire and the North entirely, and go find some other field to plow. Wood's strength, however, lay not in prudence but in nerve; he stayed put in Malton and carried on. The Guardian Society was watching, convinced of "the importance of detecting and putting a stop to an imposture which had been going on so long, so successfully, and with such effrontery."

The society soon found what it needed in Wood's successful soliciting of Rev. John King of Christ Church in the Hull parish of Sculcoates. On 9 November, it turned out, the same day that he had visited Newman Hall, Wood had called on King and actually obtained a cash donation of £1. This, and the return to England of his old African acquaintance, Consul Hanson, was to prove his undoing. At Christmas time, he was re-arrested at Malton, on a charge of defrauding King. He petitioned Home Secretary Lord

Palmerston on Christmas Day, complaining of harassment and pleading for relief.

Malton, Dec. 25th 1852 –

To the Hon The Secretary of State
My Lord,
I beg to inform you that I am from West Africa, on a Mission to this Country in behalf of the Providence Church of this City—I was maliciously arrested at Hull, on the 14th day of November, was Imprisoned, and twice remanded, on a charge of Attempting to obtain Money under false pretences, by Newman Hall. He failed to prove his charge, and I was discharged. I returned from Hull to Malton, and was again Arrested on the Same Charge, by the same party, (Maliciously) and I pray in the Name of Queen Victoria (whose Lawful Subject I am) that [I] may be protected by the Laws of the Realm, from such unjust, and Malicious treatment.
I am now to be conveyed to Hull from Malton, to be imprisoned again. I have proofs of my coming from Liberia, West Africa—but all the proofs I have has been thrown out of the Scale of evidence, and having a Wife to provide for, I am grievously torn from her and caused to Suffer as a fellon, Simply for Calling on the Inhabitants of England to aid in the completion of a Chapel in Africa.
Thus your humble Servant will ever pray in the name of my Queen –

Alfred Thomas Wood

The Home Office received the petition on 27 December and ordered that enquiries be made of the magistrates at Hull about the facts of the case. The report, dated 8 January 1853, was not at all favorable to Wood. Even had it been, it came too late.

On that Monday, 27 December, he appeared in Hull police court—Mayor Blundell again presiding—to hear King, Hargreaves and Newman Hall formally depose against him. The Guardian Society then asked that the case be put off until the next day, when Hanson would be on hand. On 28 December, Wood returned to court for Hanson's deposition. "I was Her Britannic Majesty's Consul in Liberia in the Year 1851 and part of the Year 1852," the latter began. "I am not now—I left Monrovia on the 2nd May last and Africa on 18th May last."

I resided in the Town of Monrovia, in the County of Montserado. I had known prisoner from my arrival on 11 Nov. 1850 until he left about the month of June 1851. So far as I knew, he was Pastor of the Providence Baptist Church. I believe he preached in that Church. Before the time of my leaving, there was not a Church in Monrovia calling themselves "the Providence Independent Church of Christ," nor was there a Church called "the Providence Protestant Church of Monrovia." I knew the prisoner personally in Monrovia. I remember his leaving Liberia about June 1851. I had some Conversation with him relative to his going to England. So far as I recollect, about a fortnight before he left, prisoner called upon me & said he was going to England. He mentioned that the object of his going to England was to obtain Funds in connection with the Chapel in which he was then officiating. That is my Impression. I expressed my own Views upon the matter, which were different from his. I received the Letter produced, from the prisoner. I replied verbally that I should be glad to see prisoner. In consequence, he called upon me. I gave him reasons why I declined to give him Testimonials—and I did not give him Testimonials. He left, and I think I did not see him again in Africa, certainly not again on that subject. I have no doubt I received that Letter now produced, marked E, upon the 9th June 1851.

The Government of Liberia is a Republic with a President and Vice President. There are quarter Sessions and Judges. From the time of my arrival in Liberia up to December 1851, there was not a Secretary of State—no one fitting that post. Prisoner stiled [*sic*] himself "Dr. Wood" in Liberia. I am acquainted with his Hand Writing and have seen him write. There is no County in Liberia called Monsterado. The name is "Montserado". On examining the Document produced, marked A, I believe the Writing is that of prisoner—I do not refer to the Signatures. The Republic of Liberia had not such a Seal as that upon this Document. In my official Capacity, I had Occasion to know the public Seal. So far as I know, the Seal at the bottom of the Document is not genuine. I believe there is no such Seal. Joseph Jenkins Roberts was president of the Republic on the 17th June 1851—He was then actually president—I knew him. Mr. Anthony D. Williams was Vice president.—I knew him personally. There was then no Secretary of State. I knew a young man named Johnson—I believe he was William Johnson. He was private secretary to Mr. Roberts. There was a Mr. W.W. Stewart a Clerk of the Court of Quarter Sessions—I had official intercourse with him in that Capacity in Monrovia. I knew a Mr. Brander and I believe his name was Nathaniel. I did not know him in any official Capacity. I did not know him to be Secretary, of any public Body. I knew Mr. James C. Minor. He was Collector of Customs. I have seen the President, Vice President & Mr. Minor write and am well acquainted with their Hand Writing, especially with that of the President & Mr. Minor. The Signature is like Mr. Roberts' Writing; I believe it is not his Writing. I believe the Signature is not that of Mr. Williams. Positively and distinctly, the Signature "J.C. Minor" is not the Signature of that Gentleman. I know Mr. Stewart's Hand Writing,— the Signature to the Document is not Mr. Stewarts Hand Writing. The signature "W.A. Johnson" is not the Signature of the Secretary of Mr. Roberts.

I hold a Document marked B, now produced. I believe the Document is the writing of prisoner. The Signature is not the Signature of the Mr. Stewart whom I knew as Clerk of Sessions. I never saw such a Seal in the Republic as that to this Document.

I hold a Document marked D, now produced. On the 17th June 1851, there was not in Monrovia a Church called the Providence Protestant Church. I believe I know every Building in the Town of Monrovia—there was no Building called Government Chambers at that time. I never saw such a Seal as that affixed to this Document. I certainly should have known if the Government used such a Seal as that affixed to this Document. I know a Mr. B.V.R. James—He may be a Justice of the Peace. I know Mr. Beverley R. Wilson & believe he is a Judge of Quarter Sessions. I don't know Mr. James's Writing. I believe it is not Mr. Wilson's Writing. He spells his Name with only one L. It is not the Signature of Mr. Stewart, Clerk of the Court of Quarter Sessions.

The type of the printing is very different from any that I ever saw in Liberia. I believe the Inhabitants of Monrovia do not possess the Means of printing such a Seal.

I believe the Writing on the inner Cover of the Book produced, marked C, and the Signatures of A.T. Wood in 5 places, are prisoner's Hand Writing.

At the end of the day, Wood was committed to stand trial in the Hull Court of Quarter Sessions on a three-count indictment charging him with defrauding the Rev. John King by falsely claiming that he had been asked by the congregation of the "Providence Protestant Church" of Monrovia on 17 June 1851 to collect funds to help complete the building of a church; by falsely claiming that he was authorized to collect such funds; and by showing King a forged document purporting to be a licence from the Liberian government authorizing him to travel to England to seek contributions.

The trial was set for that Thursday, 30 December, but it was then put off for one more day because a necessary witness from Liverpool could not be present until Friday, the 31st. As the trial would focus on the specific £1 fraud committed on King in Hull, with the aid of Liberian and other "documents," the problem of summoning witnesses from farther afield that had frustrated earlier attempts to prosecute Wood did not arise. Most importantly, Hanson, deemed a competent witness to pronounce on the authenticity of Wood's Liberian credentials, was in England—no need to try to call witnesses from distant Liberia, with all the difficulties, costs and delays that would entail. After certain preliminary arguments on the Friday, the trial proper before newly appointed Recorder Samuel Warren took place on Saturday, New Year's Day 1853, and lasted until slightly past midnight. Wood was represented by barrister William Digby Seymour, the newly elected member of Parliament for Sunderland. Hanson offered much the same testimony as he had given in his earlier deposition. Once the evidence was in, the jury took about 25 minutes to return a verdict of guilty, just before midnight.

In a brief statement he delivered before being sentenced, Wood protested, hand on heart, that he had always acted in good faith –

> ... and the jury having now pronounced their opinion that I am guilty of a crime for the way in which I have acted, I have only to say that, however various and complicated may have been that testimony upon which they have recorded their verdict, and whatever may have been right in the eyes of this honourable court (placing his hand upon his heart, and elevating his voice with earnestness)—no pain or remorse lies here. Under these circumstances I have but one word to add. It is simply in the discharge of a duty to my poor church that I have come and endeavoured to solicit aid from those who in England could give it. Upon that I have been convicted. I humbly submit, and merely crave your lordship's mercy.

Rebuking Wood for persisting in playing the innocent lamb when the evidence had shown him to be an altogether different beast, Recorder Warren observed that his offence was punishable by as much as seven years' transportation.

"Oh! I beg your mercy on behalf of my poor companion," Wood cried out, not at all relishing the prospect of banishment beyond the beyond to Australia, and separation from his wife. Warren replied that as it was now Sunday morning, and the dawn of a new year, he felt inclined to be merciful, and sentenced Wood to 18 months at hard labor in the House of Correction, the first and last months in solitary confinement.

Warren felt less charitably inclined on the Monday, when Wood returned to court to dispose of the outstanding charges against him relating to his approaches to Revs. Newman Hall and Hargreaves. Little more than a Sunday had passed since Warren had pronounced sentence, but in that brief time, the *Hull Packet* of 7 January reported –

> he [Warren] had been put in possession of information respecting the prisoner, which, if he had previously known, would have induced him to have transported him beyond the seas. As it was, he had it now in his power to do so—and even on Saturday he hesitated as to whether or not he was justified in not doing so then. He should not allude to the intelligence which had been conveyed to him respecting certain passages in his past life—and having publicly sentenced him he should not alter it now, but desired the prisoner to consider that he had been very leniently dealt with.

Whatever information Warren had received between the wee hours of Sunday and the sitting on Monday, it was not evidence presented in court. Perhaps it was information that the Guardian Society had obtained in its communications with the Foreign Office and the London police. A clue of sorts is found tucked away in the report requested by the Home Office on Wood's petition of 25 December. The report by William Ayre Jr., clerk to the magistrates at Hull, summarizes the prosecution of Wood, offering a glimpse of the activity that had gone on behind the scenes:

Town Hall

Hull 8th Jany 1853

My Lord

I am directed by the Visiting Justices of the Gaol of this Borough to inform you in reply to the Petition of Alfred Thomas Wood inclosed [sic] that this Individual was arrested & twice remanded as stated in the petition on a Charge of obtaining Money under false pretences, the pretence being that he was commissioned by the Providence Independent Church of Monrovia to collect Subscriptions in aid of a Church at that place.

Tho' the Justices entertained no doubt of the falsehood of these pretences, there was not any Evidence before them of their being false & so the man was discharged. After this the man put forward his acquittal before the Justices as a Testimonial in favor of his Truthfulness and he was again apprehended but not until abundant Evidence had been obtained to convict him. In fact Mr. Wood's Documents, purporting to be under the Seals of the President and other officials of Liberia were sent to the Foreign Office & placed in the Hands of the Revd. Augustus William Hanson, recently H.B.M.'s Consul at Monrovia and this Gentleman came down to Hull and proved that Mr. Wood's Testimonials were forgeries & himself an Impostor. The Jury at the Sessions found him guilty and our learned Recorder sentenced him to be imprisoned & kept to hard Labour for 18 calendar Months. Subsequently to pronouncing this Sentence Wood was called upon to plead to two other Indictments, upon which no Evidence was adduced & the Recorder stated to the prisoner that if he had known when he pronounced Sentence what he subsequently learnt he Should have felt it his duty to have transported him. I understand the Recorder had heard of two previous Convictions of the same man for similar offences.

Perhaps Ayre was wrong about the information that had reached the ear of the recorder. If not, then perhaps Recorder Warren had been misinformed: As we have seen, Wood had been jailed for debt at Lancaster in October 1851 and arrested twice subsequently—at Liverpool in January 1852 and at Hull in November—but freed for want of evidence. There is no known record of previous criminal convictions.

In reporting the news of Wood's conviction in his newspaper, the confused editor of the *Leicester Journal* could not refrain from tacking on a question: "Is this the 'man of colour' who was preaching and making collections at Melton, and several other places in that part of the county, a few months ago?" The editor of the *Leicestershire Mercury* undertook to enlighten him: No, he replied in his own newspaper, that "coloured clergyman" from Liberia who had visited the Melton area was Rev. Elie Stokes, and he was safely back in Liberia.

8. LET THIS BE A LESSON

Wood's appropriation of the characters from *Uncle Tom's Cabin* helped, in a very small way, to promote that anti-slavery novel and, by extension, the anti-slavery cause. At the trial, Recorder Warren, himself a published writer of fiction and of books and articles on the law, had indicated that he had not yet read the U.S. bestseller. He did read it soon afterwards, however, and wrote a long, favorable review of it for *Blackwood's Magazine.* Perhaps the subject came up in the conversation when, on an inspection tour of the borough jail a few days after Wood's trial, he visited the latter in solitary confinement.

For a Virginia newspaper editor with a light touch, Wood's Uncle Tom howler proved an opportunity to poke fun at him and at author Beecher Stowe as competing spinners of tall tales. "Mrs. Stowe must look to her laurels," he said. "The English parson [Wood] exhibits capacities of invention which, if properly cultivated, would throw our American story-tellers into the shade." More vexed and ham-handed, New Hampshire-born George Wilkins Kendall, an editor of the New Orleans *Picayune,* sought to make the point that the gullible English who had fallen for Wood's tale were the same dupes of Abolitionist propaganda who ventured to meddle in the debate about U.S. slavery without understanding anything about it. On leave in Paris, Kendall wrote to his paper on 27 January 1853. His letter ran in the *Picayune* a month later:

> The American in England is often amused, and at times highly gratified as well, when he sees how easily John Bull allows wool to be pulled over his eyes occasionally—in plainer terms, permits himself to be cheated and humbugged by the most arrant impostors. A case

in point—one which should afford amusement to all Americans and gratification to the greater number—occurred a few days since at the good old city of Hull, where a colored gentleman, the Rev. A.T. Wood, was brought up as a regular swindler and knave. From the evidence at the trial, where the reverend rascal appeared in the prisoners' dock dressed in black and with a white cravat, it appears that for some time past this fellow has been levying taxes in different English cities by pretending to be a preacher from Liberia, and that to prove his position and standing he produced a long list of certificates and documents, all of which it was ascertained were rank and bare-faced forgeries. One man in Liverpool was victimized to the extent of £15, others were "sold" for smaller amounts, and for a space the Rev. A. T. Wood drove a profitable trade right and left. One of his stories was to the effect that he was the incumbent of the Providence Protestant church of Monrovia, in Liberia, and he had papers to prove that he had been sent to England to solicit subscriptions in aid of said church. In other cases he would give out that he was an Episcopal Protestant, again that he was an Independent, and still again as a Baptist—he had an easy faith, and one which could accommodate itself to the creed of any person or party he might single out to operate upon. But his most money-making dodge—the card which always won with the Rev. A.T. Wood—was when he gave out that George and Eliza Harris, from "Uncle Tom's Cabin," were members and communicants of his church in Liberia, and that at the death bed of the unfortunate Cassy, another distinguished member of Mrs. Stowe's colored family, he had administered the last holy offices of religion to the departing saint. Wherever he told the latter story, British hearts and British pockets, especially pockets, seem to have bled freely, and the Rev. A.T. Wood would undoubtedly have realized a handsome sum had he not unfortunately come under the suspicion of a clergyman of Hull, who eventually found him out to be an impostor. At last dates the Rev. A. T. Wood was serving out a period of eighteen months, at hard labor, in the work-house at Hull, and during that time George and Eliza Harris, with their numerous progeny, are likely to be deprived of his spiritual advice and ghostly counsel. Mrs. Stowe's admirers should subscribe liberally for some one to go out and take his place as pastor of the Providence Protestant church at Monrovia, in Liberia, to look after the spiritual concerns of George and Eliza Harris during his unavoidable absence. But seriously, is the fact that a portion of the English people should allow themselves to be gulled by such a flimsy imposture, tolerably strong evidence of their ignorance upon a subject which seems to enlist all their sympathy—that of slavery in America. A colored scoundrel, who appears to have thoroughly understood those with whom he had to deal, selects a couple of characters from a popular novel, pretends that they are under his spiritual keeping in Liberia, and on the strength of such a transparent tale succeeds in reaching the pockets of his dupes by appealing to a philanthropy which turns up its nose at objects of real charity nearer home.

Kendall was too quick to gloat over the naiveté of the English. He did not realize that his "reverend rascal" had earlier left a long trail of dupes in the U.S. and would return to deceive many more. The English at least had the merit of having put a full stop to Wood's game in their country. How would the American game end?

Kendall's us-vs.-them tack reflected the irritation that many Americans felt at what they considered the holier-than-thou pose struck by the British public who, spurred on by a stream of visiting Abolitionists and ex-slaves, were forever pointing out how abominable it was that the boasted land of freedom harbored 3 million slaves. In that context, had Wood posed as one of those pillars of Abolitionism, who knows what damage his antics might have done to the cause? As it was, he may have helped crank up public skepticism of alms-seekers generally—and made life more difficult for legitimate canvassers, Black or White, in England—but he did little harm to the anti-slavery effort because his stated purpose was to raise funds for his church in Liberia, not to champion Abolition in the U.S. He never did go so far as the remarkably cheeky character who, in England in 1846, passed himself off as Frederick Douglass, even as Douglass was touring the British Isles and Ireland. "Greater scoundrels do not live than many of the coloured promoters of missionary labours in Africa," the *Hull Advertiser* opined.

Kendall was not the only one to reflect on how easy it had been for Wood to snow the British. For the perspicacious editorialist of the London *Patriot,* the case highlighted the vulnerability of the kind-hearted generally to cunning schemers:

"RELIGIOUS" IMPOSTORS AND THEIR DUPES.

[...]

A remarkable instance of religious imposture, or, rather, of imposture under the cloak of religion, has just been detected, convicted, and, we are happy to add, punished at Hull. We congratulate the newly appointed Recorder on this useful commencement of his judicial career. Both parties, deceivers and their dupes, may, and we trust will, learn a useful lesson from this exposure. The rascal [...] rejoices in the name of "the Rev. ALFRED THOMAS WOOD, Doctor of Divinity." For the sake of a race in whose cruel wrongs much has of late been done to revive a too languid sympathy, we regret to add, that this learned divine is a man of colour. In the autumn of 1851, he did us the honour of setting foot upon our shores, arriving at Liverpool in the Clyde-side, direct from the Republic of Liberia, where he seems to have been known as a Baptist minister [...] The bare circumstance of finding himself in a city where Episcopalian clergymen occupy the most influential position, converted him at once into a regular descendant of the Apostles. He lost no time in conferring upon his British brethren the honour of his acquaintance; and they proved so sensible of the privilege, that, in due course, he was enabled to exhibit, in addition to his "credentials," a whole batch of Masters of Arts and Bachelors of Divinity, in attestation of their being "genuine and satisfactory." Thus armed, he did not fear to invade a cathedral city; but, with a modesty which so much success might well have destroyed, he passed by both Chester, and Manchester, and, as the Presbyterians say, "condescended upon" Bangor [Wales]. The Bishop, we suppose, was not at home; but half-a-dozen of His Lordship's clergy, including the Very Reverend the Dean, fell into the snare, decoyed, no doubt, by the seductive testimony of their Liverpool brethren. [...] Astute Newcastle, thrown off its guard by the interposing vouchers of so many respectable and even dignified clergymen, never thought of scrutinizing the Doctor's original "credentials," but received him with open house and open purse, and forwarded him to Sunderland with accumulated marks of perfect authenticity. By this time, indeed, he felt himself so secure, that he gave Dissenting ministers an opportunity of sharing in the privilege of his acquaintance, hitherto bestowed upon the [Anglican] clergy only. In a charming spirit of accommodation, he dropped the exclusive character of an Episcopalian, and deigned to present himself as an "Independent," wherever he had reason to suppose that, under that guise, his visits would be more welcome. [...] Having made a collection at Bethesda Chapel [in Sunderland], he proceeded with the proceeds to Shields, where, again, he was permitted to make a collection, this time in a church, besides the gleanings at a public meeting. [...] It appears that he was now more than a match for even Scotch caution; for a "kirk" was the next place which yielded a collection towards the "Independent Protestant Church at Monrovia." [...] And, in short, before he was quite *seen through*, he had victimized a belted Earl, and had no greater achievement left to perform, unless, indeed, black mail could be levied on a sceptred Queen.

[...] How could the Earl of CARLISLE give the fellow 5*l*. under the silly impression that he was really the pastor of Mrs. STOWE'S "GEORGE and ELIZA HARRIS," and had actually attended that lady's "CASSY" on her death-bed? His Lordship, like the rest, will probably throw the blame upon the Liverpool gentlemen, who, on the arrival of the impostor, furnished him with "a clean bill of health." But, were this a sufficient excuse, how came it to happen, that a Liverpool certificate did not pass current at Hull? [...] True, Dr. WOOD committed the mistake of endeavouring to engage the sympathies of the Colonial Missionary Society, under the impression of its being connected with the Established Church, and thus unconsciously committed that act of self-betrayal which is the merited fate of the most successful impostors. [...]

[...] The "credentials" which passed muster with the Liverpool clergy, and on the faith of which those sapient gentlemen gave the impostor a passport to every town in the Kingdom, were, on examination, manifest fabrications. [...] It is to be hoped, at all events, that this case will prove a lesson to impostors, whether black or white, and to dupes, whether gentle or simple. The Press, as we have had ample experience, can do little in the matter. We are generally called upon to close the stable-door after the steed has disappeared; and, besides, Newspaper cautions cannot compete with testimonials signed by Liverpool Bachelors of Divinity and Deans and Prebendaries of Bangor. Let this, then, be a "caution" once for all. If not, why then, *qui vult decipi, decipiatur*.

"*Qui vult decipi, decipiatur*." That, as the professed linguist A.T. Wood might have said, can be loosely translated as "Suckers will be suckers." The journalistic sermonizing above drew a swift response in defence of the dean of Bangor. It suggests that Wood had had a close call in North Wales in May 1852:

Sir, – Being at the Deanery in this city this morning [12 Jan], I had an opportunity of directing the attention of the Dean of Bangor to your Article on "Religious Impostors and their Dupes," which appeared in the last Number of the *Patriot* [10 Jan].

All who have the pleasure of being acquainted with the Dean, know him to be an estimable man. The Dean has desired me to inform you, that he was induced to give ten shillings to "Dr. Wood," because he had been recommended to him by a venerable Welch [*sic*] Independent Minister; but, from the way in which the donation was received, he immediately suspected that the man was an impostor. He likewise desires me to correct a mistake into which you appear to have fallen, and to assure you that he "signed no testimonials in favour of Dr. Wood." The Dean is glad to find, that the deceiver has at length been convicted and thinks that the prison is the best place for such a man. Your exposure of the case will, I trust, prove serviceable.

I may just tell you that, as far back as last May, "Dr. Wood" was exposed in a journal published in this neighbourhood; and, if he had not made his escape from this city (nobody knows how), he might have found himself lodged in Carnarvon Gaol.

To this, the newspaper subjoined an explanatory paragraph:

We have seen a printed copy of the impostor's "testimonials," one of which is dated "North Wales, Bangor, April 27, 1852," ... and purports to be signed by six clergymen whose names and degrees are appended, "the Dean of Bangor" coming last of all. It ought to have occurred at once to the first observer that the Very Reverend gentleman would never subscribe any document in that form.

It ought to have occurred to many in the U.S., Liberia, England, Ireland and Wales that Wood was not who and what he pretended to be, and that his supporting "documents" were flawed. It rarely did. Like a performing magician, he was a master of patter, trickery and distraction.

In Portland, Me., Asa Cummings' *Christian Mirror* of 1 February 1853 published a fuller account than those in most U.S. papers of Wood's trial and conviction:

AN IMPOSTOR. – A negro, calling himself the Rev. Alfred Thomas Wood, D.D., has been traversing England and Ireland the past year, collecting subscriptions professedly for completing a new church at

Monrovia, in the Republic of Liberia. He imposed upon the good people of several cities and towns, even after a caution had appeared in the public prints against trusting him. Once he was arrested and confined for a week, but released by the officers for want of proof to convict him. He was again taken, and brought to trial Dec. 30th [*sic*], when he was convicted by the most unquestionable proof. It turned out, as had been suspected, that his credentials from President Roberts and others, were all forged. He had also represented that he was pastor of a church in Monrovia of 2000 members, including "George and Eliza Harris of Tom's Cabin memory." Her majesty's Consul in Monrovia, a colored man, testified that the town did not contain so many inhabitants including children in the enumeration. He was perfectly familiar with Pres. Roberts's signature, and that of others, which the culprit had forged. When the evidence was all in, and a most able defence made by Mr. Seymour, the Recorder summed up, and gave the case to the Jury, who after retiring for twenty minutes returned a verdict of guilty. The prisoner, however, declared his innocence, and said, "he could exchange worlds that moment with a clear conscience." The Recorder (it was now midnight of the 2d day), said, "that the [several words illegible], in the face of such evidence, made his guilt the more flagrant;" and spoke very impressively on the aggravated character of the offence, saying, "that he had power to transport him for seven years;" and did sentence him to eighteen months' imprisonment with hard labor.

Yet there is nothing to suggest that anyone in Maine, not even Hacker of the *Pleasure Boat,* recognized in "Rev. Alfred Thomas Wood, D.D." the wolf that had troubled the state as recently as four years before. So, the *Mirror* missed a chance to toot its own horn as the first paper to have exposed this world-class impersonator, and to let the world know that before going off to gull the English, he had honed his skills in Maine.

Geschichte

der

Republik Liberia,

seit ihrer

Gründung bis zu ihrer Unabhängigkeitserklärung;

nebst

Bemerkungen über den Zustand der Landestheile und der bürgerlichen und religiösen Verhältnisse der Eingeborenen und Eingewanderten.

Von

A. T. Wood,

(einem Farbigen)

Prediger an der Providence Independentenkirche zu Monrovia,
der Hauptstadt der Republik.

Aus dem Englischen übersetzt

von

Dr. A.

„Thatsachen sind hartnäckig."

~~~

1854.

Im S...

Title page of the German-language *Geschichte der Republik Liberia*
(*History of the Republic of Liberia*) by A.T. Wood, "einem Farbigen"
(a colored man), published in Hamburg in 1854.

9. PUBLISHED IN HAMBURG

"It's a bad job," Wood had muttered when arrested at Hull in November 1852. "I don't know what my poor wife will do if she comes to know of it, but I must do the best I can to get out of it." In the end, he did not get out of it, and we don't know how Frances, his wife, reacted and how she made out on her own during his confinement. If he served out his full sentence, he would have walked free in July 1854. Together again, they would have left for Hamburg, for surely Frances was the *"hübsche Engländerin"* (pretty English lady) who accompanied him there.

Hamburg? What ever for?

To oversee the translation and publication of his book?

Book!? Booklet, really.

Geschichte der Republik Liberia (*History of the Republic of Liberia*) ran to 96 pages. It was apparently published by G.W. Niemeyer, a reputable firm. The text consisted of misinformation, boilerplate, fantasy, non-sequiturs and pious invocations à la Wood. Take Chapter 5, entitled "The City of Monrovia"—from which we learn nothing of significance about Monrovia but a little about the author's belief in the importance of religious schools to banish the "deathly heathenism that has so far ruled Liberia." (*See Appendix.*) Supposedly a history of Liberia, it is more of a misleading promotional brochure, minus illustrations, its author identified as A.T. Wood, *einem Farbigen* (a colored man), preacher in the Providence Independent Church of Monrovia.

In an afterword by the translator, Dr. A, readers were informed that:

> The author, who is now in Hamburg, was born in London and is 37 years of age. He studied in Halifax, at Neadia College from 1834

to 1838. His father, a Negro born in Jamaica, was a London merchant, and his mother a quarteroon. His new wife is a pretty English lady. This work was originally published in 1853 by J. Samson at York. The author is thinking of soon returning to Monrovia and has promised to send us further information on the present state of things.

This information, like the rest of the book—like any statement from Wood—is far from trustworthy. We can probably take as fact that he was in Hamburg then, and intending to return to Liberia, which he did. The reference to his wife as a "pretty English lady" should probably be read as meaning that she was White. As for the biographical details about Wood, his stated age of 37 is more or less consistent with his age as given on other occasions, but the identification of his parents appears to be a renewal of his dodge that he was an Englishman born to ease. From 1834 to 1838, that is, between the ages of 17 and 21, he had supposedly attended "Neadia College" in Halifax. Considering that he never once mentions British North America in his booklet, that he claimed to be London-born and that his soliciting had taken him to Halifax in West Yorkshire, we must assume that Halifax was the English town of that name, not the capital of Nova Scotia. There was no "Neadia College" in either place.

An English version of the work, said to have been published at York in 1853 by J. Samson—a reference to York book-seller, news agent and stationer John Sampson—is nowhere to be found. Did it ever exist? Probably not. Sampson did not publish books. Besides, it would have been odd for a publisher at York, in 1853, to invest in a work by an imprisoned confidence man whose Liberian credentials had been discredited in a recent trial that had unfolded only 55 kilometres away. Who would buy it? Anyone in England with interest enough in Liberia to purchase a book about the place would have known, through the press or from communications with like-minded souls, of the writer's want of veracity.

There is, in fact, reason to suspect that the German translator worked at least in part from a manuscript rather than from a printed text. It is highly improbable, for example, that any English-speaking person, however careless with a pen, would have written Russworni for Russwurm, as the *Geschichte* calls the well-known

Jamaican-born governor of the colony of Cape Palmas (Maryland in Liberia), or rendered the name of the Liberian county of Sinoe (sometimes Sinou) as Sinon, as it appeared consistently in the German. Someone unfamiliar with those names, however, could easily have misread them if they were handwritten. Perhaps Dr. A misread Wood's handwritten notes, or perhaps the German printer mistook Dr. A's handwriting. The same goes for "Neadia" College. Changing the first two letters of this name yields "Acadia." Could that be what Wood had written in a biographical note for the translator? There was an Acadia College, a Baptist institution, in Nova Scotia. If Wood was claiming to have studied there from 1834 to 1838, however, this would have been one more lie: Acadia College in Wolfville—founded as Queen's College, name changed to Acadia College in 1841, today Acadia University—opened its doors to students in 1839—and there was not one Black scholar among them, nor anyone named George Andrew Smith or Alfred Thomas Wood.

But why a German translation of his prose in the first place? It is not as if he were a renowned authority on Liberia, who would have been invited to prepare such a work for the benefit of German readers. Fresh out of an English prison, why would he have wanted his prose translated? Was it with the idea of touring Hamburg and perhaps other German states, fishing for donations with his book as bait? To do so, he would have needed an interpreter-assistant, or an accomplice, since he spoke no German. It is conceivable that, flat broke after his incarceration, he was ready to try his hand at any scheme that might pay his living expenses and provide him with a ticket back to Liberia. The last line of the biographical note in his booklet—that he had promised to send back to Germany more information on the state of Liberia—might hint that the publisher and/or the translator had advanced or promised funds to help him fulfill that pledge.

"*Thatsachen sind hartnäckig*"—Facts are stubborn, says the epigraph on the cover. If this was Wood's way of signalling the contents of the book, it was singularly ironic, coming from one who twisted *Thatsachen* out of shape for a living. On the same page, for example, he masks the true name of the Providence Baptist Church he had served, making it an "Independent" church, as he had done in England and Ireland. (For all his efforts to pass for an Independent pastor, the Liberian missionaries he mentions by name in the booklet are mostly his former Baptist colleagues.) Billing himself as pastor of this church in 1854 was either a lie or a stubborn refusal to face *Thatsachen*. After more than three years away, he had to know the church would have found someone to replace him.

The stubbornness of facts works against him in the text as on the cover. From his account of Liberia's beginnings, for example, a reader would infer that the American Colonization Society was founded in 1820; it was, in fact, founded in December 1816– January 1817. "The first contingent bound for Africa sailed from Norfolk (Virginia) in September 1822," he says; the first emigrants actually sailed from New York on the ship *Elizabeth* on 6 February 1820. A man named "Ashman" led that first group, he says; Rev. Jehudi Ashmun did become the leader of the settlement at Monrovia, but he sailed with a contingent of emigrants from Hampton Roads, Va., aboard the *Strong* on 26 May 1822, and arrived at Monrovia on 8 August that year. In distinguishing the parts that Whites and Blacks played in the colony's early strug-gles, Wood allows that the ACS spent money, but Ashman and his companions, "who were all coloured persons," spilled their blood. Ashmun was, in fact, a White man, from Champlain, N.Y.

Ashmun was in charge of the settlement when native warriors attacked in force on two occasions in 1822. With little regard for *Thatsachen* or chronology, conflating events that took place before and after Ashmun's arrival, Wood provides a fanciful description of the decisive battles of 11 November and 1 December (together with skirmishes of the previous spring), setting them all on 5–6 November. He depicts the Africans as a howling mob of spear-chuckers and archers panicking at the blast of a small brass can-non, grossly inflates the number of settler casualties, and inflicts more wounds on Ashmun than the natives ever did. The natives, in fact, were armed with muskets, as well as spears, and as to their never having seen or heard a cannon before, Ashmun reported in his *History of the American Colony in Liberia, from December 1821 to 1823:* "None of the kings on this part of the coast are without cannon." True, the Africans were impressed with the speed and dexterity of the settlers in loading and firing their cannons, but it was not as if the thunder and lightning of cannons were unknown to them. It also puts a different spin on the encounters to know that, besides the small brass cannon mentioned by Wood, the settlers had five "great guns" (iron cannons) plus two small swivel guns. Regarding Ashmun's injuries, Wood went into detail, as if he had been present on the battlefield: "Ashman himself had suffered three wounds, to the arm, the loins (from the chief's lance) and, the worst one, to the hip, where a non-poisonous arrow had struck him." Here is Ashmun describing his "wounds," (speaking of himself in the third person): "The Agent received three bullets through his clothes but providentially escaped unhurt."

Five days after the battle, Wood says, a ship arrived from the States bearing food, supplies, 83 new settlers and a doctor named "Lugenbeal," to the great relief of "Ashman" and his battle-weary companions. The ships that reached the settlers in the aftermath of the battles in November and December were none of them American; they brought no immigrants and no "Dr. Lugenbeal." The schooner *Cyane,* the first U.S. ship to reach the settlers after the battles of the fall of 1822, arrived on 31 March 1823. It carried no immigrants, but it did deliver welcome supplies, and a surgeon named Dix, who promptly died. Dr. "Lugenbeal" of the ACS— James Washington Lugenbeel—would not set foot in Liberia until November 1843, fifteen years after Ashmun's death.

On and on it goes. The same sloppy flaws noted in Wood's letters to Jeremiah Hacker in Maine in 1849 and in the forged official documents produced at his trial, are much in evidence—the inaccuracies, the misspelling of names, the bogus precision and resolute vagueness, the use of more or less plausible minutiae to give a lie the ring of truth, etc. In the brief preamble, we find this: "The publisher hopes that any shortcomings of this work—and he is painfully aware of them—are offset by the accuracy of its contents, which could only flow from the pen of one who has spent some time actively employed in the place and who is mindful of the interests of the colony." Whoever wrote that was either blind to the book's failings and to the character of its author, or fibbing.

The *Geschichte der Republik Liberia* seems to have been a random anthology of lectures Wood had delivered in England, Ireland and Wales. It covers much the same ground as his known Irish lectures of 1852. One he gave in Dublin on 13 July 1852, for instance, was titled "Idolatry in Liberia," while Chapter 6 of his book was headed "Idolatry of the Natives." His Dublin lecture of 29 July 1852 (see chap. 7), touching on Liberia's past, resources, climate, native religious practices, missionary work, education, as well as on the slave trade, slavery and colonization, etc., was like a digest of his book, plus a few details he had improvised to suit his particular Irish audience. Unlike in that performance, he does not claim in his booklet to have spent 13 years in Liberia or to have worked on the drafting of a Liberian constitution that barred Catholics from citizenship. But he does pretend to be a linguist, able to speak a native dialect and versed as well in ancient Greek and Hebrew; and, without claiming the title, he plays doctor, claiming to know, better than physicians, the causes and proper treatment of "acclimating fever." He lets slip that "The Grace of God directed me to this country [Liberia] in 1850, after I had sojourned in the West Indies," from which a German reader might have inferred that, since the book was said to have come out in English in 1853, he had spent at most three years in Liberia. Yet, with muddying inconsistency, he seems to boast in the same breath of having been God's "tool in obliterating darkness and ignorance" in the heathen land over a 10-year period.

Internal evidence suggests that the work was largely put together in 1851–52, as Wood went a-wooing John Bull. This accounts for its fawning pro-British tone and its pronounced anti-American, anti-ACS slant, which was also a feature of his Irish lectures. One nugget, however, appears to have been added as late as the eve of publication. In a section on Sinoe County in his last chapter, he resorts to a variation on the Uncle Tom line he had used in England: "In this city, the engineer George Harris, the same one as in 'Uncle Tom's Cabin,' whom German readers know, is the owner of a fine establishment where he conducts a machine-building business on a large scale." The fictional George is now represented, not as a member of Wood's church in Monrovia, but as a pioneer builder of steam engines in outlying Sinoe! Wood could not have written that in 1851—the conclusion of Beecher Stowe's serialized novel, the part where George and Eliza Harris decide to move to Liberia, was not published until 1852. That this passage was added even later is revealed in the identification of George Harris as someone *"whom German readers know."* This nod to German readers would have had no place in an English-language publication in 1853. It might be supposed that the translator had slipped in the phrase, but we have Dr. A's assurance in the Preamble that he "has not deviated from the original text." In that case, we must assume that Wood inserted the phrase in preparing the German publication in 1854, meaning that it was not in a published English text. However he may have tinkered with the text after 1851–52, he made no serious effort to update it: At the end of the work, he speaks of Governor John Brown Russwurm of Cape Palmas as still in office—Russwurm had died on 9 June 1851, shortly before Wood had left Liberia for England.

If Dr. A produced a faithful translation, he could not refrain from adding an occasional note expressing some reservations or bafflement. How could it be otherwise in dealing with an author so careless as to speak of Liberia as divided into seven counties— there were three: Montserado, Grand Bassa and Sinoe—who goes on to discuss eleven places, leaving readers thoroughly confused as to which is a town or a city, which a district, which a county.

"Two works about Liberia already have been presented to the public, at least in English," the preamble states. By 1854, Liberia was the subject of many works in English each more readable than Wood's opus. Wood's work is scarcely a valuable addition to the list; it's a significant element in his life, but not in the life of Liberia. Few copies exist, and it is, after all, the only published work on Liberia, in German, by a Black Nova Scotian of the 19th century.

Whatever Wood's purpose was in visiting Hamburg, whether he had ambitions beyond publishing his book as may be suspected, he did not tarry. By the early fall of 1854 at the latest, he was off again to Liberia. Did his *hübsche Engländerin* tag along? We hear no more of her.

10. PUNISHED IN MONROVIA, REDEEMED IN MONTREAL

News flashed across the U.S. and across Britain in 1854, thanks to the telegraph, but it did not yet flash between the two countries, or across the seas to Africa. Still, it did travel, as fast as ships could carry it. Wood acted as though it did not. What was he thinking in returning to Monrovia—that the Liberians would welcome him back with open arms? That they would not have heard of his doings abroad? Perhaps he really thought he was still the pastor of Providence Baptist Church, or perhaps he had heard that Hilary Teage, who had succeeded him as pastor, had died in 1853. Either way, he acted as though the pulpit were his.

He was anything but contrite on his return. From Monrovia on 19 December, he wrote to the Foreign Mission Board of the Southern Baptist Convention in the U.S., demanding back pay for his services to the church during his three-and-a-half year absence.

Dear Brethren,

I beg to lay before you the sad state of affairs here at Monrovia. I was elected pastor of the Prov. Church here in Septr 1850, was appointed on Mission to England to raise Money to complete the Church Building. the Church here being torn by Faction and goaded on by 2 ignorant but selfish members of its own Body who has for years sought to be ordained Ministers at length after violating all trust and the obligations imposed in them, they took illegal steps with my property, and sold the same under a pretense that I owed some debts in the place. I hold their obligations to pay me $500.00 per Annum during my stay. this they have wholly refused to do. I have suffered for them, have returned, and they refuse to pay my wages. I have not for the whole 4 years I served received one years payment. my Bill against the P Baptist Church of this Town amounts to $1211.90, which sum I pray you to attend to. For if the Board has paid half the salary of $500 for 4 years, I assure you I have not received one cent of money from the Church since the year 1851, and then a half years pay was due me. I am in deep poverty and distress. I love the Baptist Cause and wish not to unite with any other people. pray send me relief, and order the Church to pay my wages. Rev. J. Day has a hand in the whole vile scheme.

    I remain Your Suffering Servant.   A.T. Wood

The mission board ignored the pleas of its "Suffering Servant." It had cut its ties with Wood as he sailed to England from Monrovia in 1851. His implied threat of leaving the Baptist fold—"I love the Baptist Cause and wish not to unite with any other people"—fell on deaf ears. He miscalculated, too, if he thought that blaming John Day, of whom he had spoken favorably in his booklet, would help his cause in any way.

The Baptists turned their back on Wood, but not the Liberians— they locked him up. "The renowned A.T. Wood was indited [*sic*] last court for forging Sundry papers and obtaining money by false pretenses, was found guilty and sentenced to five years imprisonment at hard work in chains, and a fine of $500," Day informed Dr. Lugenbeel of the ACS in March 1855. At the same time, Day conveyed his personal news that he was now pastor of Providence Baptist Church and chief justice of Liberia.

No account of Wood's trial has survived. All we know is the verdict and his sentence. True, it had been reported in Monrovia in 1852 that "It is supposed, by many persons, that Wood obtained, while here, several sums of money under false pretences," but was there more to it than a supposition? Had a crime been committed? Was there really evidence of his having defrauded Liberians, or was this more or less a replay of the case brought against him in England? It is difficult to avoid the suspicion that there was an element of double jeopardy to the proceedings against him in Monrovia, that justice was perhaps tainted with vindictiveness for the way he had traduced Liberia and some of its leading figures abroad. Wood, of course, had brought his troubles on himself, but it is disquieting to find Day, the ex-colleague he accused of plot-

Watercolor painting of an unnamed Liberian village.
(Library of Congress, Prints and Photographs Div., LC-USZC4-8196,
American Colonization Society Collection)

ting against him, ensconced as both pastor of Wood's old church and chief justice of the republic.

One accusation that Wood faced, and that Day failed to mention in his letter to Lugenbeel, certainly suggests the government's prickliness on the subject of Liberia's image, and its determination to take him out of circulation. As the *African Repository* reported in January 1856, almost a year after the fact,

> We learn from the Liberia Herald that Alfred T. Wood has been tried at Liberia for forgery, for obtaining money by false pretences, and for a "libel on the Republic," and found guilty, and sentenced to five years imprisonment and 500 dollars fine. This "Rev. A.T. Wood, D.D.," as he called himself in England, came from the British Provinces to Boston, flourished largely for two or three weeks, when the colored people found out his true character, and he ran away to

New-York, and thence found his way to Liberia. He soon went to England and begged money to erect a house of worship for his Church in Monrovia, of which, he told one of his dupes, George Harris and his wife, mentioned in "Uncle Tom's Cabin," were members. He was finally arrested, tried and found guilty of obtaining money on false pretences in England, since which nothing has been heard from him till now he has turned up in Liberia, where he seems to have met with his deserts [*sic*].

That charge of a "libel on the republic" is intriguing. It is the kind of accusation we think of as a tool used by arbitrary governments to stifle dissent. While the details of Wood's case are unknown, we at least understand that he stood accused of defaming the government, or its representatives, in some of his written or published utterances. It is highly unlikely that his *Geschichte der Republik Liberia* was the focus of attention. That leaves the published reports of his lectures (echoed in the *Geschichte*) or other reported statements he made abroad, and his "documents" bearing the forged signatures of President Roberts, Vice-President Anthony Williams and others. In his lectures as in his book, Wood certainly could be faulted for making false and inaccurate statements about Liberia, past and present. But just as certainly, he was no critic of the fledgling republic, no dissident badmouthing this experiment in Black self-rule and fomenting rebellion or inviting foreign interference. His criticisms were aimed at pre-independence Liberia under the rule of the ACS. If anything, he seemed bent on promoting the now independent country, often at the expense of the truth. He practically invited Europeans to move there by seeking to allay their fears about the climate, by denying that its constitution barred Whites from citizenship, and by boasting of its agricultural, commercial and industrial potential waiting to be exploited by the entrepreneur and the capitalist. There was nothing malicious there about Liberia, nothing meant to bring the republic into disrepute. The charge of libel seems more likely to have sprung from his forgeries. He had used bogus testimonials and certificates, some stamped with a counterfeit seal of Liberia, to con people into believing that Liberian officials, from the president down, endorsed his activities. In associating them with his fraudulent begging abroad, he could be seen as having dragged their names, and the name of their country, through the mud.

There is one other striking feature of the above account of Wood's conviction by a Liberian court. The article, which seems to have been published first in the *Boston Traveller,* is one of the few ever printed that reflects some awareness of his antecedents. His early escapades in Maine escaped the writer's notice as did his wish, expressed in England, to be sent as a missionary to China or the West Indies, and his recent business in Hamburg, but at least someone, somewhere, in the mid-1850s, was aware that Alfred T. Wood, the Monrovian convict, was the same Wood from the "British Provinces" of North America who, once chased out of Boston, had run off to New York, then Liberia, and then England, where he had posed as a doctor of divinity and the self-styled pastor in Monrovia to George and Eliza Harris. Curiously, while the writer seemed to know something of Wood's travails in Boston— he rather abbreviated his stay—he said nothing about his unmasking there as George Andrew Smith of Nova Scotia. Several publications, including the *New York Times,* carried the story, yet no one who dealt with Wood thereafter seems to have had an inkling of his shady past.

Few people could have survived five years at hard labor, in chains, in a Liberian lock-up of the 1850s. That was a virtual death sentence. Fortunately for the former senate chaplain, he was not called on to roast in that particular hell. There was life in Wood after Liberia, as we shall see.

In December 1856, Stephen Allen Benson, who succeeded J.J. Roberts as Liberia's president, invoked Wood's name in outlining his legislative agenda to the Senate and House of Representatives at the beginning of the 1856–57 session. Benson believed there was an urgent need for a new citizenship law:

> I have also to recommend the passage of a law defining citizenship of this Republic; that is, as to what shall constitute one a citizen of this Republic; as well as making provisions for carrying the same into effect. The passage of such a law should not be delayed longer, if we would obviate serious difficulties, not only among ourselves,

Beverly Page Yates, vice-president of Liberia, in charge of education.
Wood reported to him when working as a teacher in the spring of 1857.
(Library of Congress, LC-USZ6-1927 DLC, part of American
Colonization Society records, 1792-1964)

but with foreign powers: a warning against which we have had this year, in the attempt of the notorious A.T. Woods [*sic*].

The *Liberia Herald's* report on Benson's speech did not elaborate on the nature of this move by Wood, and no explanation has been found of it elsewhere. It is possible that Wood, incarcerated, had tried to call on the assistance of a foreign power—Britain, perhaps, on the plea that he was a British subject. Whatever the case, Benson's reference to Wood's move as an "attempt" implies that it failed. And whatever impetus it gave in Benson's mind to the need for a clearer definition of Liberian nationality, no new citizenship law was enacted at that time.

It is not clear whether the "notorious" Wood was still behind bars when Benson delivered his speech at the end of 1856; if he was, he soon went free. By the spring of 1857, he was a schoolteacher, and answering as such to Benson's vice-president, Beverly

Page Yates. From Farmerville in Sinoe County, he wrote to Yates that June: "Dear Brother, I have the honour herein to transmit to you my school report; it is in a prosperous condition: present attendance fourteen." The scarcity of qualified teachers must have led the authorities to set this "learned" man to work for the state rather than let him rot in jail at the state's expense.

That is the last we hear from A.T. Wood in Liberia. He may have remained in West Africa, part of that time perhaps in neighboring Sierra Leone. But when we pick up his trail again two years later, he is hustling a world away, in Canada.

• • •

For his Montreal debut, Wood shed his divinity degree, even the title of "Rev.," as well as his Liberian identity. While clinging to his well-worn alias, "Mr. A.T. Wood" now laid a new claim to the world's attention and respect as superintendent of public works in Sierra Leone. This is how he billed himself in the *Montreal Gazette* of 9 June in advertising a lecture he was to give at the Montreal Mechanics' Institute:

A PUBLIC ADDRESS
WILL be delivered at the MECHANICS' HALL, on MONDAY, 13th, by Mr. A.T. Wood, Superintendent of Public Works in the Colony of SIERRA LEONE, W. AFRICA.

Subject:
The State and Condition of the Aboriginal Tribes from Cape Palmas to the Rio Pongo.
The Progress of Missionary Enterprise and Civilization in the Colony of Sierra Leone.
The Astounding Increase in Slavery among the Natives of these interior parts.
Doors open at 7:30 P.M. Chair taken at 8 P.M.
TICKETS to be had at the Door – price 25c.

The *Montreal Transcript* observed in its editorial columns that "Mr. Wood is Superintendent of Public Works in the colony of Sierra Leone, is himself of African lineage, and, have no doubt, from his long residence in the country and the position he held in it, will be able to give most interesting information on the subjects

Map of Montreal, 1863, by Charles Magnus & Co., NY.
(Library of Congress, Geography and Map Div., G3454.M8 1863.M3)

which he is to treat." The *Montreal Witness* of 15 June observed that "Mr. Wood, a colored gentleman from Sierra Leone, gave an interesting lecture on Monday evening in the Mechanics' Institute, upon the native tribes, missionary efforts and slave trade of the West coast of Africa, in which much important information was communicated. We will give some of the most prominent points of the lecture in our next." No such account has survived.

It is probable that, between 1857 and 1859, Wood had visited, or moved to, the British colony of Sierra Leone, Liberia's northwestern neighbor, and ventured as far north as the Rio Pongo in the present-day Republic of Guinea. But his claims to a "long resi-

INSTITUT DES ARTISANTS—MONTRÉAL.

The Montreal Mechanics Hall. Wood's first public engagement in Montreal was a lecture he gave here on 13 June 1859 about Liberia and Sierra Leone. (From *Relation du voyage de Son Altesse Royale le prince de Galles en Amérique*, Montreal, Eusèbe Sénécal, 1860, between pp. 60 and 61)

dence in the country and the position he held in it" were pure gas. Just how much make-believe time had he spent there? Another advertisement in the *Transcript* at the end of July answered that question, more or less:

A. T. WOOD,
ARCHITECT AND BUILDER

Begs to inform the Public that, having recently arrived in Montreal, he will be happy to serve in his line of business whoever may favor him with their patronage. Having served for ten years in the African Colonies as CIVIL ENGINEER, ARCHITECT and BUILDER, as well as Superintendent of Public Works, he pledges himself to give ample satisfaction.
Please address

No. 70 St. Antoine Street.
N.B. – Great discount allowed on Plans and Specifications.

A.T.W.

For a carpenter/joiner like Wood to pose as an architect, civil engineer and superintendent of public works was perhaps more daring and difficult to carry off in practice than his earlier self-elevation to the status of doctor of divinity. And lecturing on Africa, in English only, in the Montreal of that day did not hold out much promise of financial reward. This was particularly so when his lectures were free of charge, as was the two-parter he advertised in the *Montreal Herald* of 9 and 16 August on the "Characteristics and Capabilities of the Africans." Notably absent from his self-identification in these early advertisements of his presence in Canada were religion and racial advocacy, two staple features of his career of the past decade. The first published references to him as a man of the cloth came in September when "Rev. Mr. Atwood [*sic*], Missionary from Sierra Leone," joined forces with visiting Boston prison reformers Charles Spear and his wife. The press carried only cursory reports of Wood's part in these free lectures. At a meeting on 8 September on the Spears' work with prisoners, "Rev. Mr. Atwood [*sic*], missionary from Sierra Leone, commended the work to the public in a very feeling manner." At another meeting on 18 September, "Rev. A.T. Wood gave some description of the prisons in Sierra Leone, and other appropriate remarks." Was his description based on personal immersion or pure fiction?

Rev. Wood was invited to give the closing prayer at a temperance meeting on 2 October focusing on the ravages of alcohol among "the Indian tribes of the coast and the interior." He may not have been personally acquainted with the subject, but this did not dim his eloquence. The *Herald* reported: "The meeting was closed with prayer, by Mr. Wood, from Sierra Leone, a pure African, who alluded beautifully to the fact of black, red and white men meeting there to worship and serve the same common God and Father and Saviour, who had made of one blood all these races, however much they might differ in appearance."

He seems to have been treading as softly as his bold imposture would allow, testing the waters, unsure as to the pose he should strike in Canada East (Quebec), uncertain of how long he would stay. The place was a British colony, but its population was largely French-speaking and Roman Catholic—not exactly his element. Unlike in Boston or Monrovia, there was no Black church he could aspire to lead. And, as he now had quite a history, there was always the risk that someone might recognize his face or his name. It could be an English or Irish immigrant, a clergyman or a missionary, a British army or naval officer or some colonial official who had served in West Africa, or the Spears or any one of several Black refugees from American slavery who had lived in Boston during Wood's brief tenure at the First Independent Baptist Church.

He had, however, formed some early ties with Black Montrealers who, at this time, were almost all English-speaking. The street address he gave in touting his services as a builder, 70 Saint-Antoine, was the home of Mathew Bell, an enterprising Black carpenter and building contractor from South Carolina. Three months before Wood showed up, Bell's partnership with White architect and builder James Nelson had ended. Bell may have seen in Wood a potential new partner.

But Bell and Wood formed no partnership. And by the fall, surer of his footing, "Mr. Wood" had reverted to type, as we saw: As Rev. A.T. Wood once more, he took a leading part in the organization of meetings in support of anti-slavery martyr John Brown, captured that October during his famous raid on the U.S. federal arsenal at Harper's Ferry, Va., and sentenced to hang.

EXPRESSION OF SYMPATHY FOR MR. BROWN. – A meeting of the coloured inhabitants of this city was held on the evening of the 24th instant [November], for the purpose of considering the propriety of setting apart the 2nd day of December, (the day fixed for the execution of John Brown), for fasting and prayer to Almighty God in his behalf, and in demonstration of their deep sympathy with and for that suffering hero of the oppressed man's cause: –
Resolved : That the second day of December be observed by the friends of the slave in this city, in an appropriate manner. That, at nine o'clock, a public Prayer Meeting be held in Bonaventure Hall, for the purpose of supplicating the Almighty God that He will impart unto John Brown His sustaining grace, and the comfort of His gracious spirit, during the fearful trial which awaits him in meeting the extreme penalty of the law, in consequence of his attempt to release our brethren in bonds: That, at 10½ o'clock, A.M., the Rev. A.T. Wood be invited to deliver an appropriate discourse: That, in the evening at 7 o'clock, a public meeting be held for the purpose of giving expression to our sentiments in relation to slavery, in which Dr. Howe and

John Brown (foreground, 3rd from left) and fellow Harper's Ferry raiders
in court at Charlestown, Va., 26 October 1859. Wood played a leading role
in Montreal meetings in support of the abolitionist martyr.
(*Harper's Weekly,* vol. 3, no. 150, p. 721)

Mr. Stearn, and other distinguished speakers of Boston, will address
the meeting: That, at these meetings, a collection will be taken up
for the purpose of aiding the funds for the support of John Brown's
family, and that the following Committee be appointed to carry out
these resolutions : – Messrs. Thomas Cook, C.F. Seldon [Selden], and
Mathew Bell.

Thomas Cook, Clarence Francis Selden and Mathew Bell were
all Black U.S. expatriates. The Boston speakers, Dr. Samuel
Gridley Howe and businessman George Luther Stearns, were
White Abolitionists and secret backers of Brown. They had fled
to Montreal after the failed raid, but they were no longer there on
the evening of 2 December.

On the morning of 2 December:

... At half past ten the Rev. A.T. Wood delivered an eloquent discourse
appropriate to the occasion. He took for his text the second book of
Samuel, third chapter, and a portion of the thirty-eight [*sic*] verse:
– "Know ye not that there is a prince, and a great man fallen this day
in Israel." ... For over an hour Mr. Wood occupied the attention of his
audience.

The Montreal *Pilot* of 2 November and the *New York Times* of 5 December reported on this meeting, but the *Montreal Herald* of 3 December gave the most detailed account of Wood's "eloquent discourse":

I trust that your minds, through what you have heard, will spread the mantle of charity over the faults of the hero of liberty, and oh, how insignificant will they appear when we measure them with the magnanimity that has cost him his life; for the motives which led our hero to death were Heaven's legitimate offspring. The character of John Brown is pourtrayed [*sic*] by his own people. From boyhood it was noticed that whenever he fixed his mind upon what he considered just and right, his whole soul became bent upon the attainment of that object. There are those who now clamour for his blood, but that have not produced nor can they produce from his history anything at all to show that he ever was a hasty, an irritable, a headstrong or a careless man. From those who knew him best we learn that for 20 years he was maturing his plans of liberty for the oppressed; and for that which he considered right he was ready to risk his life. [...] I, though born in England, have visited the Southern States to satisfy myself as to the reports I had heard about Slavery, and I never shall forget the impression made upon my mind, by the celebration of the Lord's Supper. A number of individuals came forward to commemorate the broken body and shed blood of the Lord; and when they had passed, the coloured communicants came, and when I saw this I could not but feel deeply when I thought that these latter could at any moment be turned into dollars and put into the pockets of the former. Oh the disparity between this and the gospel of Christ which proclaims liberty to the captive and the opening of the prison doors to those who are bound. The gospel of the Slaveholder insinuates nothing but duty and oppression. [...] The hero who suffers to-day, no doubt, has long prayed to God for his country's deliverance from the sin of Slavery; and felt it an imperative duty to labour for the oppressed man's cause. Embittered by wrongs which were also inflicted on himself, he steps from being a mild abolitionist to be an ultra abolitionist, and at length by grievous wrongs that noble mind was led out of its proper channel. But his intentions were not to shed blood; his object was plain—it was to enter into the State of Virginia, and to surprise the population in such a manner that he could just have cars and boats ready to take the coloured people from the plantations and run them across the

lines without firing a rifle bullet at an individual. He meets an igno-
minious death to day, and for what? [...] for an act of righteousness
imparalelled in the annals of history. [...] Brown did not undertake
what he did for aggrandizement, for his motives were pure; and he
only wished to see carried out the sentiments of the Declaration of
Independence—that all men are born free and equal, endowed with
certain inalienable rights, to life, liberty, and the pursuit of happiness. If we connect the trial of this man with his sufferings and his
motives, they raise him higher in human estimation than any other
one. I know of no one who ever made such sacrifices on the side of
the oppressed? He is the truest model of magnanimity that has ever
been recorded in the pages of time, since the days of our Saviour; and
he may well be termed a martyr, for he has suffered death in the
cause of liberty. They may execute him, but his blood will not be shed
in vain, and God will raise other Browns to proclaim from East to
West against the sin of slavery.

At the anti-slavery meeting held that evening in the same venue,
Wood proposed "That an Anti-Slavery Society be established as
soon as convenient in the city of Montreal." It was one of several
motions approved unanimously, but nothing came of it.

Religion and racial matters were back on the agenda. Wood
had found no pastorless church to lead, but he had found a Black
flock of 200 or so, and cast himself as its shepherd. If that was not
clear from his part in the John Brown meetings, it was so a month
later, on New Year's Day 1860, when, as the *Pilot* of 5 January
reported, he and his followers descended on Rev. John Cordner's
Unitarian Church of the Messiah in a friendly raid:

> The members of the Unitarian Church were agreeably surprised on
> last Sabbath evening, by an occurrence which happened after the
> usual evening service. The large number of colored people in the
> pews was remarked, and it was not until the close of the service that
> the object of their presence in such force was explained. Immediately
> after the Benediction, and when the Rev. Mr. Cordner had descended
> from the pulpit –
>
> The Rev. Mr. Wood, rising from the pews of the church, came
> forward, and addressing the Rev. Mr. Cordner, said that it was his
> pleasing duty, on behalf of the colored inhabitants of this city, to
> present a copy of the Holy Scriptures, as a slight testimonial of their
> esteem for the noble and fearless manner in which its holy principles

on behalf of the down trodden had been asserted, and vindicated from the pulpit of this church. On their behalf he also expressed a fervent wish that Mr. Cordner might long be spared to set forth before the world these principles. And some further appropriate remarks, he concluded by hoping that all should be so guided by the principles in this sacred book, that in the Father's Mansion above, we should meet and rejoice together in the presence of God, who made of one blood all nations of men.

...

During the whole ceremony the whole body of colored people remained standing, and appeared very much affected by the proceedings.

The book is a handsomely bound copy of the Oxford edition of the Holy Bible, and bears the following inscription: –

PRESENTED
to
The Revd. John Cordner,
By the
Colored People of Montreal, as a sincere
testimonial of their esteem for his
efforts and sympathies in the Cause
of Human Freedom.
January 1, 1860.

Wood had now shelved his credentials as a public works expert and resolutely donned his clerical mantle. He did not lay claim to a university degree or to a privileged acquaintance with fictional characters who happened to have passed through Montreal on their way to Liberia and literary fame. He appeared to be doing good works, for which he had community support. The *Witness* newspaper, mouthpiece of Scottish-born merchant and publisher John Dougall, as firm an evangelical Protestant and temperance crusader as he was anti-Catholic, anti-French, anti-Irish and anti-slavery, noted on 3 March: "An effort is making under the auspices of Mr. Wood, recently from Sierra-Leone, a recognized minister of the Wesleyan Church, to get up a reading-room and evening classes for the colored population of this city; who, being for the most part escaped slaves, stand much in need of education. The scheme is a benevolent one and we trust will work well." This was rather tepid well-wishing compared with the endorsements of a group of the city's leading evangelical ministers published in the *Transcript* of 1 March:

I heartily agree with this movement to provide a Hall and Reading Room for the use and benefit of the colored inhabitants of Montreal. Such an institution will, I believe, be of great service, in promoting their religious and intellectual welfare, under the care and management of those who have taken this matter in hand. I deem it worthy of all encouragement from the various denominations of Christian people in this city.

ALEX. KEMP
Minister St. Gabriel Street [Presb.] Church
Montreal, 27th February 1860.

The contemplated movement is eminently desirable, seeing there are somewhere near 200 colored inhabitants in our city. The Rev. Mr. Wood, a recognised Minister of the Wesleyan Church, of whom I have a very favorable impression, seems admirably qualified to superintend it. The determination is to conduct the whole matter on Christian and catholic principles. Surely our brethren of African descent, who, as a race, have suffered so much, ought to have our help. I concur with Mr. Kemp in his recommendations.

HENRY WILKES, D.D.
Minister of Zion [Congregational] Church
Montreal, 27th February 1860.

I concur with my respected brethren in the sentiments expressed above. In the cities of Canada West the colored inhabitants are provided with schools and churches, but in this city they have nothing of the kind. Why is it so? As there is likely to be a rapid increase of this class of our population for some years to come, it seems the more necessary that something should be done.

W. TAYLOR, D.D.
United [Erskine] Presbyterian Church

I heartily concur in the above recommendations.

JAMES S. BONAR
[American Presbyterian Church]

Wood had the wind in his sails, so much so that he was blown away, never to be seen again in Montreal. Considering the trust that so many had placed in him, and the public attention he had drawn, it is odd that not a word appeared in the press about his absquatulation. Had the impostor been found out? Had someone detected that the "recognized minister" was nothing of the sort? It seems that he may have left Montreal as he left Monrovia in 1850, under the pretext of going abroad to raise funds for his "flock."

He had undoubtedly used forged documents, as he always did, to prove his standing as an accredited minister, but there is no record of his having been publicly exposed, prosecuted or jailed in Montreal—only a puzzling silence. His name never appeared in city directories or on municipal assessment rolls. Had he still been on the spot in August, he surely would have taken a hand in the drafting of an address that Black Montrealers intended to present to the visiting Prince of Wales. He did not (the address itself was never delivered). And he was not counted in the census of January 1861.

In that headcount, Mathew Bell, about 33, and his Montreal-born wife, Marie Catherine Eulalie Coffin, were found still living at 70 Saint-Antoine St. Living with them were Bell's recently married 18-year-old sister-in-law and her French-Canadian husband, both natives of Montreal. Neither couple had children, yet two were recorded in their home. Jane Elizabeth Williams, a 6-year-old "mulatto" schoolgirl, Roman Catholic, was practically an orphan. Her father, Samuel Williams of Virginia, had died two years earlier, and her Irish mother, Margaret Furlong, was at death's door (she died 2 April). The identity of the second child is a poser. On the census form, Bell identified him as 4-year-old George Smith, a native of England, a Methodist like Bell and his wife—like George Andrew Smith, alias A.T. Wood, for that matter.

11. ILLINOIS AND "THE FALL OF MAN"

Two curious instances of "Liberian" hustling took place in the border states of New England after Wood's disappearance from Montreal. In reviewing the highlights of his own activities for the year 1860, the Rev. Franklin Butler, the American Colonization Society agent for northern New England, noted in the society's annual report of 1861 that in Maine –

> Some funds were diverted from us by two colored men, who traversed the eastern part of the State, lecturing and soliciting aid to go to Liberia, as they said, 'on their own responsibility.' One of them was about to apply to this Society for passage on our ship, when the other unfortunately made his acquaintance, and persuaded him to go by the steamer to Liverpool, and thence to Monrovia. After collecting some hundreds of dollars, chiefly from our friends, the impostor disappeared, and had not since been heard of; the other feeling that he must go *somewhere,* shipped for Hayti.

Wood? He would not have dared dip his line in Maine a second time, would he?

The following spring, on the outbreak of the Civil War, a similar canvassing took place in Vermont. "Beware of Impostors," warned a front-page notice in the *Burlington Free Press* of 3 May 1861.

> The undersigned has good and sufficient reasons for publishing this note of caution against placing undue confidence in the representations of certain colored persons who are abroad in the country asking charity.
>
> By information easily obtained from reliable sources, the parties solicited for aid may be saved from bestowing their benefactions upon unworthy persons.

> JOHN ORCUTT,
> Travelling Sec'y Am. Col. Soc.

The Civil War had broken out on 12 April. At first glance, Rev. Orcutt's vague caution against Black beggars might seem to have targeted sharpers capitalizing on the tumult of mobilization to mulct the public, perhaps by claiming to be destitute freed slaves or fugitives from Southern slavery. But the ACS would not have targeted such frauds unless the persons involved were poaching on its preserve. Reading between the lines of Orcutt's warning, it is clear that "certain colored persons ... asking charity" were claiming to be raising funds in aid of Liberian emigration.

There was "reason to believe that at least one of these impostors has been at work of late in Vermont," Butler was quoted as saying in an accompanying note. The paper did not identify the suspect, or indicate where he had struck; neither did it spell out the nature of his imposture or why the ACS was concerned. Butler, however, was more forthcoming in his yearly report to the ACS board of directors, published in the society's 45th annual report in 1862:

> A colored impostor, under the cloak of zeal for inducing his brethren to go to Liberia, and with a long array of names of good men in Maine and New Hampshire for his commendation, made his appearance in Vermont last March, and induced some clergymen to afford him facilities for lecturing, &c. At the last we heard of him he was in rapid flight, with a *sister,* to parts unknown.

It is conceivable that the miscreants of Maine in 1860 and Vermont in 1861 were one and the same, since the one who struck Vermont had come armed with testimonials bearing the names of reputable men of Maine as well as of neighboring New Hampshire. But Butler's report was mum on the point, and no published account named the culprit.

Wood would have rated as a prime suspect were it not for the fact that he had an ironclad alibi. On leaving Montreal in the spring of 1860, he had made straight for Cincinnati, across the Ohio River from the slave state of Kentucky. Known as the "Queen of the West" for its cultural sophistication, the city was also blessed with the less regal nickname of "Porkopolis" for the remarkable quantity of pork it produced and the running of herds of pigs through the streets to the slaughterhouses. Wood was up and running there by the beginning of May, and he remained in Ohio for the next three years. In March 1861, when Butler's impostor was roaming Vermont, he was ministering to an African Methodist Episcopal (AME) congregation in Cleveland on the shores of Lake Erie.

On his first outing in Cincinnati, in the columns of the *Cincinnati Daily Commercial* of 5 May 1860, Wood seemed ready to play the same cap-in-hand game he had played in England, only this time he began by visiting Black churches, not White ones, ostensibly fundraising for a chapel in Montreal rather than a church in Liberia:

> DIVINE SERVICES. The Rev. Alfred T. Wood of London, England, late of West Africa, now resident of Montreal, Canada East, will preach at the following places on SABBATH, May 6th at New street Chapel 11 A.M.; at Allen Chapel 3 p.m., and at New Street Chapel at 7½ o'clock in the evening. He is on an agency to collect funds to purchase a small brick Chapel in Montreal for a place of worship, as well a school and reading room for the people of color in that city, and comes appointed and recommended by the White Wesleyan and Presbyterian Churches of that city. He has been ten years on mission service in Africa.

Nothing came of his pretended plans for Montreal. This was the last time he played that card and invoked the endorsement of Montreal clergymen. He then turned once more to capitalizing on his African experience. The *Daily Commercial* of 8 May informed its readers:

> We are requested to announce that Rev. A.T. Wood, formerly of England, but lately from Liberia, will lecture this evening in Baker street Church, upon his "Ten Years' Observation and Experience in Liberia." Mr. Wood is a colored Englishman—born and raised in England, where he studied and practised law, and afterwards went to Liberia as a Missionary. He is reputed a man of real ability.

So ran the notice of a talk he was to give at the African Union Baptist Church in Cincinnati. Wood introduced himself to Cincinnati, as he had to Montreal, through lectures, this time billing himself, not as a high functionary from Sierra Leone, but as a London reverend with a background in law and a decade's experience in Liberia. We may suppose that in his "Porkopolis" lectures, Wood recited his old lines about Liberia—home of our fathers, refuge of a persecuted race, Edenic landscape, as healthy as any place on Earth, great agricultural, commercial and industrial potential, etc., etc. But that was the tune he sang before Liberia had punished him for his imposture. There is no record of what he told his audience in that first advertised lecture on 8 May, only that "his auditors were well pleased with him." In another lecture he delivered at the same church six days later, he took a decidedly different tack than he had in any of his earlier productions. The man who had promoted emigration to Africa now reportedly viewed it as certain death (he was living proof that it wasn't!). Where he had formerly denounced the ACS as the handmaiden of slavery, he now praised it for its honorable intentions.

> Rev. A.T. Wood, of London, England, delivered a lecture, last night, in the Baker-street Church, which was quite largely attended, on the subject of the Colonization of Colored Americans in Africa. The speaker had spent a number of years among the African Colonies, and gave his experience in the form of an address, from which he drew the conclusion that emigrating from this country to that was a species of suicide.

> He stated that three hundred and forty-seven persons went over in the ship in which he sailed, and in thirteen months from the time they landed in Monrovia, only five were left. He described the effect of the African fever upon the system, and gave physiological reasons why persons born in this, must necessarily die in that climate. He praised the spirit of philanthropy which had suggested and kept up the colonization movement; but insisted that it was death to those who emigrated, and furnished statistics showing that the number who survived the acclimatizing process was only $7\frac{1}{2}$ per cent.

> The speaker does not believe that Africa ever can or will be colonized, and if civilized, it must be done in some other manner than by emigration thither. In Freetown, a city of 72,000 inhabitants, there were only 230 of European birth; and this fatality among the emigrants existed all over the county [sic]. The lecture was very long, but somewhat interesting, and was listened to with attention until the close.

He was lying, of course, when he counted 347 passengers on the ship that had taken him to Africa in 1850; the *Liberia Packet* had carried precisely 56. And Freetown, the capital of Sierra Leone, had nowhere near 72,000 inhabitants in 1860—more like 16,000–17,000. Here as elsewhere, Wood displayed his gift for needlessly twisting the straightest facts out of shape. His statements about emigrant survival were so much pap.

Only the sketchiest information has been found about his time in Cincinnati, and indeed about his Ohio years. He did wander about the state; whether by choice, from necessity, or at the request of certain churches or church officials is not known. For a few months in 1860, he was associated with the New Street AME church in Cincinnati and the *Daily Commercial* named him as one of two speakers at a ceremony held to cap the stone monument erected to the memory of local hero John Isom Gaines at the celebration of West Indian "Emancipation Day" on 1 August.

> Mr. Wood proceeded, and gave a very curious commingling of sermon, lecture and stump speech in manner and matter. He spoke in Wendell Phillips's style, (duly mitigated by difference in capacity), of the institution of slavery. He made one point forcibly. He said the white men pretended to believe the negro inferior in intellect. They really believed no such thing. If they were not afraid of the powers of the negro's intellect, why did they not give him or allow him educational facilities? He was very severe upon the "hydro-headed" [Hydra-headed] prejudice against the coloured race, which he pronounced "God dishonoring and man degrading."
>
> He proceeded into history to prove the greatness of Africa in other ages, and after quoting a passage from Herodotus, claimed all the glory and grandeur of ancient Egypt, from the founding of Grecian civilization to the building of the Pyramids, for the African race. The Reverend orator missed it there, however, for though there are passages in Herodotus from which it might be implied that the Egyptians were of the African race, the proof is conclusive that they were of the Caucasian race. The mummies are clear upon this point. The old Egyptians had not woolly heads, nor were their skulls shaped on the African model, nor were they of African thickness.
>
> The reverend orator spoke in high terms of the fact of emancipation in the West Indies, and drew a hopeful picture of the negro race in the future, exhorting all most earnestly to live pure lives, and

devoting themselves to their people, never to forget those in bonds, nor cease to pray and labor for their freedom. He spoke of Mr. Gaines as a type of nobleman of the African race.

By 19 August, he was at Columbus, the state capital, preaching at the Congregational Church in Broad Street, where his credentials were judged to be "of a highly satisfactory character," and by the end of the year, he had moved north to Cleveland, where "Rev. A.T. Wood, D.D., of London, England, and late of Sierra Leone," could be found preaching at the Bolivar Street AME church at Christmas time. The last pastor of the church, Rev. Samuel Williams, had died on 1 December after less than six months in office. By early January 1861, Wood had succeeded him. But his pastorate was as short-lived as Williams', as we see from a letter in the *Cleveland Morning Leader* on 20 May:

EDS. LEADER. – Gentlemen: Please tender to the Bolivar street A.M.E. Church (through your paper) my thanks for the many favors conferred on me while I had the charge of said church, and especially for the timely aid afforded by a festival got up for my benefit, through the untiring exertion of Sisters Jones, Lynch, Garrison, Green, and others. May that church and society receive an hundred fold reward by the hand of Him who promised to recognize the gift of even a drink of *"cold water to one in the name of a disciple."* God bless the labors of their present pastor beyond their present expectations, is the prayer of

Your obedient servant,
A.T. WOOD

It is odd to find the pastor taking leave of his congregation in this way rather than in person. It suggests that his departure from the Cleveland church was one more precipitate move.

Just as intriguing was his composition, published in the *Leader* of 4 February 1862, eulogizing a young Cincinnati woman who had recently died:

A tribute to the Departed.

The subject of these brief lines is one of whom I formed an acquaintance in Cincinnati during my pastoral charge of New street Church. Through the whole of my career as a public minister of the Gospel, never before had my attention been so forcibly attracted by a mortal being, who, to all appearance in life and action, did possess that grace, purity, dignity and beauty, as an angel of heaven, robed in a mantle of human clay.

All that could be conveyed in the words of "mild, gentle, obedient, kind, chaste, and beautiful;" all appeared to harmonize in the human creature I here attempt to describe. It was Miss Frances Ellevia Leach, now the departed joy and hope of her bereaved parents! At the time of my first introduction there appeared such dignity, blended with affability, purity and easy deportment of life, such childlike reverence for her parents, combined with a mature sense and love of duty, that I was led to the conclusion that she was far above the ordinary standard of persons in her years and position. A sense of *propriety* was dominant in her thoughts; *modesty* appeared as her natural habiliment; *duty* her first impulse, and *goodness* her native element. A brief interview with her at a tea party, among the most pious and respectable citizens of Cincinnati, convinced me of her extraordinary power of intellect, and I took pride in the idea that she was one of God's own models for society in days to come. Would we had more such models in our young female societies on earth! What a power of renovation to our moral world would such be in the coming years of our race.

A year and a few fleeting months have passed away, and lo! she is numbered with the silent assembly of the dead. Yes, that beautiful star, which had but risen in our human horizon, was to sit in the sombre shades of death ere it reached its meridian!

How bitter the cup of disappointment and sorrow her dear bereaved parents are called to partake! Yet, thank God! there is a ray of Heaven's consolation in this sad allotment of Providence. That unfettered spirit basks in the light of God's throne now, and Hope sings from the azure skies the hour of a future and glorious meeting, when we shall have accomplished our earthly studies in this varied school house of human probation. Farewell, loved one! Rest in peace.

Shout, Francis [sic] Ellevia, thou heroine, at last
The mantle of clay from thy spirit is cast;
Thou art loos'd from this planet of tombs;
Thou hast gone to a world ineffably bright,
Where the cloudiest day, or serenest night,
In the lap of Eternity blooms.

I long to behold thee in that blest abode,
Where, with Parents, and Angels, our Saviour and God,
Ever freed from all sorrow and pain.
There we shall shout glory, yes, glory to God,
Sav'd through the rich merits of Jesus' blood,
We shall never be parted again.

A.T. WOOD, D.D.

Just who Miss Leach was and what she had meant to Wood remain a mystery. Had she really driven him to versify? Perhaps he truly had been smitten. But as he was never known to expose his vulnerability by baring his soul in public or revealing his innermost thoughts and feelings, we cannot help but doubt the sincerity of this very public show of grief, and wonder whether A.T. Wood, D.D., for some reason, was not seeking to impress his classmates in the "varied school house of human probation" with a display of his literary prowess or just padding his clippings file.

The next confirmed sighting of him comes nearly a year later at Leesburg, about 160 kilometres east of Cincinnati, as a new era dawned in the war-torn States:

REJOICING ON THE FIRST OF JANUARY.

The colored citizens of Leesburg, Highland County, Ohio, met at Oak Grove school-house, January 1st, 1863. A. Williams was appointed Chairman, and G. Foster, Secretary.

The Chairman said that this being the day on which the President of the United States issues his Proclamation to emancipate the slaves of all States, in rebellion against the government, we have met to express our congratulations in view of that event.

A hymn was then sung by the congregation, and prayer offered by Rev. A.T. Wood, in which he feelingly invoked the Throne of Heaven to bless our government, the President and his Cabinet, and all due authority; that all things may be done in accordance with the will of the Most High; that the time may soon come when peace will be restored to our distracted country; and that liberty may be proclaimed to all the inhabitants thereof.

After some remarks by different gentlemen present, the following preamble and resolutions were read by the secretary, and unanimously adopted: –

Whereas, believing that slavery, in all its forms, is a violation of divine law, and the degradation of human nature; and that wherever it has been tolerated it has been the means of destroying the peace and happiness of that race or nation encouraging so heinous a sin, and has brought down the judgment of the Supreme Being;

And whereas, the institution of slavery has existed in the United States ever since the year 1620, and has been a great and growing evil ever since its introduction, and the cause of a wicked rebellion against the government of the United States, to the destruction of thousands of lives;

And whereas, in consequence of said rebellion, Abraham Lincoln, President of the United States, has issued his proclamation that on the 1st day of January, 1863, emancipation shall take place in all the States in open rebellion against the government; therefore,

Resolved, That we, the colored people of Leesburg and vicinity, have assembled this day for the purpose of expressing our thanks and congratulations in reference to said proclamation.

Resolved, That we regard this great decree as the most import-ant, in behalf of the colored race, that has ever been issued in America, and we hope that, as this war comes to a close, it will be the means of freeing every slave on this continent.

Resolved, That should all this be accomplished, the name of Abraham Lincoln will ever be gratefully remembered by the colored race of America; and the 1st of January should be celebrated to our latest posterity as the most important event in all our history.

A sumptuous dinner was then served to the congregation, for the preparation of which a vote of thanks was returned to the ladies, and the meeting adjourned.

That report appeared in the *Liberator* of 16 January. Thirteen years earlier, a notice in that Boston-based paper had unmasked A.T. Wood, the pretended Englishman, as George Andrew Smith of Nova Scotia. But auld acquaintance was forgot and no one in Boston, or among the *Liberator*'s readers, now recognized the name. It may also have occurred to Wood, as he blessed sweet Emancipation and tucked into the feast cooked by the Leesburg ladies, that on this day 10 years before, in an English court, he had had to down a much more bitter cup.

The Baptist pastor from Boston and Monrovia who had passed for a "recognized minister" of the Wesleyan Church at Montreal

Bishop Jabez Pitt Campbell of the African Methodist Episcopal Church.
(New York Public Library digital collections, from William J. Simmons,
Men of Mark: Eminent, Progressive and Rising, Cleveland, Ohio,
Geo. M. Rewell & Co., 1887, p.1030)

was now a minister of the African Methodist Episcopal Church. That August in Chicago, he attended the annual meeting of the AME's Indiana Conference (encompassing Illinois). A participant noted of the program of 16 August: "We had a very good time on yesterday (Sabbath) in the churches. ... At night, the Rev. A.T. Wood preached an excellent sermon." At the conclusion of the conference, Wood was assigned to the Charlestown, Ind., circuit.

From time to time in the course of the next year, his name appeared in the *Christian Recorder,* the church's national organ, as the author of obituary notices about members of his flock—none as effusive as his tribute to Frances Ellivia Leach—or as forwarding financial contributions from members. In May 1864, he was promoted to Bethel Church in Chicago, a posting that was confirmed at the annual conference in Indianapolis in August that year. Early in 1865, he was among 28 churchmen ordered by

Bishop Jabez Pitt Campbell to prepare addresses to be delivered at the next annual gathering scheduled for that August in Springfield, Ill., President Abraham Lincoln's hometown. Wood's assigned topic was "The Fall of Man."

Bishop Campbell, as it happened, was the stepfather of Montreal barber William Henry Medley. A chance communication between stepfather and stepson about any misstep by A.T. Wood in Montreal in 1859–1860 and his jig in the AME would have been up. This was the kind of bolt from the blue that could have struck him at any time, just as the appearance of a Halifax acquaintance had done in Boston in 1850. No matter how far he wandered, he had to be constantly on his guard—or preternaturally unconcerned.

He was in Chicago between 3 January and 7 February 1865 when the Illinois legislature repealed the "Black Laws" that had denied civil rights to Blacks and had sought to bar them from moving into the state. A celebration was planned for 13 February at Metropolitan Hall. "The public, as well as the friends of freedom, are invited to be present, and listen to addresses from Rev. A.T. Wood, Rev. D.G. Lett, Rev. R. DeBaptiste, and our fellow townsman John Jones, Esq., who was the bearer of the petition to the Legislature praying for the repeal of those laws," read the notice in the *Chicago Tribune*.

Wood came through in style: "Rev. A.T. Wood, an Englishman of color, read a funeral sermon upon the Black Laws. He traced their ancestry and rejoiced over their repeal. He was received with applause." Yes, as one participant observed of Wood's oration, "unlike most funeral sermons, there was not a tear shed." Wood himself gleefully reported on the episode to the *Christian Recorder*:

Chicago, Ills., Feb. 16th, 1865.

DEAR EDITOR: – I write to inform you of what our people have done, and are doing in the State of Illinois.

In the month of December last, we formed an association for the repeal of the infamous Black Laws of this State. That association was composed of every colored person of brains and means, so to speak, irrespective of sectional or denominational differences. At the head of the cause stood the indefatigable John Jones. He carefully compiled the Black Laws in pamphlet form, and strewed them broadcast in farmer style. Said Mr. Jones was appointed as general agent, to attend the sitting of the Legislature at Springfield and present the petition of the colored people of Illinois. He did present it, with 11,000 signatures. He took his stand at the door morn, noon, and evening. Every copperhead who entered the State House, ere he entered, was brought in contact with a powerful kinkyhead. You know both races meet in our worthy representative, Mr. Jones, so there was no evading him. With his presence and address, he carried his points so far as to make good use of his time. The petition was presented, lobby-work began, the Democrats raved; Republicans looked as solemn as at a funeral. Then came the "tug-of-war." Postponing, calling the House, suspending rules, and all the tactics of the times were resorted to, but there lay the great, mammoth petition, the negro-budget on their hands. The day arrives for its disposition. The Bill is called up. The vote taken.

The Honorable Senate cast 13 votes for the Repeal. On the Budget rushes to the Representative chamber. Filibustering rages, intense anxiety reigns supreme; the question is put; and in that body, 49 members, (a large majority,) vote the Black Laws *Repealed*.

Mr. Jones returns home to Chicago the happiest man I have seen for years. 100 guns were fired at Springfield in honor of the event. At Chicago, 13 were fired for the Senate, 49 for the House of Representatives, and 13 for the Governor, [Richard J.] Oglesby.

A grand Jubilee was held at Metropolitan Hall, on Monday night the 13th inst., and a glad time the citizens had. Speeches were delivered by Rev. J.B. Dawson, John Jones, Esq., Rev. Mr. Lett and Rev. De Baptiste, also a tried friend to our race, Rev. Mr. Roye [Roy], (white.) Your humble servant delivered a funeral eulogy over the corpse of poor old *Jacob Black, Law*. He is dead. God grant him an eternal sleep. Amen.

Yours, faithfully,
A.T. WOOD.

There may have been a hint of reproach in the remark of the pastor from Galesburgh concerning the quarterly meeting of his church in mid-January, that "the Rev. A.T. Wood, our presiding elder, was present. We would have been glad if the elder could have stayed longer with us, but his business at Chicago called him away." No matter.

The Rev. Elisha Weaver, editor of the *Christian Recorder,* was one of Wood's
supporters when the storm broke at Chicago in 1865.
(Credit: From James Handy, *Scraps of African Methodist Episcopal History*
(Philadelphia, A.M.E. Book Concern, 1902), p. 203.)

Affairs were once more prospering for Rev. Wood. That March
he launched a fundraising campaign to buy a lot and build a permanent home for his church, which then occupied rented premises.
The target was set at $11,500 and, a few months later, the need was
said to be pressing: "The congregation is very poor, freedmen con-
stituting no small portion of the members, and their lease has now
almost expired." He had a supporter in Rev. Elisha Weaver of
Philadelphia, editor of the *Christian Recorder.* "Rev. Dr. A.T. Wood,
of the Indiana Conference, arrived in our city, last Sabbath morning," Weaver reported that June. "He came to our residence while
we were engaged in family devotion, and took a seat until after
prayer, after which we had a hearty shake hands. He preached a
very fine discourse on Sabbath morning, in Bethel Church, and in
the afternoon in Wesley Church." Bethel Church, on 6th Street in
Philadelphia, was and still is the mother church of the AME.

If Black preachers were faulted, sometimes by their own church, for a lack of education and sophistication, the well-travelled Wood was not one of them. Witness the short piece he sent to Weaver that summer disputing the notions propagated by the "scientific racism" of his day. It is not without some elegance of thought and expression.

THE AFRICANS.

In all nations throughout the regions of this earth, however opposite in their characters, inclinations, and habits of life, all are united in one grand essential point, viz. an adoration due to a Supreme Being, and means resorted to for giving public evidence of such a belief. In every country and clime we will find altars, priests, sacrifices, festivals, religious ceremonies, and places set apart for the worship of a Deity, or a plurality of them. They also manifest an awe for the divinity, and confess an entire dependence on him, both in their undertakings, necessities, adversities and dangers. While they find futurity veiled by an impenetrable darkness to their mental powers, we find them intent upon some mode of consulting this Deity; and in order to merit his protection they offer vows, prayers, and sacrifices.

Upon this fact alone I draw the eternal line of distinction between the human and the brute creation. God has planted this innate principle in the homo species only, for no other but man adores and aspires. The doctrine, then, of "connecting links," is, to say the least, connecting nonsense; and no other than minds clothed in ignorance and sanctified to human devilism will harp upon such absurdity.

In order to demonstrate such as true, you must show me a dog at sacrifice, or an ape at its prayers.

A.T. WOOD.

The issue of the *Christian Recorder* that carried these musings also published a report on a meeting held in Philadelphia on 17 July in support of Black voting rights, where Wood's eloquence drew warm applause:

Rev. Dr. Wood, a native of England, spoke next, and said, with great force and eloquence, he thanked God that he had always enjoyed this heaven granted right, the franchise. He sympathized deeply with his brethren in America who were without it. America owed it to all her colored subjects by virtue of organic law, they being truly

Americans. Convicts and paupers from England, Ireland and Germany might come here, and, no matter how degraded, after a very short time they could vote simply because they had white skins. The colored man would not, as some pretended to think, abuse his right to vote; he only wanted to be able to vote good men into office— men who would not endeavor to crush him. He hoped there would be a qualification that only such men of whatever class as could read might vote; that ballots would be deposited by men whose heads, hearts, and minds are right. The speaker sat down amid great applause, and evidently made a good impression.

But it was summer, the Civil War was over, U.S. slavery was dead, if far from buried, and John Wilkes Booth had killed the president—time to reflect on "The Fall of Man." The annual conference of the AME churches of Indiana and Illinois was to open on 19 August in Springfield. A week before its scheduled start, the *Christian Recorder* published this jarring note about Brother Wood:

REV. A.T. WOOD.

We have received a note from Bro. D. Cooper, of Greenville, Ohio, desiring information as to whether the above named worthy divine is authorized to solicit funds to go to California, and whether he has been released from his charge by the Bishop.

In reply, we would say, that Bro. Wood's personal honor would not allow him to make any misrepresentations, especially of himself. It may be an oversight on the Bishop's part not to give official announcement through our columns, but that does not materially affect the case. Bro. Wood has our most sincere good wishes for success.

This matter did not immediately occupy the conference, but another complaint against Wood came up in the session of Tuesday, 22 August:

... There was before Conference a somewhat difficult case—a difficulty between Rev. A.T. Wood and James Curtis. Brother Curtis was silenced or suspended on the Charlestown [Ind.] Circuit, by the Quarterly Meeting Conference, until the sitting of the last Annual Conference, when it seems that the Conference referred it back to the Quarterly Meeting. Brother Curtis brought a charge against Brother

Wood for having, as he claimed, excluded him from the Church, without giving him due notice. Rev. Richard Bridges, acted on behalf of Brother Curtis, and Brother Wood acted as attorney for himself.

There the "somewhat difficult" matter rested, inconclusively as it appears, at the end of the day.

On the morning of Thursday, 24 August, "the case of Brother A.T. Wood" was the first item on the agenda, but business of a more general interest took precedence and Wood's case was put off until the following day. That evening, however, yet another complaint against Wood, was brought up, tried, and settled:

> Complaint was made against Brother Wood, by Brother Davis, on behalf of another brother, not present, who sent a letter stating that Brother Wood had made certain remarks in reference to his mission. Bro. Wood emphatically denied the charge. There was no proof furnished by either plaintiff or defendant—but one brother's word being considered as good as another's, the Conference decided that he was guilty of the charge—and that, too, without proof.

Irritatingly vague, Weaver was suppressing facts and mystifying all readers of the paper who had not attended the conference. He would not say what objectionable "remarks" Wood had been accused of uttering, or to whom, but he was prepared to go so far as to report that Wood had been convicted by his fellow churchmen without a shred of proof.

Those churchmen cannot have been pleased by the imputation. And if Weaver's idea was to shield Wood's reputation, he was going about it the wrong way. Anyone not in the know, trying to follow his reporting, would have thought that Wood was a troublemaker, the subject of an endless string of complaints. As it turned out, the one complaint disposed of at the Thursday evening session was the allegation by Brother Cooper of Ohio that Wood had tried, without authorization, to raise money for a run to California. Weaver's coyness on this subject is difficult to fathom since his paper had reported the source and substance of this charge only two weeks before.

Then on Friday, "the case of Brother Wood" took up the entire morning and afternoon sessions. Now, what was this case about? Weaver's report on the proceedings offers a few details but he

again does his level best to withhold the substance of the accusation and the nature of the evidence:

Friday Morning, Aug. 25.

Conference in session assembled, Bp. Campbell presiding, assisted
by Bishop Quinn. ... The case of Brother Wood was again brought up.

Elder Wood had been tried in the presence of Bishop Quinn by a
committee, who decided that he was guilty of imprudent conduct,
and further recommended that he be removed from his charge and
receive a severe reprimand. He left the charge by order of the Bishop,
and was in fair standing.

The document having been sent to Conference, it was read before
the members, after which the case of Dr. Wood was attended to in a
proper manner.

It was now twelve o'clock. The defendant had secured Rev. H.J.
Young and Dr. Revels for the defence, and the plaintiff had engaged
Revs. R. Bridges and John Wilkerson for the prosecution.

2 o'clock, P.M.

Conference again assembled. The case of Dr. Wood was taken up,
and the arguments pro and con were heard.

Rev. John Wilkerson led off with an argument against the
accused, and came down on him very severely, while he also advocated the purity of the Church, and showed the necessity of keeping
it from corruption.

Elder Young then followed in a most eloquent defence of the
accused, and showed most conclusively, that Dr. Wood was not lawfully nor justly proved to be guilty, to which we heartily acquiesce.

The next who spoke, was Dr. Revels, who, with wondrous tact
and ability, unraveled the whole affair, and, we believe, showed to
the satisfaction of every unbiased and candid mind that Bro. Wood
was entirely guiltless of the charge made against him.

Rev. Richard Bridges was next called upon, who arose and said
that Dr. Revel's argument had considerable weight with him, &c.
Brother Bridges made a very strong and plausible speech against the
accused.

These formalities having been gone through with, the Bishop
then remarked that the prisoner had the benefit of a doubt in his
mind, &c. The motion was taken, and Dr. Wood declared to be not
guilty of the charge. He was finally cleared and then suspended from
all official standing for one Conference year.

The "prisoner"? Surely this was a reporting error by Weaver or a slip of the tongue by Bishop Campbell: The AME was not in the habit of taking prisoners. The charge had apparently been aired some time before in Chicago at a hearing before Bishop William Paul Quinn. Now, the "formalities" had been resubmitted to the full conference, and Wood had been acquitted—yet suspended for a year?

Bishop Campbell, the founding editor of the paper, found Weaver's reports highly misleading, and on 13 September, he wrote him an indignant letter:

> Mr. Editor: – By the last number of the *Christian Recorder,* Sept. 9th, the readers of that journal are informed that two charges were preferred against Rev. A.T. Wood, for immoral conduct in the Indiana Conference, and that he was condemned and suspended from all official standing in the Church, without being found guilty of any crime. Such is the substance of the article.
>
> I deny the statement, and assert that it is not true. Two charges were preferred against that brother, of a nature sufficient to exclude a man from the kingdom of grace and glory. There was evidence, and too much evidence of his guilt before that Conference.
>
> Rev. A.T. Wood was found guilty upon the evidence of facts produced in his two trials before the Conference. For some reason best known to the Conference they applied the law and inflicted the very least instead of the most severe punishment upon him. The matter may end here, but I have serious doubts of that being the fact. If Conferences will not punish men for the highest crimes under heaven, the people have reason to thank God, that the laws of the country will sometimes punish them. It is neither just nor true that the Indiana Conference condemned or silenced Rev. A.T. Wood without evidences of guilt being found against him. On behalf of the Indiana Conference, I call upon you for the insertion of this correction, which is in accordance with her published minutes.

In a rebuttal, published in the same issue of the paper, Weaver clarified matters slightly. Two charges had been preferred against Wood, one of soliciting funds to enable him to absquatulate to California, for which he was tried and found guilty by the conference on Thursday, 24 August; and a second, which he left unspecified, for which Wood had been previously tried and convicted by

Bishop Quinn's committee in Chicago, then retried and acquitted by the conference on Friday, 25 August. To Weaver, the fundraising charge was small potatoes compared to the one Campbell had called one of "the highest crimes under heaven." Still, Weaver did not give it a name.

In light of Campbell's harsh language and of Weaver's obdurate opacity on the subject, we suspect that Wood's alleged "immoral conduct" involved sexual misconduct of a possibly criminal nature. The church's proposed way of dealing with the problem tends to support that inference. As we learn from Weaver, in remarks he published on 30 September, Bishop Quinn and his committee had recommended that Wood be severely reprimanded, dismissed from his post and banished from Chicago.

THE EDITOR'S ANSWER TO THE BISHOP.

In relation to the action of the Indiana Conference in the case of Dr. Wood, relative to the various charges preferred against him.

As will be seen by his article in this number, our worthy and distinguished friend, Bishop CAMPBELL, has seen proper to give a flat denial to certain statements made by us in the RECORDER of August 9th [read September 9th]. Coming as it does from a Bishop—one occupying as high a position as can be exercised in our Church—we are completely astounded at the unmistakable contradiction. We can scarcely believe that the Bishop would make use of such harsh and unkind language towards us as may be found in his communication in our columns—and especially so, if he has taken the precaution of *carefully considering* our article in the issue of September 9th, No. 36, where the objectionable remarks in reference to the case of Dr. Wood are made—made, not in a spirit of criticism, but in good faith! We demand that Bishop Campbell shall read our entire article—not merely a stray sentence here and there. In justice, this, at least, is due us. Now, let it be fully understood that we were an eye witness and close observer of the whole affair, and feel confident that we can fully sustain each and every statement made by us in reference to the action of Conference. The RECORDER of September 9th shows that Dr. Wood was charged with collecting money on false pretenses, (purporting to be sent to California.) This much was couched in a letter sent by a good and honest minister of the Ohio Conference. Upon its being read, Dr. Wood most emphatically denied the charge.

Now, then, there was no one else present at the Conference who had ever heard Dr. Wood admit that he was guilty of the charge,—and therefore, until a man is proved to be guilty of libel, one man's word is as good as that of another. This the Bishop must admit.

Nearly all the testimony given was in reference to the good character of the brother who had sent the charge against Dr. Wood. There was no witness to prove the truth of the allegation—and even the complainant himself was not present, the thing being done by proxy. But for all this, Conference decided him to be guilty, as stated in our article referred to. The strangeness of the proceeding rather struck us; and as the unfortunate plaintiff [accused] stood, with pitiful face, almost without an advocate, in the "house of his friends," we could not but express our sympathy (not criticism of the decision of Conference) in his behalf. For this, we have been made the subject of Bishop Campbell's severe and totally uncalled for language. Let the calm reader decide whether or not we have overstepped the limits of our editorial jurisdiction.

The next mark made against the Doctor was in relation to his former case, which had been tried in Chicago by a committee, before one of our Bishops. The said committee, in view of what had been alleged against Dr. Wood, recommended that he should be reprimanded by the Bishop, and then be removed from the charge which he was at that time holding—this being the prescribed penalty. The Bishop was then to give him another charge, which, we think, was to be New Albany, Ind.; but it appears that he did not get it.

The Conference tried the whole affair over again. Dr. Wood chose Dr. Revels and Rev. H.J. Young as his counsel, by whose ability and unswerving sense of honor and justice he was cleared. Now, then, they wished to locate him, but could not, from the fact that the Conference had already decided him to be guilty of collecting money to go to California, which was but a small bill of indictment compared with the one on which he was tried in Chicago. One came off on Thursday, and the other on Friday. A motion was made, we think, by Brother Bridges, that, as Conference had decided him to be guilty of wrongfully collecting money to go to California, the charge be reconsidered,—which was put by the Bishop, and carried. Now, we ask our good Bishop, Did not the Conference, by their own action, clear him of every charge which had been made against him? Most assuredly so. The Conference then, by resolution, moved that Dr. Wood be removed from all official standing for one year.

In No. 36 of the RECORDER, we merely stated that Conference cleared him. We think the Bishop will find that we have said nothing but the truth.

Now, as regards the guilt of Dr. Wood on any of the specified charges, we have never expressed our opinion. We have our own private belief in the matter.

Readers of the *Recorder* never did learn the nature of the mysterious charge against Wood, neither were they told whether Wood got to read "The Fall of Man," but he lived it. At the end of this ordeal, he did not wind up behind bars, as he had in Maine, England and Liberia, but the ministerial career of Dr. A.T. Wood had certainly taken a very public hit.

There may have been an implied denial of his pretensions in an item the *Christian Recorder* published the following spring. In a sketch of the life of AME Bishop Daniel Alexander Payne, the paper of 7 April 1866 noted that Payne was "the only colored clergyman in this country, on whom the degree of Doctor of Divinity has been conferred." Perhaps by then, editor Weaver had come to appreciate the true nature of the friend and colleague he had known as Rev. Dr. Wood.

12. RECONSTRUCTION

If ever there was a time for Wood to retire to his dressing room, change his costume and makeup, and recast himself in a new role, this was it. Hadn't he taken the character of Rev. A.T. Wood about as far as it would go? Besides, if, as Bishop Campbell had suggested, the civil authorities might want to consider prosecuting him for committing some of the "highest crimes under heaven," he had good reason to make himself scarce. He left Springfield before his church trial ended and quickly exited Illinois.

It was a wide world he travelled—Africa, Europe, North America—but it was also a small one, in which someone could pop up at any turn to rattle the skeletons in his closet and show him up as a fraud. It had happened in the U.S., in England, Liberia ... Still, he persisted in his impostures, undeterred by the ever-present risk of exposure, clinging all the while to his tainted alias. After that debacle in Illinois, where would he spring up next? In what guise?

The notice he placed in the *Colored Tennessean* on 13 January 1866 answered those questions and raised more:

Dr. A.T. Wood,

A GRADUATE of Cambridge University, late Missionary to Africa, and a member of the Indiana Annual Conference, is now a practising Physician in this city. His thorough education, and success in medical skill, has raised him to eminence among his colored brethren and friends, as well demanded respect from the whites both North and South. Dr. Wood will be found at his office on Gay street, between Vine and Spruce, residence of Mr. Jerry Stodard.

Private diseases promptly attended to in strict confidence. Terms quite moderate. Colored friends patronize your own Physician.

DR. A. T. WOOD,

A GRADUATE of Cambridge University, late Missionary to Africa, and a member of the Indiana Annual Conference, is now a practising Physician in this city. His thorough education, and success in medical skill, has raised him to eminence among his colored brethren and friends, as well demanded respect from the whites both North and South. Dr. Wood will be found at his office on Gay street, between Vine and Spruce, residence of Mr. Jerry Stodard.

Private diseases promptly attended to in strict confidence. Terms quite moderate. Colored friends patronize your own Physician. jan13–6m

Shortly after his arrival in Nashville, Wood advertised
his services as a physician.
(*Colored Tennessean*, 24 March 1866, p. 2)

Physician now, Cambridge graduate, in Nashville, commanding respect from Whites North and South. Really!

That was quite the self-reconstruction—a selfie as deceptive as any item in his arsenal of "documents," a bundle of falsehoods capped with a self-serving appeal to racial solidarity—and in a rather surprising locale. From caring for the souls of Black inhabitants of New England, Africa, England, Canada, the North and the Midwest, he now turned to mending their broken bodies in the war-battered U.S. South. He had no family, no roots to lure him there. He could have gone to California, as he had been set to do when stationed at Chicago; he could have made his home almost anywhere, other than in the places where he had already exercised his ministry. He chose to go South.

Drs. Amos Aray and Joshua Byers Young, the two other Black medical doctors in Nashville in 1866, would have been curious to meet this paragon who claimed to command respect across the color line. Surely, they would have wanted to share experiences, consult, or just talk shop. Aray, who practised a form of alternative medicine and who prided himself on compounding "his own medicines from *carefully selected material*," had set up his practice in Nashville around July 1865. A year later, he opened a drug store on

Cherry Street, across from the post office. Young first offered Nashville his medical expertise, along with his Nubian Hair Elixir "for the prevention and cure of baldness," around March 1866. The three of them were carpetbaggers, newcomers to the South. Aray and Young were Northerners. And Wood? He persisted in his role as the Englishman. Given their common professional interests and outsider status in a racially fractured society, it would have been natural for them to club together. Perhaps Wood and Young were guests at Aray's wedding that December; his bride, Leonora E. Ball, a young teacher from Ohio, another outsider, would be one of the first members of the teaching staff at Fisk, Nashville's Black university, incorporated one month after their wedding.

In terms of medical practice and experience, Aray and Young were ahead of Wood, both having served in medical posts on the Union side in the bloody operating theatre that had been the Civil War. Michigan-born Aray, in his late 30s—roughly ten or twelve years Wood's junior—had studied medicine at the University of Michigan in 1852–54, without taking a degree, then at the Eclectic Medical Institute in Cincinnati for a few months in 1854–55. At the end of the winter of 1855–56, he had set up in practice at Chatham, Canada West (Ontario), and then closed up shop in 1858 to join Dr. Martin Delany's projected Niger Valley Exploring Party as surgeon. But budget cuts had obliged him to withdraw from that venture before Delany left for Africa in May 1859, and he had resumed his practice at Chatham. He returned to the U.S. during the Civil War. In late 1863, Delany, then a recruiter for the Union army, called on him to screen Black recruits. Young, a Pennsylvania native in his midforties, 20 years married, had long lived in Ohio where, on the eve of the war, he had been practising in Mercer County. In the last year or so of the war, he served as an assistant surgeon in the 15th Regiment of Ohio Infantry. Could these two seasoned hands have failed to diagnose a case of terminal imposture in their "eminent" colleague? If they did sense something suspicious, they did not broadcast the fact.

Another outsider whose presence might have rattled Wood was the Rev. John Seys, a White West Indian who had spent the last thirty years bouncing back and forth between Liberia and the

U.S. He had arrived in Nashville at the beginning of January 1866, shortly before Wood's advertisement appeared in the newspaper. From 1834 to 1845, he had served as superintendent of Liberian missions for the Methodist Episcopal Church, and later as an agent of the Maryland State Colonization Society, special agent in Liberia of the ACS and, for much of the last decade, the American government's agent for the care and resettlement in Liberia of Africans freed from slave ships intercepted by the U.S. navy. His church had assigned him to post-war Nashville, swarming with freedmen crammed into makeshift dwellings and sorely in need of care—spiritual and physical—to minister to the newly freed slaves and teach them the 3-Rs. He may not have subscribed to the *Colored Tennessean*. He may not have known of Wood's sorry reputation in Liberia; his time there and the days when Wood's notoriety was established did not quite coincide. And Dr. Wood's publicity, including puffs in the *Colored Tennessean* vaunting his "superior knowledge of medicine" and his "extensive experience in Europe and the United States," made no specific reference to Liberia. Still, tuning in to the needs of the freedmen, Seys surely would have heard of this Black doctor with the remarkable credentials. Wouldn't he have been curious to meet the Cambridge-educated physician who, like him, had known Africa? But Seys' time in Nashville was short. Duty called him away in October, when he was appointed U.S. consul general to Liberia.

From the land of Lincoln in September 1865, Wood had made his way to Tennessee's capital within a month. As he had done at Montreal and Cincinnati, he introduced himself to the public through lectures, a good way to display his oratorical gifts and moonshine erudition, gauge the reactions, make connections and weigh his prospects. The *Colored Tennessean* encouraged him in its issue of 14 October:

COURSE OF LECTURES.

The Rev. Dr. Wood, of the African M.E. Church, is at this time delivering a course of lectures in this city. The subjects of these lectures are as follows, viz: "Africa and the Africans;" second, "The Bible and Slavery," third, "The necessity of giving the colored man the elective franchise."

The first of the course was delivered on Tuesday night last [3 Oct], at St. John's Chapel. A large and appreciative audience was present and the Doctor enchained their attention for over two hours. Interesting statistics concerning the inhabitants of the different governments in Africa were given, and the subject of climatic changes was handled in an entirely new and original manner. The second lecture of the course was delivered at the Christian Church, on Tuesday night [10 Oct]. Our reporter was not present, but we have heard the lecture highly spoken of. Lectures of this kind should be patronized by our people, as they instruct, elevate and enlighten.

Wood then seemed set to resume his preaching career, suspended in Illinois two months earlier, but he soon changed course. By the beginning of 1866, Rev. Dr. Wood, D.D., had morphed into Dr. Wood, M.D. In the advertisement for his services reproduced at the beginning of this chapter, he still identified himself as a former missionary in Africa and a member of the "Indiana Annual Conference" (a cryptic reference to the AME that might have puzzled some readers—why not come right out and name the church?). From then on, however, he was no longer routinely called Rev. but Dr.—and doctor of medicine, not divinity. As the topic of his third lecture suggested, he also showed an interest in politics, his ambitions in that field flowering as soon as Tennessee granted Black adult males the right to vote in 1867.

As to why he decided to let his religious "calling" slide to focus on the practice of medicine, it might be supposed that he wanted to make himself useful. That might be true of anyone but Wood. All his efforts so far had been directed at his own survival and advancement, not at bettering the lot of Blacks in general, and he did not change directions now. After Chicago, he may have thought it wise to ease out of the preaching game. If he had wanted to offer Nashville Blacks the kind of practical help for which he was suited, he could have taught school or set up as a house carpenter. He seems to have quickly sized up the situation and concluded that, while there were carpenters and preachers and teachers a-plenty, there was a crying need for Black doctors. Doctoring carried prestige. It has been suggested that Blacks saw their physicians as "race leaders" in the postwar struggle to better their lot. Cue the eminent Cambridge graduate.

But Wood remained Wood at heart as well as in name. He held on to his well-travelled alias, and his middle initial may as well have stood for Trouble because Trouble had been his close companion for 20 years—and trouble did surely come in the fall of 1866.

On 18 August, the Probate Court had given Wood permission to adopt Mary Jane Myrick as his heir and next-of-kin. Three months later ...

A COLORED PHYSICIAN IN TROUBLE – ARREST OF DR. ALBERT WOODS ON A CHARGE OF SEDUCING HIS ADOPTED DAUHTER [*sic*]. – There was considerable excitement created among our colored population yesterday afternoon, caused by the arrest of one of their leading and influential physicians, on the heinous charge of seducing a young girl whom he had adopted as his daughter.

The arrest was made at the instance of Sarah Merrick [*sic*], the mother of the girl, who says her daughter is about fifteen years of age; that she has for a long time been living in the family of Dr. Albert Woods; that the Doctor has taken advantage of her youth, and the circumstances by which she was surrounded, and succeeded in compassing her ruin.

The defendant is a fine looking old man, and has the appearance of more than ordinary intelligence. He is probably sixty years of age. His victim is a mere child, in appearance, and is in an advanced stage of pregnancy.

The prisoner was carried before Esquire Mathews, and at the request of his counsel, the examination was continued until to day [14 November], at 11 o'clock A.M.

"Dr. Albert Woods" was unmistakably Alfred T. Wood. Sarah Merrick or Myrick? An acquaintance. Her daughter? Apparently she was Wood's lawfully adopted daughter, but whatever disquiet Black Nashvillians may have felt at the arrest of one of their "leading" members would have subsided the next day, 14 November, when he was acquitted:

EXAMINATION OF DR. ALBERT T. WOOD – HIS ACQUITTAL. – We noticed in yesterday's paper the arrest of Dr. Woods, a colored physician, on the charge of seducing a young girl whom he had adopted as his daughter. The examination took place yesterday, at eleven o'clock A.M., before Esqs. Mathews and Patterson.

The magistrate's office was crowded to excess by persons of every hue, the majority of them no doubt drawn there by a desire to satisfy a morbid anxiety to hear the disgusting details generally brought out in trials of this character.

A number of witness [sic] were examined but no evidence was adduced to show that the prisoner had been guilty of the offense charged. On the contrary, the girl testified that her ruin was accomplished by a negro man named Thomas, who belonged to one of the colored regiments stationed in this city; that the prisoner had at all times treated her with great kindness, and never made any improper proposals to her.

A number of witnesses testified to the good character of the defendant, and official documents were produced showing him to be a regularly ordained minister of the gospel.

The case was argued by Guild & Smith for the prosecution, and by E.W. Parker and Alexander B. Hoge of the prosecution [sic].

After a careful review of the evidence, Esquire Mathews announced the decision of the court to be that the prosecution had failed to sustain the charge, and the defendant was therefore discharged, the prosecutor to pay the costs.

The one Black person who had cause to rue that outcome was Sarah Merrick or Myrick. Not only had she failed to make her charge stick, she was saddled with the costs of the prosecution.

The court ruling settled the matter of Wood's guilt before the law, but it leaves us with a question: Could Mary Jane Myrick, said to have lived in Wood's home "for a long time," have been at the heart of the unspecified AME charge against him in Illinois in 1865? If, back in Chicago, she had passed for his adopted daughter, and he was thought to have seduced her, he would have been suspected of incest, or close to it, which would explain Bishop Campbell's condemnation of Wood's offence as one of the "highest crimes under heaven," behavior of a kind "sufficient to exclude a man from the kingdom of grace and glory." The jury is still out on that one.

The case shows once more how quickly Wood found his niche and won acceptance, accompanied by a dash of controversy, in practically every corner where he alighted. As always, his "official documents" helped, as also did his appearance—he was now a "fine looking old man" with an air of "more than ordinary intelligence." As to how he could so easily pass for a physician, this would have been a cinch for a man with his cheek and talents. He needed no

licence, only an actor's ability to play the part, plus some knowledge gained from observation, experience and a little reading.
The Medical Society of the State of Tennessee had held the exclusive right, since its founding in 1830, to issue medical licences, but
no law required practitioners to be licensed—and no medical society in Tennessee was yet willing to admit Blacks. Under the circumstances, no medical body had a right to poke its nose into his
business. Besides, for most of Wood's patients, medical care would
have amounted to little more than "bleed, puke, purge and starve,"
with now and then a poultice, all of which he could manage as well
as anyone. Had he not given an indication of his "superior knowledge of medicine" long before this, in his *Geschichte der Republik
Liberia,* where he had claimed to have a better grasp of the causes
and treatment of malaria than physicians did?

His so-called daughter was to make one more splash in the fall
of 1867, when his political career was in full flight. A report of this
new difficulty brought renewed suggestions of a quasi-incestuous
relationship:

A SABLE ESCULAPIUS IN TROUBLE.

"Dr." Wood and His Protégé at Columbia –
Big Fuss and a Gay Lothario.

The last issue of the Columbia *Herald and Gazette* has something
dramatic in regard to the negro Wood, who cut so much of a figure
in the late State election. It says:

"During last summer much to do was made over one A.T. Wood,
a free man of color, by the Radical leaders of this and some of the
adjoining counties. He was quite a toast among the negroes, and
celebrated as an orator, physician and divine, and we are told claimed
to be a graduate of Cambridge College. All went well with the
"Doctor" until last Friday morning, when misfortunes dire and disgraceful overtook him. It seems that the course of his love has neither been true nor smooth; but we reck not the past—nor does the
"Doctor." On Thursday night or Friday morning one of the town
police was applied to, to look up an erring daughter by adoption of
the "Doctor," whom some gay Lothario of the colored persuasion
had enticed from safe keeping and fatherly care. Early Friday morning the daughter in question made her appearance at the negro
Bureau, followed soon by the Wood-be father. High words soon arose

between the two about a child of the daughter, and mayhap of the father. The "Doctor" finally snatched the child from its mother's arms, whereupon she made gght [?], flew at him and snatched him vigorously, but all in vain. He carried off the child in triumph, she following, abusing and pounding him. The law stepped in, in the person of Capt. Frael, and summoned the parties to appear before the Recorder. On Saturday morning the case was tried, and the "Doctor" and should-be father was fined $3 and costs, and the child remanded to the mother in lieu of any acknowledged father.

In the course of the quarrel and trial it leaks out that this A.T. Wood is a precious fellow, who deserves what perhaps he may yet get—a berth in the penitentiary for subornation. We are told that the woman whom he claims as his adopted daughter has been living with him for a great while, and that he was tried in Nashville some time ago for living in open and notorious lewdness with her, and upon trial she swore the child—about which they had been quarreling—to some white man. From Nashville they came to this place, and this woman has been living with him until Friday last [11 October]. In the meantime, it appears that a Captain of the Radical Leage [sic] has walked into her affections, to the huge disgust and jealousy of the "Doctor." Hence the quarrel. Hence these disclosures. We hope the matter will be investigated, and if the facts are as related, this hoary-headed old sinner be brought to punishment.

The writer evidently was skeptical of Wood's medical qualifications and dismissive of his Cambridge degree, and he wanted the "old sinner" investigated for having incited at least one witness to lie under oath. Such allegations, coming from a press that demeaned Blacks, scoffed at their accomplishments and was generally hostile to Wood's Republican politics, did nothing to diminish his standing among Blacks or to impede his political rise.

Signs of that progress were evident within weeks of the opening of Tennessee's political doors to Blacks. On 26 February 1867, Republican Governor William Gannaway Brownlow, fiercely anti-secessionist and anti-Confederate, signed into law the bill recognizing their right to vote. Not that Parson Brownlow, as he was known from a previous life as a Methodist minister, was eager to groom a Black successor or to see Blacks throng the legislature and fill government offices. He and White Americans generally, not only Southerners, had grown so accustomed to looking down on Blacks

The Tennessee State Capitol became the focus of much of Wood's attention.
(Library of Congress, LOT 4388-L [P&P] Sketch
by H.P. Whinnery, c. 1880, engraved by A. Little, Philadelphia)

that looking up to them was impossible, and would be for years to come. It was as if the so-called Radical Republicans were willing to cede some rights to Blacks, confident that Whites would rule forever, while "conservatives"—those set against federal enforcement of equal rights—saw any concession to Blacks as paving the way to "Negro supremacy." But politics was politics. Brownlow's Republicans held sway thanks in large part to the disenfranchisement of unrepentant Confederate rebels. Giving Blacks the vote would strengthen the Republicans' hand: Practically to a man, Blacks would vote for the party of Lincoln, the "emancipator," the party that had made Tennessee the first among the secessionist states to abolish slavery, and the one that now gave them the vote.

The political door had no sooner squeaked open than the Davidson County Republican Committee rushed out to "embrace the most influential Negro leaders," Dr. A.T. Wood among them. These leading figures were given seats at the local party convention. They rallied Black voters—there were an estimated 5,800 in Davidson County—at the state capitol on 13 April. Dr. Wood, "all the way from Albion's Isle," was one of the speakers who addressed the crowd on that occasion. His subject was "the 'ethnological and physiological' origin and development of the Hamitic race"—not exactly "I have a dream" material, but as the *Nashville Union and Dispatch* reported, "the negroes ... seemed to drink in his 'words of learned length' on that subject." The ethnology lesson ended, Wood tackled the nitty-gritty of politics:

> He said God raised up Abraham Lincoln to carry out the work of emancipation. He had chastised the country, and slavery was destroyed; but he [Wood] did not wish to see those elected to office who would disinter its putrid remains. We have to look after our own interests. We must vote with one eye open. The land-holder will tell you if you do not vote his way, he will not allow you to live on his farm; don't fear that; be quiet, keep still, and when the day of election comes go to the polls and vote, and when you go home he will increase your wages. Go for no man who abuses Brownlow, Congress or the Radical party. Brownlow is a Southern man; so is Trimble; so are we all Southern men.

Notwithstanding this endorsement of native son John Trimble, a former state Assemblyman, senator and attorney-general, as the prospective Republican candidate for Congress in the 5th Congressional District, Wood and other Blacks walked out in protest at the party convention that nominated him a month later. Staging their own convention, the dissidents nominated Northerner John Lawrence, superintendent of the Davidson County Freedmen's Bureau (who later withdrew from the race).

Wood was also called on to carry the "Radical" torch outside Nashville. On 20 April, "Dr. Wood, a talented colored physician of Nashville," as an out-of-state reporter dubbed him, was one of several speakers to address a rally outside the court house in Gallatin that drew most of the Black population of Sumner County.

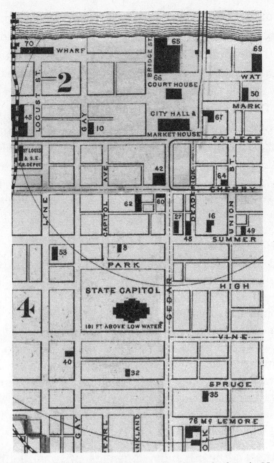

Map of the area around the Capitol. In Wood's early days in Nashville,
he lived and practised on the block behind the Capitol, on Spruce St.,
between Gay and Cedar streets.
(Library of Congress, Geography and Map Div., G3964.N2 1877 .F6)

An estimated crowd of 5,000 turned out. The hoopla and speech-
ifying began at 3 in the afternoon and lasted until midnight, with
one brief intermission.

On 11 May, he spoke at a Black rally at Clarksville in
Montgomery County, by the Kentucky border. The *Clarksville
Weekly Chronicle* generally ignored the substance of his talk, but
dwelt on the style of his presentation, suggesting that "Dr. Wood,
with a full sense of the important trusts he had held as a delegate

from Exeter Hall, England, to Honolulu, in the Sandwich Islands, and elsewhere," had not forsaken those self-important airs that Hilary Teage had sniffed at in Liberia years before:

> His stately presence then made its way to the speaker's table and then his right hand leisurely took hold of an inch wide guard and drew from its honored resting place near his heart a glittering gold watch. Upon this his piercing eye rested for something like a minute. Then replacing it with easy grace and throwing his head a little back, Cicero opened out upon us in all his matured and meridian splendors. With more than the facile handling of that distinguished Roman, he aired his profound learning and research before the starting eyes and gaping mouths of his colored "fellow-citizens," who wondered "whar dat nigger ever larnt so much." Regardless of the Scriptural injunction that "you cast no pearls before swine," Dr. Wood slung his Latin and Greek and Hebrew around with lavish hand among those who knew nothing about the value of such gems. He is not only a ripe scholar, but one that is rotten ripe, for he utterly discarded Anthon and Leverett and Fulton in the use and meaning of the classic vernaculars. He said, over and over, with that fervor that belongs only to originators and discoverers, that the word Radical came from the Latin word *Radi*. What cared so independent a linguist as Dr. Wood that *Radi* could not be found in any known Latin dictionary? He also translated the Latin word *Conservo* by "to stand still." What recked this sable Dr. Parr that no other man, Roman or modern ever translated it thus? But we have not space to dwell upon other exhibitions of his superhuman lore, or to give that synopsis of his matchless effort which it deserves.

As biased and dismissive as the reporting was, this snapshot of Wood lecturing freedmen on ethnology and wonky Latin etymologies rings true. His urge to act magisterial and show off often did get the better of him. But a similar report in Nashville's *Republican Banner* elicited a rebuttal from Wood, of which the most interesting feature is perhaps the *post scriptum,* containing some biographical factoids—false, of course:

> NASHVILLE, Tenn.,   15th May, 1867.
>
> EDITOR REPUBLICAN BANNER – *Dear Sir:* As you have published an anonymous communication, from Clarksville, Montgomery county, in regard to myself and a speech I made there.

I take the liberty to denounce the whole communition [*sic*]. My *watch guard* is not half an inch wide; it never had a *gold occupant* attached to it. I did use the Latin word *Radix,* and not the word used by my assailant.

As he slanders my watch guard and watch, so he slanders the whole proceedings of the meeting.   Yours truly,

A.T. WOOD, M.D.

P.S. My mission was to Africa, from May, 1842, to April, 1859.

I graduated at Cambridge University, in 1841, from which I received my diploma.

On the Fourth of July, he was in Fayetteville, near the Alabama line. Shots rang out. A report that Wood had been the target of a Rebel assassin was dismissed by his opponents. The *Fayetteville Observer* suggested that Wood, who was unhurt, and his Radical associates had seized on an unrelated offstage incident to add lustre to his image:

> The [Nashville] Press and Times of the 6th says an effort was made by a Rebel to assassinate the negro "Dr. Wood," while speaking at the courthouse in this place on the 4th. The statement is a *falsehood* in its length and breadth, in detail and in the aggregate. We have the evidence of a leading white Radical, who says he was in [*sic*] five feet of the belligerents, and saw the whole affair. He says the difficulty was a private matter between two negroes, and had no reference whatever to the speaker, or the subject under discussion ... – The assertion that one hundred dollars was offered by the Conservatives, or any one else, to shoot the "nigger speaker," is a *lie* of Dr. Quinine's own begetting.

While the Nashville city directory for 1867 listed Wood as a physician at 179 Gay Street, the report of his run-in with his "daughter" that fall indicated that he had recently moved to Columbia, in Maury County, southwest of the capital. He did not stay there long. About the time of his dispute with his "daughter," he relocated to Murfreesboro, in Rutherford County, about 55 kilometres southeast of Nashville. *Freedom's Watchman,* the local Black newspaper, announced in its editorial columns on 16 October: "Dr. Wood, the eminent colored physician of Nashville, has determined to locate in this city for the purpose of practising his profession." A week later, Wood blew his own horn in that paper, in terms similar to those he had used on establishing his medical practice in Nashville in 1866. This time, he claimed to have been practising as a physician for more than 30 years:

NOTICE!!

DR. A.T. WOOD, THE EMINENT colored physician, formerly of Nashville, Tennessee, is now located at the corner of Lytle and Academy streets, in the city of Murfreesboro.

All diseases, both common and private, attended to in strict confidence. Terms very moderate.

Dr. Wood is a graduate of Cambridge University, England, and a practitioner of over thirty years standing.

All chronic diseases promptly attended to, with assurance of success.

At the end of November, he also appears to have married again. At least, county records show that on 22 November, a colored man named A.T. Wood obtained a licence to marry a colored woman identified as Mary Jane Wood—would that, by any chance, have been Mary Jane Myrick, his adopted "daughter"?—but it is not clear from the surviving register that a wedding actually took place.

In leaving Nashville, he did not abandon the political career on which he had embarked. No sooner had he settled in Rutherford County than he sought election as county clerk:

"Dr." Wood, a colored Solomon from Nashville, who has some pretensions in the way of physic and Latin, and whose Latin, by the way, is a most effectual physic, is one of the aspirants for the County Clerkship, and wants to be attorney for all the deluded darkies in the State who have been swindled by claim agents. The latter appointment he expects to get from the "State."

Whether he angled for his own appointment, or simply advocated that the state name someone to protect the freedmen from exploitation, he did at this time make a public show of concern for them. In a letter to *Freedom's Watchman,* he explained:

In considering the present state of things in regard to the *contract system* as carried on at present, and the advantages taken of the freedmen by their employers, I am of opinion that the State ought to make some provision for a colored *Attorney at Law;* to take up and investigate all such cases where the complainant is too poor to fee a lawyer. This would blockade this wholesale swindling of the colored man out of the amount due for his year's labor. The [Freedmen's] Bureaus are crowded with hundreds of such cases, and no white Attorney will attend to them unless he gets his fees, and then it is hard work for him to prosecute a white man for a negro. All his sympathy is with the white man, and his prejudice against the black. I have already suggested this state of things to Headquarters, hoping thereby, in doing my duty, to relieve much suffering and inconvenience.

A.T. Wood, M.D.

He had sent a memorial to Rutherford County's representative in the General Assembly, proposing the passage of a law creating special colored attorneys, but the House Judicial Committee judged a law "unnecessary, as any person, whether white or colored, can now practice law as an attorney, provided they are otherwise qualified according to law."

Wood did not gain the county clerkship or an appointment as the freedmen's attorney, but he was not entirely left out in the cold. On 18 January 1868, the Rutherford County Republican convention chose him as a delegate to the state convention taking place in Nashville four days later. At the latter, he was selected one of two alternate delegates from Tennessee's 4th Congressional District to the national Republican Convention to be held in Chicago 20–21 May.

Soon after his selection, his opponents spread a rumor that he had turned his back on the Radicals and sold out to the Conservative Republicans. The *Nashville Union and Dispatch* of 20 February reported:

"NOT SO" – Under this head, the Radical organ on behalf of "A.T. Wood, M.D.," (colored,) denies that he has gone over to the Conservatives and says he is "a straight out Republican." It is not a matter worth a baubee one way or the other, though the individual in question has taken great pains to define his position. In a letter before us he says he is a Republican but adds: "I do not believe in placing our offices in the hands of Northern men who never loved the negro at home sufficient to vote there for his franchise." Is that the "straight-out" article?

Delegates arrive in Chicago for 1868 Republican National Convention of May 20-21. Wood had been selected as an alternate delegate from Tennessee's 4th Congressional District, but he had died a week earlier.
(*Harper's Weekly*, 6 June 1868, p 360)

Another paragraph on the facing page repeated the charge of betrayal, and this time it claimed, on the authority of a Radical source, that Wood had been bought:

> A QUESTION OF VERACITY. – "Dr." Wood, the colored educated physician who has so long figured with the Radicals and slaughtered Latin on the Tennessee stump, says, through the immaculate Press and Times, that the statement to the effect he had gone over to the Conservatives is "a damnable lie." However that may be, we got the information from Simon pure Radical of Rutherford, who also stated that the Radicals had offered the "Dr." fifty dollars to stump the county for them, but that the Conservatives had secured him at seventy-five dollars.

It is striking that a certain press that was all too eager to discredit Wood never succeeded in doing so. Rather than look seriously into his credentials and background, it contented itself with mocking him and making snide insinuations, parsing his faulty Latin and going out of its way to be gratuitously offensive. It seems to have made no effort to probe his past, and never came close to uncovering the truth about the "educated physician" from Albion's

Isle. More than a century would pass before James Summerville, a fact-checking historian, ascertained that while Wood claimed to have studied at Cambridge, Cambridge had never heard of him. His name was nowhere to be found in the 10-volume *Alumni Cantabrigienses: A Biographical List of All Known Students, Graduates and Holders of Office at the University of Cambridge, from the Earliest Times to 1900.*

The *Union and Dispatch* was clearly not convinced by its own reporting. Witness this item it published on 14 May, as Wood was preparing to leave for Chicago and the national Republican convention: " 'Dr.' A.T. Wood, a negro Radical stump orator of some note, died at Murfreesboro day before yesterday, of apoplexy." The one-sentence report was headed, "Death of a Prominent Negro Radical." Radical to the end, then.

13. OBITUARY

Was it true? Had he really died that 12 May? Wood being Wood, you want solid proof that this wasn't just another absquatulation. You want the *corpus delicti,* but you won't find it. There is no record of a funeral, his grave site is unknown, and no paper other than the *Nashville Union and Dispatch* seems to have noted his passing. It is on record, however, in the Rutherford County archives, that on 7 July 1868, county authorities approved the payment of $5 to Cole Brown for "making coffin for Dr. A.T. Wood, Dec'd a Pauper." There is nothing there to confirm the exact date, place or cause of death, but for want of a proper certificate, this entry in the county minutes and the 20-word notice of his passing in the columns of the *Union and Dispatch* will have to do.

So, the great impersonator died a pauper, on 12 May 1868, buried God-knows-where in Cole Brown's pine box, generally ignored and soon forgotten, but firmly lodged in history's hard drive, with no possibility of parole.

Like Wood, Cole Brown had been one of Rutherford County's 25 delegates to the state Republican convention in January. Is it possible that, in making Wood's coffin, he acted out of friendship for the man? Not likely. It seems clear that Wood never had a friend; dupes certainly, batches of them, and acquaintances but no friends. The games he played made it impossible to let anyone into his confidence and pretty well ensured that his life of imposture would end more or less as friendless as it had always been. Another truth that would have made friendships impossible to maintain is that he never stayed long in one place and generally did not revisit a place once he had left it, or maintain contact with acquaintances he had formed there. The one notable exception to

From 26 February 1867, when black Tennesseans were allowed to vote and
run for political office, Wood went into full-steam electioneering mode on
the Republican side. A Nashville newspaper described him as a "a negro
Radical stump orator of some note" when he died in May 1868.
(*Harper's Weekly*, 25 July 1868, p. 468)

the rule of no-return was Liberia. He had gone back there. He
shouldn't have.

If his life's goal had been to get rich, he failed—he died poor. But
there is ample evidence that he was not driven by the lust for riches.
Take, for instance, his known marriages, all to women of no great
wealth or exalted social standing. Commenting on his marriage in
England in 1852, one newspaper had remarked that, "if he had only
made the most of the graces of his person," instead of marrying "a
respectable young woman, of no family, and with no fortune," he
might have won the hand of an English heiress, an unconventional,
upper-crust Arabella or Georgiana who, idealistic and soured on
the high life, wished to dedicate herself to saving the world.

If what he sought was not money so much as substance or
standing, as the titles and diplomas and airs he gave himself suggest, he made out slightly better. He would have relished that last,
laconic press notice saluting him as a "prominent Negro Radical"
and an "orator of some note." This could be taken as praise, coming as it did from a newspaper that showed little regard for Blacks

in general and none for him in his lifetime. Certainly, "orator of some note" sounded a thousand times better than all those names he had been called in all the nooks of the world he had visited—a wolf in sheep's clothing, a fornicator, a fraud, an impostor, a liar and a swindler, perpetrator of some of "the highest crimes under heaven," etc. He had slipped out of most of those places under a cloud, but from Tennessee, where the Ku Klux Klan was born shortly after his arrival in 1865, he exited on a surprisingly positive note, not entirely unblemished, not so "eminent" as he claimed to be, but acknowledged in some quarters, both friendly and hostile, as a political figure to be reckoned with, someone who mattered.

As I pursued Wood, an old outlaw named Henry More Smith occasionally came to mind, perhaps because he and Wood had covered some of the same territory in northeastern North America, although at different times, and because their personalities presented similarly tantalizing puzzles. More Smith, a remarkably crafty white thief and Houdini-like escape artist, believed to be an Englishman, first surfaced in 1812 at Windsor, N.S. After plaguing Nova Scotia and adjacent New Brunswick for the next few years and marrying, then abandoning, a young woman, he went on his thieving way to Maine, Connecticut, Maryland, New York, Upper Canada, etc., under various aliases. His enigmatic character, baffling skills and clever ruses so mystified and fascinated High Sheriff Walter Bates of Kings County, N.B., who had had him in custody in 1814–15, that he spent a great deal of time and effort in tracking and chronicling his progress, hoping against hope that he would eventually give up his devilish ways. He did not, any more than Wood did, and the force that drove him remained a mystery.

As I wondered aloud about the mystery of Wood and his motives, it was suggested that perhaps he was simply "born bad." That brought me up short. Are there such people? Isn't every child innocent until proven adult-ish? I could not believe, and still do not, that Wood never had a choice in the matter, that if he did not behave as a "good" man should, it was because he had been programmed from birth to be "bad." It does, however, seem probable that the great impostor in him was born out of experiences in his childhood or his youth, about which we know nothing.

He was anything but a role model. Yet throughout his career, he showed that he had the wits and persistence to achieve what most people would consider success. He could have been what he pretended to be, and more. There is no denying that Blacks in 19th-century North America lived and labored under crushing disabilities, but a man with the nerve to pass for a doctor of divinity among clergymen and missionaries in England and Ireland, the United States and Liberia, as an architect in Montreal, and as a Cambridge-educated physician in Tennessee, had something going for him, a formula that seemed to dissolve disabilities. Wood could have qualified as an ordained clergyman, like Augustus William Hanson or any number of "preachers," risen to be a bishop in the African Methodist Episcopal Church like Jabez Pitt Campbell, or operated a medical practice as legitimate as, if not more so than, those of his Nashville colleagues Amos Aray and J.B. Young. As one British newspaper put it, after his conviction at Hull on New Year's Day 1853, "With proper culture, talents such as his might have placed him at the head of an Episcopal Chapter, whereas, now he is but a poor, petty-larceny rogue." That, in fact, was rather an underestimation of the might-have-beens. A good part of the fascination he exerts lies there. He was a very able man, if rather careless, as he showed in producing documents, with names of people and places misspelled, that he tried to pass off as official Liberian papers. Able as he was or could be, he acted on the principle that the way to succeed was to pretend to have done so. To act successful was to be successful. It was all about the act. People fell for his.

If ever there was a self-made man, he was it. He was his own invention, the unscrupulous improvisation of his imagination and intellect. Carpenter, preacher, pastor of this denomination or that, missionary to Liberia or Hawaii, shipwreck survivor, doctor of divinity, author, teacher, lecturer, superintendent of public works, graduate of this university or that, architect, physician, lawyer, political orator, advocate of Black rights in the Illinois of the Civil War era or in post-war Tennessee, he conjured his various selves out of thin air and those "documents" he carried everywhere. He would not have been pleased to learn that, for his sins, he was to spend his afterlife trapped in the set of documents presented here.

On the score of documents, a word of explanation is in order. The sources of information about Wood are limited. No memoirs or reminiscences cite his exploits. Virtually none of the persons who knew him would have cared to record the experience in a written account of their lives. No institution with which he was associated would have been eager to see the connection noted in a house history. He had hoodwinked virtually all the persons he had known, including those closest to him, and none of them felt proud of it, particularly those who had recommended him to others as trustworthy or who had stood up for him in the face of attacks. He was an embarrassment, a bad dream to be forgotten. As for the "documents" that he used at every turn to establish his credentials, none has ever turned up.

Newspapers, therefore, are the indispensable tracking device. They are the phone records and social media of the day, often providing the only indications of his whereabouts and activities. Newspapers proliferated throughout the Victorian Era, making it possible for us to reconstruct the lives of "newsmakers." Not only did they print the odd "tweet" and notice about Wood, but he himself used them to further his ends, submitting advertisements or notices of his lectures, articles that showed him to advantage or, as we saw when he was prosecuted in Maine and in England, letters to the editor defending himself against imputations of wrongdoing. We might picture him keeping a scrapbook of newspaper notices of his triumphs, letters of reference and other documents. At times, as in Wales or in his Ohio years, we might even suspect that he wrote to the newspapers to pad his *curriculum vitae,* publishing notices and letters that inflated his status, creating the clippings he would use later to establish his bona fides in some other locality, in other words, writing his life on the go. Since he built his life on documents, fabricated or authentic, it is only fitting that a tale of his exploits should consist largely of documents, that might help to set the record straight.

Setting the record straight in his case is a somewhat quixotic exercise because from head to toe, Halifax to Nashville, he was not who he was. He was who he was not. Rest in peace, then, Alfred Thomas Wood/George Andrew Smith (ca. 1815–1868), whoever you are.

HISTORY OF THE REPUBLIC OF LIBERIA

The following text is a translation by Montrealers Marie-Elisabeth Morf and Louis Bouchard, two experienced literary translators, of A.T. Wood's German-language *Geschichte der Republik Liberia seit ihrer Gründung bis zu ihrer Unabhängigkeitserklärung; nebst Bemerkungen über den Zustand der Landestheile und der bürgerlichen und religiösen Verhältnisse der Eingeborenen und Eingewanderten.* It is in fact their retranslation into English of a booklet or collection of lectures that was rendered into German in the mid-19th-century. No copies of the original English work survive, if it ever existed as a book. The translators worked from a copy of the German text in the Schomburg Center for Research in Black Culture of the New York Public Library. The reader should bear in mind that as a retranslation, the work does not contain Wood's exact words. The text should be seen as *what* Wood said, and not exactly *how* he said it, although the word choice, it is hoped, is close to what his might have been.

It may seem paradoxical to reproduce in an appendix a "history" that is of little, if any, historical value. While it has found its way into the odd bibliography of Liberian studies, it should not have, at least not without a caution about its unreliability. Its only value lies in what it can tell us about Wood, not about Liberia. It is included here because (a) this is the proper place for it, and (b) students of Liberian history who have heard of it but who are unfamiliar with old German may read it without themselves going to the trouble of trying to decipher it or getting it translated.

The translators found the phrasing of the German text to be rather rough and awkward, convoluted and verbose, to the point that meaning was obscured. It was not the work of a polished, experienced writer, they thought. Whether the fault lay with Wood or "Dr. A," who had translated the original English into German, it is impossible to tell. In reviewing the new English version presented here, efforts were made to puzzle out the fuzzy passages, which required playing with words and expressions, recombining clauses and sentences, smoothing them out, and creating links between seemingly disjointed sentences or paragraphs, all without straying too far from the language that Wood might have used. The idea was to convey the sense of the German version in English that the general reader would find intelligible.

The only footnotes accompanying the text are Dr. A's. All but three footnotes—nos. 7, 9 and 11—begin with the words "Translator's note." But even the three notes that are not so identified are believed to be the translator's work. For clarity's sake, it should be said that Dr. A's Note 6 in Chapter 7, quoting Shakespeare but without identifying the work from which the words are drawn, is thought to refer to the lines in the play *Richard III* (Act 1, Scene 3) that have the murderous Richard saying:

> *And thus I clothe my naked villainy*
> *With old odd ends stolen out of holy writ,*
> *And seem a saint when most I play the devil.*

Note 8 in the same chapter, concerning a war in progress, refers to the Crimean War of 1853–1856. Finally, in the segment on Bexley in Chapter 8, Note 11 identifies camwood as "African redwood." It is more properly African sandalwood, which yields a red dye. African redwood is another plant[1].

---

1. This translation was made possible by my son, Daniel. He paid for it at a time when I was strapped for cash. For that, I will always be grateful.

History of the Republic of Liberia

History of the Republic of Liberia from its Founding to its Declaration of Independence; together with Remarks on the state of its various districts and on the civil and religious condition of its native and immigrant populations, by A.T. Wood (Colored man), Preacher at the Providence Independent Church of Monrovia, the capital of the Republic. Translated from the English by Dr. A., Hamburg, 1854.

"Facts are stubborn"

Preamble

Two works about Liberia have been presented to the public, at least in English. The author of this sketch, while not wishing to deny their merits, has every reason to believe that they were the work of writers not personally acquainted with Liberia who, never having ventured to the coast of Africa, were of necessity dependent for their descriptions on second-hand accounts.

The publisher hopes that any shortcomings of this work—and he is acutely aware of them—are offset by the accuracy of its contents, which could only flow from the pen of one who has spent some time actively employed in the place and who is mindful of the interests of the colony.

Should this brief essay serve to some degree to excite the benevolence of Europe toward this land of refuge for Africans oppressed by American slavery, the author will have achieved his purpose.

The translator has not deviated from the original text, nor has he changed the order of the chapters, although he would have preferred that the seventh be the fifth.

Chapter I: The Founding of the Colony of Liberia

In the year 1820, the government of the United States of North America was confronted with the pressing issue of slavery, and the traders in human flesh[1] in the southern states used all

---

1. Translator's note: As is generally known, Blacks treated as human merchandise were euphemistically called Ebony!

conceivable means to foil efforts to settle the question of what justification there could be for keeping humans in bondage. But slavery has taken on such importance at this critical time that the most hard-hearted slave traders could but shudder at the consequences that the presence of an ever increasing Black population was bound to bring. What is more, the Negroes were so extensively interconnected with the Whites through racial mixing and the resulting ties of kinship that many farseeing owners who gave the matter any thought, realizing that slavery depended for its perpetuation on making room for a steady supply of new slaves, had to consider how to dispose of the overflowing colored population in an orderly manner. At the same time, leading statesmen, as well as spokesmen for the churches and civil society, felt a repugnance at the entrenched injustice of slavery. Their united efforts led to a marriage of Church and State that produced a child named "Colonization." Studying the features of this creature, we find a wondrously precocious child whose parents, Congress and Church, had not only to see to its upbringing and ease its growing pains but also to ensure that it enjoyed every possible advantage. So minded, they deemed that a region of Africa infamous for its slave trade would best accommodate their offspring.

The west coast of Africa had long been visited by American seafarers who, lusting for gold, cared not how it came into their hands, any more than they scrupled to consider how they acquired animals, ivory, plants and, most notably, humans, whose progeny they thereby condemned to a life of bondage.

To satisfy North America's requirements, a portion of this African territory was chosen as a convenient and secure place to send freed Blacks as well as slaves worn out and crippled by their labors, a place that could also serve as a *Barracoon*[2] for the trade in fresh young slaves. Cape Mesurado, at 8° 33' 15" North latitude, was considered particularly appropriate, situated as it is near two major rivers and possessing a good harbor, in an area encompassing part

---

2. Translator's note: This word, unknown to us, is thought to mean an underground holding area for slaves.

of the Grain (or Pepper) Coast and the Ivory Coast, and bordering on the Gold Coast.

Appeals were then made to freed Blacks, holding out to them the gleaming prospect of liberty. The merits of this scheme were also vaunted abroad, to assuage the feelings of foreigners who looked with scorn and revulsion on the continued existence of slavery. The organizers sang their own praises and spoke of their work as helping to free the slave. In reality, it was never their intention to give up such a valuable article.

A Society was founded that solicited funds to undertake the work of emptying America of its native-born Blacks. Those Blacks allowed to remain in America were left to wonder how far their one-time masters might respect their rights.

The first contingent bound for Africa sailed from Norfolk (Virginia) in September 1822 (reversing the journey that many thousands had made earlier). They landed on a small island near the mouths of the St. Paul and Mesurado rivers. The natives prevented them from setting foot on the mainland, so that these poor people had to wait and suffer quietly for six weeks, starving, without fresh food or clean water. They did manage at times to draw some fresh water by venturing close to the shore at night, more often than not under a hail of arrows from the natives. One hundred and thirteen persons landed on the island. They soon bore the brunt of the climate and a good many fell victim to it. It was an appalling scene, misery and hardship were everywhere, with children dying, parents grieving, the air filled with the tears and lamentations of souls tormented by disease and barely surviving!

The captain of the company, Ashman, who had sailed as chaplain to this small band, tried to appease the warlike natives. Failing in this, he called together the immigrants, whose ranks by now had been thinned by half. He spoke of the dire peril they faced and warned that, in such straitened circumstances, all might die. If this was God's will, it could also happen if they ventured to land. "But it is also possible that we may succeed. If it is ordained that we must die, then we will do so in loyal devotion to His will! Under God's protection, we wish to attempt a landing this afternoon. We would sooner die in the attempt than waste away ignominiously here!" His hour-long speech ended with deeply solemn and moving prayers to the God who guides us alike in fortune and misfortune.

All the men, women and children who were not disabled by illness were so heartened that they seized up their weapons, ready to engage the enemy.

The fatal afternoon arrived and as Ashman and his small band attempted to land, a large enemy force greeted them with a volley of arrows. But the settlers, caught between life and death, stood firm so that after a short battle, being in possession of firearms, they carried the day. The enemy was routed, running off howling into the forest.

Having established a foothold on dry land, they tended to the wounded and the sick, and hastily buried the fallen. Ashman then instructed them to erect a rampart for their security, after which they gathered for a prayer of thanksgiving. As they sat down to a simple meal, he walked about, deep in thought. His eyes surveyed the injured, the dying and the suffering. He foresaw that the battle would resume soon enough. Breaking the gloomy silence, he addressed them in his soothing voice: "Dear distressed and friends! We have together undergone a severe trial today but heaven favored us. Because of His support, we were able to enter the land of our ancestors. Though our quest was an honest one, it proved a difficult enterprise, attended with prayers and lamentations, and ending for many in death. Some still lie here; their bloody wounds tell us that they will soon breathe their last. As much as they embraced their fate, achieving through prayers and combat what they sought, their loss will leave a deep pain in our hearts.

"But I urge you to consider this: No matter our present position, my friends, steel yourselves because the coming night will see a fearsome onslaught by our enemies! God alone knows who among us will see the light of the new day; we do not even know who will see the radiant beauty of this day's sunset. The savages will try to destroy us this very night. We can count on no support but God's. Sixty-eight of our people have already gone to their eternal rest, sent there by the hand of our cruel enemy! We will trust in God to lend us his gracious support!" Reminding them once more of the danger before them, he enjoined them earnestly to gird themselves for a battle that would prove more fierce and bloody than the one they had just won. All placed their trust in God's grace and mercy.

That night, the men stood watch in pouring rain, waiting anxiously for the enemy to attack. By 4 o'clock on the morning of the 6th November, no attacks having come, they felt some hope that the threat had passed but they remained watchful. The women and children then arose to take over guard duty while the weary men retired. Suddenly, blood-curdling shrieks heralded an attack, the enemy storming the rampart, their poisonous arrows raining down on the poor immigrants. The women fought the lords of the forest with the weapons at hand—axes, knives, clubs and hatchets, stones, bottles, and so forth. At the same time, the men discharged their weapons against the savages. Still the attackers kept coming over the rampart, inflicting a terrible bloodbath on young and old. Three men ran to the supply hut from which they took a small brass cannon which they filled with stones, nails, glass, etc., and fired to devastating effect. The natives fell in heaps, the thunderous clap and lethal power of the cannon filling them with such panic that they faltered, allowing the immigrants to reload and fire a second time. This second blast proved even more deadly than the first. In the thick of battle, some of the women turned to prayer. At last, thoroughly beaten, the screaming enemy retreated into the forest, leaving the field covered with blood and corpses. Ashman himself had suffered three wounds, to the arm, the loins (from the chief's lance) and, the worst one, to the hip, where a non-poisonous arrow had struck him. Loudly he proclaimed: "God has given us victory! His name be praised! Praised!"

The victory was decisive but it came at a dreadful cost. The bodies of dead and dying men, women and children lay everywhere. The remains of the native chief were found near those of the slaughtered women and children whom he had most probably himself immolated. Only seventeen persons were left alive in the camp and it took them four days to bury the dead, take stock and recoup, not knowing when the next attack might come. It must be said that the savages were struck with a holy fear of the Nora Deny (the powerful arrow), meaning the cannon.

Five days later, as the few remaining hands were setting the camp in order, their meager stores of provisions and powder all but exhausted, the sight of a ship in the channel filled them with great joy. After casting anchor, it sent its boats ashore. This second ship was found to be carrying eighty-three new immigrants, foodstuffs and household tools—there was even a doctor (named Lugenbeal) on board—all the necessities for a settlement. What a solace this proved to the poor souls who had been too sorely tried when they landed! They laid the foundations of a settlement which they named Monrovia, after the president of the United States (Monroe).

They looked for a site on which to erect suitable quarters for a governor, and set about building such a dwelling, knowing that this appointed official's arrival awaited the completion of proper accommodation.

Word reached them that the natives were eager now to meet the "newcomers." They nevertheless remained on guard, seeking to win the trust and confidence of the natives while keeping a wary eye on their comings and goings. Slowly the natives got to know their brothers from distant America, and as the number of immigrants grew, trading and exchanges with the chiefs began. As we became better acquainted, they wanted to know what form of government we had and what our intentions were in coming here. They seemed happy to learn that we wished to purchase lands and build houses, to instruct them in our ways, so that they could read and write, and wear clothes like ours.

After nine months, the American government sent out a governor for the colony, which they called Liberia (after the Latin word: *liber,* free). What contradictions this word contained! Indeed, the Colonization Society, as its founding charter states, had vowed not to meddle in the debate over slaveholding. As evidence of this, I submit extracts from five articles and will discuss some of their peculiarities:

1) You will understand that it was not its intention to interfere with the question of slave ownership; the rights of the owners will

be strictly respected by the Colonization Society. The point of the whole undertaking, its focus, is to assure the slave-owners, as all the Southern states, against the evil consequences that would arise from the triple mixing of our population.

2) There is no intention on the part of the Society to free the slaves or to meddle in the question of slave-ownership. To let them walk free among us would be a worse evil than slavery itself.

3) The ultimate object of the Colonization Society is to benefit all classes of society. The landowner may, by supporting these objects, increase the value of his slave holdings. Rather than reduce it, the implementation of the enterprise would increase the value of his remaining holdings.

4) The aim of the society is to relieve the country of the rapid increase in the colored population, which inspires fear in the slave states and hostility in the others. Many states forbid free Negroes and mulattoes to settle within their borders and authorize the sale of such intruders as slaves. – Not long ago, an article was made public and I intend to demonstrate clearly to you their intentions:

5) Our readers will be very happy to hear that the ordinances in question were passed by a decisive majority in Virginia's legislature. A great moral step has been taken toward achieving colonization's important goals.

The Society here described was, is and ever will be an imposition on the public. Through calculated perfidy, North America has found a way to draw the utmost from the slave trade. As a citizen of Liberia, I have had ample proof of this, and a variety of sources confirm it. We have in Liberia a government set up to rule over a people who had paid for their freedom with their blood and their lives, yet who had no part in the legislative process! That, America must do for them! A code of laws was drafted in America, without the least involvement or consent of the Africans. It was brought to the colony and made law: American ordinances, based on American legal authorities, without a single contribution—not a word or suggestion—from the people for whom they were destined. The blessed Colonization Society did it all and left them to bear the consequences.

It is under such constraints that the colony of Liberia was founded, paid for dearly by the early immigrants but then completely taken over by the Americans and treated as their preserve. I have yet to see anyone bring forward a shred of proof that the Americans fought and shed blood for Liberia's freedom. What belonged to the Negroes was appropriated by North Americans for their own purposes. If the Society paid money to further its ends, Ashman and his companions, who were all colored persons, paid in hard-fought battles with their tears, their blood and their lives.

The first efforts of the government of Liberia were directed at claiming full control of the trade of the colony and ensuring that American merchants were favored to the exclusion of the British. They gave the Americans free access to the coast, including to its inhabitants. These Americans often outwitted the patrolling English coastal cruisers, pretending to be engaged in trade with Liberia while abducting its coastal inhabitants. Certain American merchants hired Africans from Liberia as seamen for their ships, but once these unfortunate people set foot on board, they never again saw their homeland. Indeed, as America congratulated itself on its colonization efforts, it was Africa, specifically Liberia, that was being depopulated, its inhabitants being shipped to the slave states to be sold. Many whose task it was to transport immigrants to Liberia were pleased to return to America with a valuable cargo of slaves.

After the founding of the colony and the appointment of a white governor, the flow of immigrants to the shores of Liberia increased but slowly. Some slave owners freed their slaves on condition that they go to Liberia, there to act as their agents in laying hold of the country's productions, seeing to it that the slave trade was maintained and, from time to time, sending them a small cargo of Africans. It was understood that these agents acted with impunity as the valuable instruments of their masters' designs. In this way, they were able to purchase their freedom, which was a boon to them and to their owners. These poor creatures went to Liberia, an African fiefdom, purchasing their freedom at the price of enslaving others. For twenty-two years (from 1822 to 1844) there existed a peculiar state of affairs in the colony. Spanish and Portuguese visitors paid regular calls on the governor and his aides, who alone were privy to their business, until it became publicly known that these visitors, who enjoyed the most cordial relations with the American governor and the merchants, abducted persons in Liberian territory whom they sold as slaves to American captains. As much as the colonists had a horror of slavery, some of them, pledged to supply their former owners with African slaves, benefited from the abominable trade. Their fellow settlers could not shake off this yoke of colonization because many were still in debt to the Society for their transport. They were thus bound by contract to the Society, just as the others described above were bound to their former masters.

A highly mischievous and clever Spaniard came to Monrovia, married a colored woman from America and they made their home in the area called Cape Mount. Report had it that he had come from America, where he had been educated and where he had made the acquaintance of his future wife's family. For a few years, while her parents lived in Monrovia, members of his and her families were in the habit of exchanging residences. The Spaniard's home at Cape Mount was soon outfitted with every conceivable luxury, like a palace. The abundance of silver wares, the sumptuous furnishings, his many trips to the United States (on the pretext that he was a seafarer or a ship-owner), aroused the suspicions of Monrovians. Inquiries were made, and some English officers got wind of his activities. Determined to outwit them, he continued to ply the seas, always escorted by his brothers and his wife's many relatives, abducting his victims by night, loading these luckless Africans onto his ship and carrying them off to America. Notwithstanding his notoriety, he continued in this wretched line of business, amassing great riches—this in the country ruled by the Colonization Society. Eventually an English officer discovered his whereabouts. He was summoned to court but failed to appear; inquiries were made at his home but he was not to be found.

At last, a detailed search of his compound uncovered proof of his misdeeds. In an old smithy were found handcuffs and chains of recent manufacture. A side entrance led to a vast underground *barracoon* capable of holding in concealment 800 to 1,000 slaves! In an adjoining cell a mass of human bones was found, relics of poor Africans held there who had perished from mistreatment. The discovery among these of two relatively fresh corpses was evidence that humans had been penned there quite recently. All the buildings in the compound were consequently destroyed. To this day, in 1851, no one has tracked down this Spaniard; rumor has it that he took his nasty business elsewhere along the African coast. From this simple tale it can be seen that while the purpose of the American Colonization Society was supposed to be to hold out to the colored people of America the prospect of liberty, carry them to Africa and safeguard its colony, it instead maintained the slave trade and exercised a tyrannical hold over the inhabitants of Liberia.

Chapter 2: Resources of the colony

Providence has blessed this colony with great potential and a wealth of products. The soil is so fertile that it is at all times covered with a green canopy. The tremendous harvest to be had from the fruit trees that are found in profusion in the forests, the different kinds of birds in their bright plumage, and the rich mineral deposits are sure signs that this city will one day be the capital of the whole African nation. Cotton, coffee, sugar, tobacco, rice, indigo, arrowroot and other valuable plants can be harvested in quantities five times as great as in America, or wherever else slave labor is used, and at one quarter of the cost in labor and money. The facilities needed to bring these goods from harvest to market are at present lacking. Yet no place in the world is more blessed than Africa with such vital commodities, and one might rightly think that of all the products mentioned here, none can be found of such exquisite quality elsewhere. Here one finds a wild cotton plant that, if properly cultivated, would yield a harvest surpassing any average American planting. The bolls are long in shape and contain fine staples, which, if they were properly extracted and processed in a mill, must exceed in quality the American product.

The sugar cane grows quite high and much juice can be extracted from it; once planted, it requires little supervision. The different varieties of coffee trees grow quite rapidly and produce a luxuriant crop of beans; experience shows that cultivating six acres of such trees here requires no greater investment in money and labor than is required for 1½ acres in America. The forests supply an abundance of timber such as rosewood, ebony, teak, mahogany and various dyewoods. Palm trees, which are found in large supply, grow quite tall; quantities are sent to Monrovia each year to be exported. Ivory of superior quality is available to excess. The soil holds such minerals as iron, coal, copper, silver and gold.

This is a land offering ample scope to the useful professions—farmers, mechanics, mineralogists, artists, merchants; even the theologian and the philanthropist will find a place here. Crime, acts of violence, and mischief are scarce in Liberia. Pray to God they never multiply as they have elsewhere! The two major rivers offer convenient means for transporting goods from the interior, and the coastal areas are very fertile and rich. The waters contain a multitude of fish of excellent quality, and the forests an abundance of game. The climate on the coast is very healthy, especially if one abstains from intoxicating beverages. No place is better located than the city of Monrovia for trade and transportation, and the government still holds large tracts of land, which can be purchased at a minimal price. Here one can find all that is needed for trade and agriculture. The tribes of the interior flock to the markets bearing ivory, gold dust, dyewoods, rice and other valuable articles. Exporters today can count on the same well-known advantages that from time immemorial have caused the slave traders to favor this area as a base for the shipment of their wares. Even if slavery in America were to end, the fund of resources found in this area would still capture the attention of capitalists seeking a profitable investment. Such are the advantages that account for the founding of the colony in this location, and hence the reason the Americans tried to gain a stranglehold over it.

Is it any wonder that Americans should show such interest in this land? Had their constitutions been better suited to it, they would have populated the entire area within a few years.

As it happened, a steady increase in the number of immigrants led the colony's administrators to enact new rules for settlers. Each was required to purchase a plot of land from the Society on the understanding that the purchase price was to be paid within a specified time, failing which the land would be forfeited and the Society free to sell it to the next registered person who showed an interest. And if a settler wished to sell his land, he could do so only through American agents, which was not always advantageous as it tended to bring down the price. This ordinance stirred resentment in the colony and led to loud public complaints. Making a bad situation worse was the fact that the Americans had claimed the power to expel all who refused to recognize that American law applied in Liberia. They claimed the right to seize slaves here, insisting that while a fugitive slave might feel happy to reach Liberia, the governor was duty bound to send him back to his American owner. Liberians denied this and resolved that no law of theirs should ever authorize such renditions. They found the claims demeaning; their indignation aroused, all felt bound to oppose them. They swore to stand up for their freedom against the renewed assaults originating with the government of the United States and the Colonization Society.

Chapter 3: Declaration of Independence

For 22 years, the Liberian people had to engage in a burdensome and bitter contest against slavery and its daughter, Colonization. From time to time false accusations were made against them and their rights were trampled. Assaults on their integrity, they found, persisted even after they had removed to Africa. They discovered that there were many among them who acted as agents of American slave traders, some going so far as to abduct people from Monrovia. They resolved to create a state of their own, to give themselves a constitution and to declare their independence. They held secret consultations, for a period of about three months, without arousing the governor's suspicions. They chose representatives, calling on them to form two separate Houses that would take in hand the business of legislating for the people. The men they selected drafted a declaration of independence and a constitution, and chose a president. To secure Europe's official recognition of their country, they first sent delegates to England. God in his benevolence favored them, who had been so long aggrieved, and guided Queen Victoria's heart so that England became the first nation to recognize the independence of Liberia, giving the new Republic a powerful protector. The newly elected president of the Republic, J.S. Roberts, then went to France, where King Louis-Philippe also recognized Liberia's independence. Other European powers whose approval and recognition the Liberians thought it necessary to secure followed the example of England and France. Elated at seeing their love of freedom so manifestly rewarded, Liberians celebrated President Roberts' return from his triumphal trip with illuminations. The chiefs of neighboring tribes joyfully took part in the festivities and expressed a wish to unite their territory to the new country of Liberia. The offer was accepted and the tribes sent emissaries who swore allegiance to the government of Liberia. The American governor was honorably discharged and his return to America paid for. The flag of Liberia was hoisted at Cape Mesurado, and at the top of the national flagpole they nailed the English flag. The American government would not have tolerated this impertinent stroke had not Britain taken the young country under its wing. This republic arose from the sinister designs of a slave-owning country which, as one had reason to fear, intended to make of Liberia a small-scale replica of America in Africa from which to draw an endless supply of stock for its slave markets, or perhaps a land of exile for those too clever to be held in slavery, or a place to consign the lame and the aged who, like beasts of burden no longer fit to work, would be put out to pasture to await death. But Providence foiled these schemes and, astonishingly, Liberia gained its independence without shedding one drop of blood. There was no firing of cannons, no swords were drawn, no bayonets; no wails of wounded or dying men were heard, and no battlefield bore the indelible scars of some epic battle. We rejoice in a more glorious and noble triumph, and our trophy is engraved: *Deus, libertas et patria* (God, freedom and fatherland)! We see that

God's grace sustained our feeble efforts and that His power prepared a place of rest for thousands of the suffering sons and daughters of Africa. He who created light shone his light on the benighted
shores of Africa that the heathens might partake of the blessings
of our faith.

This was said to be the goal of the Colonization Society, but its
deeds belied its words, so that even God in His mercy could not
have credited its sincerity. Indeed, we no more have the Society
to thank for our independence than the children of Israel had reason to be grateful to the pharaohs of Egypt for their deliverance
from slavery and tyranny. Throughout the course of events, we
see at work only the shepherding hand of the One who resigns over
all. Africa's Savior unsheathed the sword of his will to help his
Black children. The God of Freedom set himself between
oppressed and oppressor. The God of Love guided his sorrowful
sons and daughters along the path to the peaceful home of their
ancestors. What people on Earth can with greater confidence lift
up their eyes to heaven, their hearts brimming with gratitude, and
cry: The Lord hath done great things for us! We believe in the helping hand of the One whose help is never-ending; in the Providence
that unbelievers deny and evildoers fear! We thank the noble
princes of Europe for their favors, but above all and for all time,
we thank the Almighty who meted out his sublime justice to the
downtrodden Africans.

Chapter 4: The climate of Liberia

The climate of Liberia is much healthier for Europeans than is
generally thought. Ship captains and sailors who have visited
these shores speak of the country as a graveyard for Europeans.
Speaking from experience I can state positively that the baneful
results they attribute to the climate are actually the effects of
alcohol! Could we but persuade outsiders to resist the temptation
of this herald of death, they would soon find this fertile land a
choice place to live.

Some will say this view is wrongheaded because it is so contrary to the reports of sailors who have called here. To support

my argument, I will cite the following facts: No class of people is more prone to drink than seamen. For them, spirits are the beverage of choice, and they imagine that they have a constant need of this stimulant, especially when they feel unwell. They have heard much of Africa, they probably once have been there; nevertheless they are unacquainted with the benefits of its waters or their direct effect on the human body. They know nothing of the precautions they must take to maintain life and health.

Having never lived in such an environment, they know nothing of its foods and the effects of these new foods on the stomachs and constitutions of those who are unused to them. They know only that in Africa they are subjected to a climate that is the opposite of their own, that it is known to be unhealthy for them, and that they probably will fall prey to bouts of African fever. Some of their comrades may even have died of it; but the cause of their death or the nature of the disease that killed them, remains inexplicable for them. They do not realize that their blood is not adjusted to the atmospheric, plant and mineral influences of the climate. This ignorance leads them to resort, as always, to the old habit of drinking distilled spirits in the belief that these can ward off all ailments. But, Oh! such disregard for the laws of nature only confirms the truth of the old saying: "An ounce of prevention is worth a pound of cure." By the time they realize this, it is usually too late!

In this environment, the carbon content in the blood is greater than usual owing to atmospheric, plant and mineral influences;[3] needless to say, steps must be taken to counteract this, to keep our bodily functions in order. Now, the consumption of alcohol may mask from an individual what is happening to him and keep him from taking proper measures before physical irritations and dysfunction take hold; the heart and the vascular system are over-

---

3. Translator's note: The effect of minerals cannot come into play, unless is meant through the content of the water, which will in no way contribute to the accumulation of carbon in the blood. Ever since Lind, physicians have known that the functioning of the liver is more stimulated, hence disturbed, in tropical climes.

loaded, the skin becomes dry, and natural condensation[4] or perspiration is greatly impeded. At the same time, the blood becomes saturated with gases, producing congestion in the brain that can lead to death within a matter of hours.

How can a foreigner protect himself against such a fate? Will he trust those who advise him correctly in such matters? He will readily think that they are toying with him, pronouncing him sick when he feels otherwise and is convinced of his own well-being. But he forgets that our feelings are unreliable indicators of the true state of our bodies. On the other hand, we may well wonder, what should we make of the testimony of doctors who, sailing by these shores aboard naval vessels, often greatly reinforced the sailors' reports? I would respond that one should treat their pronouncements as one does many others, that is, trust to one's own eyes. These men, it may be acknowledged, possess a rather sound scientific training but they lack the practical experience to support their testimonials. The most experienced and skilled sailor might lose his ship, not, in theory, from ignorance of his trade, but from a lack of knowledge of a specific coast, its currents, tides, shoals, reefs and banks. So it is with physicians: As highly skilled as they are in the arts of medicine and surgery, and very knowledgeable about the secrets of anatomy and physical constitutions, all the same, they require a great deal of practice to gain the experience that would allow them to speak with authority about what effects the simplest causes might produce on bodies that are so completely different from those they are used to examining in their regular clinics. One would have to station these medical witnesses at various points along the coast of Africa, in different latitudes, so that they might observe the passing seasons, the different influences produced by the earth and atmosphere, and gain from real life and acquaintance with the country the information that would lend weight to their views. Physicians on board warships are always betwixt sea and shore: On the ships, they are con-

---

4. Translator's note: The process of evaporation, or elimination through perspiration, should not actually be termed condensation because of the accumulation on the exterior of the skin.

stantly under the influence of trade winds; how different this is from being on land! What a difference of atmosphere! This is why they cannot make a credible assessment of the African climate.

To further illustrate my point, without at all wishing to disparage the physicians' abilities, I will cite one example: In 1850, a young man travelled from the United States to Liberia. Suffering from the various ills of the acclimation process and the influences which I previously described, he wished to meet with a physician aboard a warship anchored off Monrovia. The physician told him that there was no danger in eating ripe fruits; he should not entirely abstain from eating these because some—oranges and the like—would be recommended at such a time, while he was still ill. I had earlier observed the negative effects of eating oranges and pineapples in these circumstances; I therefore discounted the physician's advice, as the young man was under my supervision, and warned him of the baneful results that would ensue should he follow the doctor's instructions. But he was convinced that the physician knew best, therefore the next day, as suggested, he ate two oranges, at 8 in the morning. By noon that same day, he was a corpse. No one could have thought that the physician, by his advice, had intended to dispatch him so rapidly into the afterlife. He treated him as best he knew; but we can here see the result, and the difference between theory and practice, knowledge and experience. As I know by experience of the horrible effects of consuming the acidity found in fruits and alcoholic beverages, I make bold to let the world know of my experience, without regard to any scientific and medical objections that may be raised. If these facts were more widely known, many who now consume them and then fall victim to the climate, could return from Africa to their family and friends in a happy and healthy state.

Another question may also arise from all this: Are there not any adverse influences in Africa on our health? The answer is: Of course, there are, as many as in other parts; but I cannot say that they are found to any large extent. When an African visits England, he comes in contact with harmful influences; he is here much more closely exposed to diseases and to death than he is in his homeland. This is accounted for by the climatic and dietary changes he experiences. He must be careful and attentive to the way of life of the people who know the climate better than the foreigner; in this way he will not find a premature grave, but will adjust in time and regain his good health in that climate. Yet he will always feel the difference between this country and his own. If he were to expand on these ideas, he could conclude that England is a graveyard for Africans! And he has a right to retaliate.

But we do know that it is possible for an African to live in England, and, likewise, it is not impossible for a European to live in Africa. In Liberia, we have Europeans living amongst us; they enjoy as good health as the colored people who emigrated from the United States. And their families there prosper and thrive in the climate. I do not at all mean to say that Europeans could ever adapt and acclimate themselves to the extent that they could bear the same level of labor and hardship that they do in their country; but we seek only to dispel the delusion that a European could not live in Africa or that he is there exposed to more noxious influences than at home.

In concluding this chapter on the climate of Africa and Liberia, I beg you to read what I have said frankly and impartially. What I have written is drawn from first-hand experience, and I hope that my suggestions will lead Europeans to a knowledge that will benefit them, and prepare and beckon them to visit the shores of Africa.

Chapter 5: The City of Monrovia

Monrovia, the capital of the Republic of Liberia, is located in the western part of Africa, on Cape Mesurado, at the confluence of the St. Paul and Mesurado rivers, at 8°33'15" North latitude. The countryside in this part of Africa is magnificent, its mountains and valleys basking beneath the green canopy of an eternal summer. The air is mellow; one can almost hear it whispering as it carries on its wings the rich fragrances of the flowers and golden fruit that grace the green countenance of Nature. The city is laid out in a grid pattern about 3 miles long and ¾ of a mile wide. The houses are quite nicely built, of brick and stone. In some areas, the orange, plum and tamarind trees that ornament the city provide some shade. This site and its beautiful environs afford visitors a good idea of what, as history tells us, the Garden of Eden must have looked like. In such a country as we have just described, extending 600 miles along the coast and stretching 150 miles inland, 2½ million people live in the darkness of paganism, idolatry and superstition!

The Grace of God directed me to this country in 1850, after I had sojourned in the West Indies. I kissed the ground on the piece of earth where the first immigrants to Liberia were obliged to engage in battle and prayer and where so many had shed their blood and died. I preached the word of Life before a gathering on that holy place where today we have laid the first stone of our church. My public and sacred actions were aimed at bringing salvation to the participants. As they did not have a proper clergyman, I was there asked to be their preacher, to proclaim and spread the word of God. This I willingly did and then began my duties. I am delighted to say that all my efforts were blessed by God because I was his tool in obliterating darkness and ignorance. In the 10 years between 1841 and 1851, 783 people were converted to the light of God, proclaiming it in their creed of faith, which they exemplified by living according to God's commandments, in this country that until now lived in darkness. To this day, when the Word of God is preached, they show their appreciation by the look in their eyes, the way they breathe, by their tears and their total concentration, which shows that the Holy Spirit has entered their soul, that they might be guided to Him and know his Omnipotence.

The influence of schooling on the natives is of capital importance. On school-free days, the young pupil gathers his little book collection and returns to his native town or village, eager to show his clan what progress he has made. He reads to them what he has learned in school; he explains it in a simple way and those present desire to know more. And in this manner, he really is like a child preacher to his parents and extended family, who had never before heard of such things and had no idea that the world worships such a Being. They wish to be kept apprised of the child's progress and they go to their chief and, through his intercession, ask that our government build a school in their area.

In this way, we have an opportunity to reach the young as well as the adults so that they will receive religious instruction. This is but the first step.

The gates of darkness have been slightly opened; thus can they have access to the light of Truth and Life which banished the darkness that has for so long enveloped the children of Africa in paganism. And we may glimpse the triumph over the deathly heathenism that has so far ruled Liberia; now they can look cheerfully to the joyful realm of Faith and its blissfulness. Because this country, where pagan spirits rule, can be made fertile mission ground, but much remains to be done. That is why, Oh dear reader! you must heed the call resonating throughout this country: Come to us and help us! These unmistakable cries for help will appeal to your reason; should they go unanswered? Could the cultured inhabitants of Europe fail to find an answer to this supplication? Oh, grant us your support and let God's word fly to these nations sunk in darkness and death.

Chapter 6: Idolatry of the Natives

The condition of the natives of Liberia is thoroughly deplorable. They know nothing of the existence of the one God. This land never was neglected by seamen out to make their fortune, in gold, ivory and slaves. But no comparable interest was shown in the country by philanthropists, philosophers and Christians. I know that intelligent, religious people will be astonished at this because they read the accounts of missionary labors in Africa. I would be lying if I said there were no interesting stations planted by various missionary societies along the coast of Africa; but I challenge anyone to show me that these societies are active in the whole of our republic. They never even made the effort to send the Gospel there.

When Liberia was under the rule of the American government, there were a few stations along the coast supported by the churches and by groups of slave owners in America, but these sought to disguise and mask their true intentions rather than to instruct and enlighten the heathens. Would that Heaven had allowed such societies to achieve only one hundredth of what they claimed to have done in their missionary accounts! How extraordinarily different would have been the state of these blinkered, persecuted, exploited people! Instead we find the so-called American Christians plundering the shores of Africa of its inhabitants, selling them like animals into eternal dependence and slavery. To think, these praying predators are pious members of some congregation or other. They dare steal from parents, dare sell the parents of these children and reduce their own fellow Christians, male and female, to slavery, yet dare to style themselves children of God. Would this not cause Heaven to blush and reduce the angels to tears?

But how do we know all this to be the truth? I answer: Look to America, communicate with one of those church associations, and watch the actions of the officials of the various congregations in the slave states, and with your own eyes you will see deeds and proceedings that will shatter your soul! In my travels through America, I have seen slaves belonging to the same church as their owners take communion in that *same* church, though on a *separate* table, who, on the Monday following, were sold off by their pious owners because of some small misdemeanor they had committed. But hark, we hear the stone-hearted seller praise this same slave to buyers as a good, reliable, loyal and honest Christian who is modest but diligent!

I have seen this with my own eyes and I have distant relatives who have endured this bitter experience. Is this the true nature of their church, the wellspring of their religion? How can they be effective and succeed in their missionary work if they behave in this way?

The real state of ignorance in which the Africans who inhabit these shores must live so far remained unknown to the people of Europe. I will describe it as any visitor would who showed a sincere interest in their mores and habits. All of them are caught up in some form or other of idolatry or superstition. Every trimester or in every third month the tribes celebrate and sacrifice to their divinities. Some sacrifice to the moon, others to fire, the sun, rivers, even to snakes. But the main objects of their idolatry are rough fetishes which they make themselves or objects from wrecked ships found washed up on shore.

Let us lay aside the gods and concentrate on the abominable forms the sacrifices take. The moon worshippers, for example, wander through the forests carrying a heavy load of fruits and flowers. Once they reach the place of sacrifice, they collect dry wood for a huge pile which they set on fire. They then retrieve from a hole dug in the ground clay mixed with different colors, and with this they paint their faces, their limbs and whole bodies. They then return to the fire, howling and dancing in quick steps around it. From time to time, they cast some food and flowers into the flames. They then select a certain position from which to observe the heavens. As soon as the full moon comes into view, they let out a wretched sound and begin their dancing again, scattering their offerings until none are left and throwing themselves on the ground for a brief time, looking to the moon again. If a man believes that the moon is going to smile favorably upon him, then he is happy; but if it seems that it is cross with him, he runs back angrily to his hut, grabs the first child he sees, drags him to the place of sacrifice, smashes his skull with his club, and casts his body into the flames! By such means does he seek to appease the wrath of his god!

The same can be said of the sun worshippers. The water worshippers throw their sacrificial offerings and their children into the water, first tying a stone around their necks to keep them down and to make sure that their instinct of self-preservation is thwarted. In such horrible ceremonies are hundreds of humans sacrificed.

When one of their kings or chiefs passes away, they organize so-called *Gregre Palava* (magical talk) and designate various persons to be sacrificed in the ensuing ceremony, where horrible scenes take place. They separate the heads of the sacrificed from their bodies, collect their blood in a calabash or a coconut shell, and pour it on the grave of the dead man. It is not unusual for them to select sacrificial victims from their own tribe. When this happens, they give them a narcotic drink extracted from a plant called *Sasa* (sasawood). The chosen ones are first buried up to their arms in a hole and must then quaff the concoction. As these bloody sacrifices and cruel ceremonies have taken place for hundreds of years, we find human bones scattered everywhere that the different tribes live. One cannot visit any native city or village that does not bear traces of such painful proofs of folly, superstition and deprivation. I do not know of a single forsaken place, from Sherbrö Island near Sierra Leone to the Bight of Benin, where one cannot see such occurrences, which are generalized. The only exceptions are those placed where the influence of civilization and Christianity has led the neighboring tribes to copy and follow the wise example of their foreign neighbors. This improvement often occurs thanks to the efforts of a few people who have taken it upon themselves to instruct and intercede for such unfortunates who do not know how to face death with proper reverence.

Often I was asked to go to the hut of some afflicted person when sickness had struck them and kept them bedridden, and always I would find them surrounded by their idols. My first act was always to destroy these images. I would then talk to the sick man in his dialect, explaining to him the error of his ways, showing him the ineffectiveness of his idols and how he could acknowledge and pray to the God of Love and acquire some of his might. He thereupon begins to think and reflect upon the dark ignorance that heretofore engulfed him. In this way, he may humbly hear the word of Life. Slowly his spirit awakens to an awareness of the all-powerful Supreme Being, of human frailty and of the recognition of evil. His soul is swathed in a profound humility. For the first time, he is full of hope. What a change comes over the poor idol worshipper once he becomes convinced of the truth of the newly received doctrine, recognizes that his earlier self was given over to vanity and sin, and accepts that he can find forgiveness through the grace of God, to whom he can appeal though he cannot see Him! He acutely appreciates that he has now come under a higher power that was previously wholly unknown to him. The word "religion" now captures his full attention and he sees in it a magic that cuts through the fog that once enveloped him.

Readers have here received a truthful portrayal of the natives' character, showing that they are receptive to civilization and the Gospel.[5] Such are the inhabitants of these countries, who were robbed of their children by agents of the civilized and Christian world. Instead of working with them, to better them through education and lead them to an understanding of the true religion, they let them degenerate a thousand times, teaching them to wage wars, to kill and to sell their brothers. If only all the ships that had come to the coast had brought cargoes of Bibles and missionaries instead of rum, powder and arms, how different this area and its inhabitants would be from what one sees at this moment! When Africans turn their thoughts to the Almighty and begin to think about the Creator, life on earth and their own death, then their spirits can be moved in the same way as those of all other people. They fear, love and pray to the Almighty just as educated Europeans do. How then can their fellow men treat them as mere livestock? When did the Creator of the natural order decree that a human being should be enslaved, the property of another?

Chapter 7: Slavery in America

When one reflects upon this situation, not only does the mind recoil at those who stoop to engage in an undignified commerce born of cruelty and that is the worst affront to humanity, it recoils even more at those who profess to be teachers of Holy Writ yet have the effrontery to whitewash and justify these ghastly crimes against the will of God. They dare to call slavery an "arrangement made in heaven," and to prove their assertion, they cite verses from

---

5. Translator's note: Yet not only slave holders but also physicians in the slave states, as in the recent case of Nott in Mobile, have sought to portray black Africans as closely related to the brute beasts, citing physiological factors as evidence of this, but the evidence does not stand up before the tribunal of truth. Blacks may differ from Caucasians in cranial and facial structures, but one cannot reduce them to the status of animals on that basis.

the Holy Scriptures[6] (which they twist out of context and interpret as they please). They tell us that one particular word, which in Hebrew corresponds to servant (*Ebed*), means *slave*. Can there be anything more revolting than this? If we were to let this terrible blasphemy stand, then we would turn all positive meaning of language on its head; for if it were true, Christ, who calls himself a servant of God "who came to fulfill the will of God who sent him," would actually become God's *slave*. The angels, who we are told serve every day of every year in the eternity of light and blessing, would not be the joyous servants of God, no! but an enormous horde of *slaves!* Thus, He who says in the Gospel, "I am the *eternal Master,*" would be understood as saying that He is a large-scale *slave owner.* He who commands the veneration of all creation would (according to these theories) be the fount and origin of the basest foolishness, cruelty and wickedness ever conceived in the sullied heart of one of his creatures. In vain would we look to this eternal Being for justice, holiness, morals, purity and truth; all would be contradiction, confusion, destruction and affliction! But fortunate to know *Him* better, we feel the affront to the sublime status of He who is without fault and error. He is unwavering in desiring the welfare of his creatures; His Name and His Being are love. He is the fullness of wisdom, goodness and perfection: that is why we pray to Him and praise Him!—If we now examine the claims of those slave-owning servants of the divine Word, we find them guilty of an outrageous fraud because there is a great difference between the original words for servant (*doulos,* in ancient Greek) and for slave, the former being *Ebed* or *Abad,* and the latter *Corfu.*[7]

---

6. Translator's note: Shakespeare, that great friend of justice and morality, once said, "that the Devil will use the Holy Scriptures to his advantage."

7. The words *Abad* (to serve, to work) and *Ebed* (servant, farm laborer) themselves contain so little reference to slavery that one finds in the Bible the following when referring to days of rest: Six days shalt thou labor (expressed by *Abad*). The word generally designates hard work, and *Malacha,* light work. The Bible refers to a bound servant as *Ebed olam.* To the expert Hebrew translator, the word *Corfu* is suspect, in particular because its ending is not that of a Hebrew noun.

Reading these words and comparing their meanings, without being proficient in languages, even the ignorant can be convinced of the difference. One could almost wish that this difference was imperceptible to the people we rightly criticize—they thus might have some slight excuse; unfortunately they cannot plead ignorance in their defence. They hold too high a tangible and temporal stake in the system they have set up; that is why they seek to maintain it for their own gain. Some maintain their markets and profits by the indulgence of others who are careless of what happens to their fellow man; others defend the horrible system of slavery as a lesser evil, and even as necessary! What sin, I ask, is necessary to mankind? Will it help the soul or the body? Surely not! How can these monsters claim that any good will come of this? Will they cite the successes achieved by some of those who were raised in shameful slavery? These can only be attributed to God's mystical and merciful Providence which shield the slaves from evil designs, as happened to Joseph when he was sold by his brothers to Ishmaelite merchants, or to the Jews who were cast into the fiery furnace. If we understand correctly these preachers who defend slavery, we must assume that they encourage something that they loathe in their own hearts, and yearn to make God a participant in this highest injustice! Oh, how self-serving they are in quoting the words of the Lord that issued from the mouth of the prophet when he cried: "You considered me as one of your own!" Ah, how dark is the turpitude of these guilty preachers! How horrible their responsibility! Among the slaves now laboring under the yoke of chains and the lash in this God-fearing and God-worshipping system, there is not one who, when he faces Him, will not stand better than these educated preachers. Some of these suffering creatures, despite their ignorance, will go on to glory in the afterlife, while many who despise and oppress them, notwithstanding all their erudition and the privileges they enjoy in this world, will find eternal damnation! What a reversal is in store! The souls of the suffering slaves will ascend to heaven while they who are convinced of their rectitude, but who lie to themselves and to the world, these preachers and philosophers are doomed to eternal annihilation! Yet I implore God's mercy for them, that their soul might see the Light and be forever saved!

But it pains me now to realize that I have never heard of a single such hypocrite who mended his ways and was, by this conversion, saved! How sad and dim is the state of those who profess to live a life agreeable to God even as they drift away from the right path! We recall the names of Esau, Judas, Felix, Simon, Magnus and so many others whose sanctimonious behavior has been reproved by God, by their contemporaries and their descendants.[8] We see no comparison between the servitude of Abraham's time, authorized by God, and the devilish ways of slavery in our time.

In former times, the servant received instruction and wages for his efforts, and in time could exchange his position for another more suited to him. Abraham paid his hired hands according to the value of the work they performed and what they asked, and no one was paid to steal human beings for him and to sell them as one would an ox and a donkey. No law decreed that these servants and their descendants should be doomed to eternal slavery and cruel abuse. We do not really know how contractual service operated in Abraham's time, but we do know for a certainty that it bore no resemblance to the slavery found in America, with its iniquity, wickedness and cruelty. In our time, slaves and their families are considered wholly the property of their owners; the latter seize the infants from their mothers' beds, sell them like calves from a stable and fill their coffers with the proceeds. The laments and cries of the bereft mothers are punished with whips and chains. Thus is their unbearable sorrow, separate as they are from their husbands, their homeland and everything that is dear to them, made worse. The men, ripped from their wives' and children's embrace, are sold in distant lands, never to see their loved ones for the rest of their miserable lives. A law prohibits the forlorn slaves to marry, thus robbing them of any of the rights and consolations to which other servants are entitled. All instruction is

---

8. Translator's note: Do we not see at this moment a horrible war going on under the cloak of religion, while those in command include persons of any religion but the one in whose name we claim to be fighting.

denied them; they are condemned to live like beasts, to indulge in fornication, incest and crimes of all sorts; it is also their lot to die like animals, without any ray of light to illuminate their darkened spirit or to prepare their soul to enter the better world which the Creator has provided for them. Many will ask: Is this the state of slavery in America? Let me reply with a question of my own: Do you doubt that it is so? Others will say: We have known other preachers from America who presented a completely different view of the subject. I will explain to you why they do so. It would cast a terrible light on their characters if the nature of their activities in the slave states were known in your home countries. I have come to know how the slave-holders corrupt these preachers and get them to share their views. When a clergyman arrives in one of these states, posted to a church or to a congregation,[9] the wealthy members of this assembly present a young slave to him as a gift. If he refuses this gift, he is ousted and taunted and finally expelled from the state.

Most commonly, however, the clergyman's mind brims with anxious thoughts. He struggles against the first leanings of his heart and is inclined to follow the well-known path that has led so many into sin, saying to himself: I am caught between two evils and must either spurn their proffered gift or accept it and show myself to be their tool. Since it is the custom of this country, I will choose the lesser of the two evils—I will take the slave and thereafter act according to my conscience! So he accepts their offer, and his lips are sealed so that he may not preach against sin, as he has himself become a sinner; having taken the cunning bait that was thrown his way, he floats with the current and in this manner, he falls victim to the well-known sin of the country he has entered.

Truly very few stand up for the rights and freedom God created for everyone, and fewer still abide by the golden rule: "Do unto others as you would have them do unto you!" The sins of the worldly greatly preoccupy us, but what should we think and do about the servants of a religion that preaches humanity who

9. Congregation, actually an assembly, therefore a religious community, that does not always have its own church building.

engaged in these detestable activities? Oh humanity is so full of injustice! From early on, he will perform his devotions in a pharisaic manner, to display his deep spiritual convictions! And who can better succeed at this than he, both because of his position in society and his character?

It is no wonder that people are left with false impressions, whose effects are so much at variance with those intended by the simple commandments of the Holy Scriptures and so contrary to reason.

In America, there are numerous religious congregations whose leaders and members are the wealthy owners of vast estates and countless slaves. The churches and congregations rely on these as their principal pillars for support; but I ask, Is it reasonable that God's work should be rooted in blood and injustice? Can we allow or excuse the least connivance with such a dark and horrible system? Nevertheless, Ah! because of the previously cited reasons for maintaining slavery, they have accepted it and present it as a necessary evil. Some will agree with me that slavery is an injustice and they will raise the old question: What can I do to make it go away? I will answer: If you are a servant of the Gospels, do not stain your hands with the blood of your fellow man; raise your voice like a trumpet and let it ring against such a monstrous sin; fight it with no other weapons than those which God has provided for you, and do not cease fighting until the call resounds, from state to state, country to country: Slavery is no more!! If you are a deacon or church warden, consider your position each time you help your clergyman in his churchly functions, acknowledging the coming redemption of mankind and the community of God's people; remember your counterparts in the slave states, who may themselves be slave owners and who may have sold slaves of their own to punish them for some minor offence, slaves to whom they had previously, with their own hands, offered the sacrament of communion. At heaven's gate, you will appear together with them; can you not warn them against such sin? Now, you will say: It will do no good. But, Oh, consider the sorry plight of the country when the people loyal to God begin to pray together and rise up against this sin! Pray, yes, pray to God that He will destroy such an atrocity and banish it from the earth, and you will see what a glorious success will result! If you are a simple member of a Christian congregation and ask, what can I do? This is my answer: Open your heart and defy the arrogant rule of slavery that has come between the Most High and His faithful subjects on the one hand, and those who would rob Him of His prestige and destroy any trace of moral rectitude and human happiness; speak out against slavery, pray that it ends, shun like the plague all dealings with the slave holder! This will prod him to reflect on his crimes and to give up wrongdoing. Some will counter: Our church, its clergymen, including its deans and other church wardens, will surely entertain some doubts on this subject and I, as a simple member of that church, must remain dutifully silent until the matter is taken up by men who have more influence than me.

Elijah could have spoken thus when Elias went up to heaven and left nothing for him but his coat. Yet he did not react this way but struck the water and shouted: Now, where is the God of Elias? And behold! Elias's God was these to answer him and reveal his omnipotence.

Silence and inaction in this matter might have been in some measure justified if humans were not responsible creatures, with talents and the opportunities to use them. But having in mind the bulk of humanity, of which I know only a minuscule part, and seeing how the course of events often affects me and how, indirectly, I help to uphold slavery when I buy a product made by slaves at the cost of so many moans and laments, I feel called in all justice to tip the scales in the other direction. Do I but contribute to increase the cursed weight of my unhappy fellow man's shackles and fasten them more solidly so that he might never taste freedom in his lifetime, I cannot help to break his painful chains and guide him to liberty. If I cannot do this directly, it has to be possible to do so indirectly. There is no reason to think it impossible to help a creature gain freedom, since heaven intended him to live free. I am only doing my duty when I pursue such an honorable and praiseworthy quest for human rights and privileges. Many contend that freeing the slaves would be unsafe and productive of much evil. I can confirm that it would create some difficulties for the slave holders, but in my humble opinion, the evils they fear and talk about will never come to pass. From the dawn of time, there have always been people to raise such fears whenever there has been a question of granting freedom to the enslaved, but experience teaches us that none of these evil consequences has ever arisen. If the devilish powers bent on maintaining slavery could prove the negative consequences of a general freedom, they would draw satisfaction from doing so as this would serve to maintain mankind in affliction forever. These evil powers are creatures that take on human form, among whom one can discern some who claim to be especially religious. If humanity were stricken by some evil catastrophe or affliction, you can be sure that those who use religion as a cloak would somehow be behind it. The Savior Himself was betrayed by one of his disciples. All the evil in the present state of things springs from clergymen or some religious order. The dominion of evil is maintained with insistence and force, as happened under the rule of the Syrian king, because it is a fact: As are the priests, so are the people! The priestly class guides the people, encouraging them to commit a national sin, and the people are happy to indulge. So while America enjoys an excellent political reputation abroad and ranks high in the field of science and literature, slavery remains an eyesore, yea, a curse. One might well compare the country to a lady in a dress of pure white that bears a dark stain so conspicuous that it catches the eye of every passer-by.

Thus is America a graceful beauty in every respect, but marred by this great blemish. As long as it harbors this dreadful evil in its bosom, it will be seen as an earthly beauty defiled by ignominy. Oh, why should God's radiance be so obscured and mankind be so destroyed?

May the day soon dawn when this nightmare will end and mankind is cleansed of this disfiguring stain! Then the tears of the slave will be dried and his sorrowful chant will become a hymn. May God grant it! May He let us partake of this joy beyond words, that we may see the day of redemption when American freedom rises up to heaven! Amen!

Chapter 8: Provinces (Counties) and Cities in Liberia

The Free State of Liberia occupies a strip of coastal land bordered on its western side by the Atlantic Ocean; it is 600 to 700 (English) miles long and at its northern extremity abuts Sierra Leone. The river Cestos,[10] extending 150 miles from the ocean into the interior, forms its southern and eastern boundaries. The country is divided into seven provinces or counties (Translator's note: The author has described more than seven, as we shall see) plus an unsurveyed area located north of Cape Mount.

1. Millsburg.

Beginning at the north, the first county one comes across is Millsburg on the Mesurado. It presents many advantages for agriculture because of the richness of its soil and also because the river that flows by it is navigable. The immigrants from America founded a city here and occupied a large expanse of land. They are making important advances in cultivating the soil and in civilizing the natives, many of whom have sought to emulate the work practices of the laboring residents and to make better use of their talents for cultivation than they had until now. This district is well known for its rice and cotton production, and the sugar cane also grows well. All sorts of tropical fruits found in Africa grow in abundance here. This is an elevated area and the air is free of vapors because there are no swamps. Religious life has seen a significant development; many schools have been built which the natives attend. There are Episcopalian, Methodist, and Presbyterian churches and a Baptist congregation, each with its

---

10. Translator's note: Or Great Sestros, forming the eastern boundary, just as the river Mana marks the western boundary. But the country never did extend into Ashante territory. According to the most recent reports, Liberia is situated on the Malaghetta or Pepper Coast and stretches northwest to southeast almost 76 German miles from the Gallina to the Settakru rivers (actually from Cape Mount to the St. Andrews River). The exact width cannot be determined, but it certainly exceeds 20 (German) miles. The width in its middle amounts to 8 2/3 (German) miles.

own school. The natives can choose between them and so be instructed in a manner agreeable to them and to their religious inclinations, and each of these churches feels obligated to partici- pate in the education of the inhabitants. Indeed, it is a pleasure to peer into the snug homes of the inhabitants, whose roofs rise above the surrounding bushes and trees where, not long ago, one found only low native huts thatched with palm fronds. And the fields are covered with luscious germinating and ripening seeds where previously the soil yielded nothing but weeds and wriggling insects. After having tasted the bitterness of American slavery, the newcomers found a pleasant home here and a peaceful land where they could develop social and family ties.

2. New Virginia.

Starting from the north, this second district has a greater popu- lation of immigrants than the first. It draws its name from the origin of its first inhabitants, that is, Virginia (in North America). Agriculture and handcrafts are much more developed here because the settlements, watered by the Mesurado River, have existed for a longer time. Travelling by boat, one can see many fine planted fields and the scenery is charming to the eye. One sees large coffee plantations and the loveliest palm-covered valleys.

In the last three years, the extraction of palm oil has greatly expanded as has the cultivation of rice, so that this area will prob- ably become the most prosperous of the whole country and its inhabitants the richest, if progress continues at this pace. The natives have a stake in these improvements as civilization and education were made available to them and they embraced these wholeheartedly, seeing in better practices a way to improve their well-being. Peace and harmony pervade the land. They regularly go to church and strive to achieve the blessings of civilization. The same religious societies as are active in the Millsburg district are present here, but in far greater numbers, and the schools are very well attended. Much credit for the general advancement of this district is due to Mr. W.A. Johnson, to his efforts and the educa- tion he so graciously provided as a teacher of adults as well as of children in the schools. Visiting those schools in the course of my inquiries, I was able to see for myself that the pupils in catechism classes did very well.

3. New Georgia.

Proceeding southward, we find this district also flourishing, ranking second only to the capital in prosperity. There is a branch of the Providence Church here and society is in a flourishing way. Many natives are steady members of the different churches and, because they have accepted the ways and customs of civilized life, they form a distinguished part of society, allowing us to see well enough what Africa might become. The Sabbath and its celebrations are well observed and respected; the inhabitants cherish the enlightenment that has been provided to them; their religious feelings are strong and their devotion is sincere. Love, harmony, peace and good will prevail among them; nothing seems to shake their confidence in one another; they unite in common endeavors and aspirations and they really form a happy and prosperous people. Extensively cultivated fields and plantations, and neatly built houses offer proof that good feelings are the foundation of the advancement of these people. The outsider is moved by such a sight and is touched by the blessings of social ease, which he never could have grasped had he not seen with his own eyes what before he had only read about. So has this part of Africa been visibly saved from darkness and ruin.

4. Bexley.

This district is also in a flourishing state; its main products are coffee, palm oil, camwood,[11] ivory and rice. Its prospects are very encouraging because the soil, if well cultivated, could produce in abundance. The neighboring tribes are not only pacific but also show an inner desire for religious instruction and are attentive to it. All their chiefs have placed themselves under the protection of

---

11. African redwood

the republic and, in the cities for which they are responsible, they have done all in their power to ensure that schools are built and maintained. In the present schools, many pupils show promise that their education will bring rewards in both knowledge and piety. For many years, the schools here were under the supervision of John Day, a Baptist minister from America who has earned praise for what he has been able to achieve. The headquarters of this denomination are here, and most people here are members of it. The inhabitants greatly respect John Day because of his way of life and how he deals with people. He has a deep interest in anything touching the well-being of the district, both in matters commercial and agricultural, and in this manner he is useful to all segments of society.

5. Louisiana.

The name of this district derives from its settlement by an association of immigrants from the state of that name in America. This district also is outstanding, not for its commercial affairs, but for its unmatched agricultural sector. The moral and religious progress among the natives has been rewarding, and the schools, which had been under the supervision of Mr. Richardson, are thriving. The settlement of American immigrants in this part of the country increases every year so that the extent of land under cultivation will continue to expand.

6. Monserado.

This district of the country is the largest and most populous, and includes the capital city of the country, Monrovia. The city is under excellent administration; trade is very well developed and commercial ventures seem to be expanding. The finest harbor is found here, better than any other on the west coast. In the city itself, there are three major houses of worship belonging to the Independent, Episcopalian and Presbyterian churches, and they are at present building a second Episcopalian church. Here too are the public or state buildings, such as the High Court, the legislative assembly, a prison and a large customs house, the post office, the government secretariat, the Treasury, and the executive office building.

The laws and regulations in force here are respected by most of the people. The city has 15,000 inhabitants, including the native people, who have so thoroughly adopted civilized ways that drunkenness, theft, robbery and similar crimes seldom occur. Those who may have committed such offences elsewhere encounter high-principled inhabitants here who keep a close eye on them and steer them back onto the righteous path. Transgressors find themselves under the powerful influence and scrutiny of a moral and religious people, who, in the country where they were held as slaves, had known so much wickedness from vice and intemperance that they feel obliged, for the safety of their kith and kin, to fight such dereliction with all their might to prevent a repetition of the same evils here. For this, we have to thank Mr. B.V.R. James, rector of the Latin School. Because of his high sense of duty and his virtuous conduct, he has earned the confidence and respect of one and all. He serves as an elder of the Presbyterian Church and is also the government's Keeper of the Rolls (*Custos rotulorum*). How useful he has been to the state is evident from the positions he has held. Here I must note that all the arts and sciences known to the people of Liberia have found a high degree of perfection in this district.

One thing the republic lacks is its own legal tender or currency. For local transactions, they still do not have their own coins or paper notes. The only ones in circulation are the gold and silver pieces of foreign countries. Hard currency is always in such demand and so seldom to be had that most commercial transactions are conducted by barter, which puts Liberia at a big disadvantage. It is imperative that the government take steps to introduce a legal tender for the republic.

7. Junk District.

Adjoining Mesurado to the south, this district is known for its farming; every valley is like a palm garden, and each plantation has coffee trees. The natives of this district belong to the Kru tribe.

Above all, they busy themselves with the extraction of palm oil and the cultivation of rice and *cassada*;[12] they live happily and peacefully among the Liberians, who enjoy associating with them as they accept the habits of the Liberians and live in the same manner as they do.

As a result of earlier wars with neighboring tribes, their numbers were decimated. They do a great deal of hunting in search of ivory. Many of them are smiths and, considering the conditions in which they must work, they are very creative and dexterous. They build their own air furnaces to melt the iron ore that is widely found in this area. They make charcoal from mango wood, bellows out of animal skins, and hammer the metal with a stone that is quite hard and heavy. They forge their own spears, knives and swords with it, and also make ornaments. Others melt down gold and silver from which they make necklaces, rings and other types of jewelry which are greatly appreciated by African natives.

This district does not enjoy the facilities of water communication that the northern district of Monrovia does—only an insignificant little river runs through it, and the coast is rugged and the seas rough. All merchandise must be transported over long distances by land, then by boat, to be transferred onto larger ships anchored far offshore. Despite these drawbacks, it is developing quite well thanks to its facilities for trading in the interior. An extensive inland trade is carried on by the natives who deal in highly prized items such as ivory, rubber, dyewoods and gold, which can very well be transported by land and then easily ferried out to ships.

The capital of this district is called Hardytown and is developing nicely. On the banks of the river Junk, one finds a fine species of turtle whose shell is popular with foreign traders on the coast. There are two houses of worship, both very plain wooden huts, that are also used as schools. Education and religion go hand in hand and hold the promise of a brilliant future. A big drawback is the shortage of teachers and preachers. The congregations are seldom visited by proper clergymen because there are not enough

---

12. Translator's note: Cassava or arrowroot, Jatropha Manihoc

of these to properly serve the needs of the population. A congregation might be visited only four times a year by a regular preacher,
who will celebrate the sacraments. Under the circumstances,
these congregations depend for their survival on the faithful support of their members and the efforts of their deacons and elders.

8. Edina District.

This is the second district to the south of Monrovia. Its main city
is located on the coast. At the estuary of the Mecklin River, there
is a good harbor and the river banks are excellent, 18 to 20 miles
broad. The immigrants were drawn to this area by its scenic
beauty and its fertile soil. This city is a growing community and
has a school with a proper preacher of the Baptist Church, Mr. J.H.
Cheesman, who is aided in his work by an assistant and a teacher.
Education is making rapid strides and the inhabitants go about
their occupations with great zeal. The congregation is made up
mostly of converted natives but includes some immigrants and
Liberians. In this district, many wealthy people from America
have bought great tracts of land with the intention of removing
here as soon as they are in a position to do so.

There are four schoolhouses or places of worship, operated by
the Methodists, Baptists, Presbyterians and Independents, and
all are well attended on Sundays. Many of the settlers are engaged
in trading and much ivory is brought to market from here. The
natives are of the Oley tribe and their principal occupations are
hunting and fishing as well as rice cultivation. They live in tidy
little huts and their gardens are well kept. Some are travelling
traders or have trading connections with the inhabitants of the
interior. They belong to a peaceful and sociable tribe and are
averse to war, much more so than any other tribe on the coast.
They used to be much given to drink at the time when American
slave traders plundered this coast.

They sold thousands of their own people, yes their own sons
and daughters, into eternal slavery for rum. Now, under the protection which Liberia affords them against the incursions of
American raiders, a happy change has taken place in their lives.

The chief no longer sells his fellow men but, for his livelihood, cultivates his own fields and by this dignified and honest conduct sets an example for his people. Moderation reigns in this district, and together with the rest of the country, the tribe takes the highest interest and plays an honorable part in the life of the Liberian nation. We are confident that other tribes that once debased themselves by participating in the abominable slave trade will soon follow the shining example set by this clan which has providentially cleansed itself of this hideous sin against God and humanity.

The schools are well attended, but unfortunately there is a shortage of teachers. The day is close at hand, however, when men of faith will visit these shores to teach the inhabitants and bring the word of God to those thousands who have yet to enjoy the opportunity of receiving moral and religious instruction.

9. Bassa District.

This district is very extensive and the only one in the country that is in a disturbed state. The native populations stubbornly remain under the influence of a chief, Grando, who has until now refused the benefits of education and civilization. This leader, even after he had sold his territory to the government, signed the contract and received payment, still acted basely. He continuously incited the people of the Bassa tribe to hostilities against the immigrants and the Republic. On several occasions, they carried out nighttime attacks against the inhabitants, killing many. When this area was first settled, the natives, under Grando's leadership, attacked one of the new villages in the dead of night, killing 400 people; only 18 managed to survive. This rash attack led the American and English cruisers then patrolling the coast to intervene; the natives were routed from their hiding places, many were felled in battle and some of their leaders were captured. When asked why they had committed such horrible deeds, they replied: "Grando wished it so, otherwise he would have killed us all!" The interrogators inquired where Grando was hiding; but he had fled into the interior.

After that terrible slaughter, the small settlement was put in a state of defence, the natives, at least those who abided by their oath to the government, returned to their various villages, and soon the district was again peopled by American immigrants, notably by freed colored persons. After a few years, it was rumored that Grando had been seen among the natives of Fishtown, the main town in the Bassa district, only 2½ miles from Bexley. The government put a bounty on his head. Once again he vanished, until 1851, when he suddenly reappeared accompanied by other chiefs and a great many savages. They attempted to destroy the towns and villages that the Liberians had built. The result was a horrible battle in which the Liberians suffered great losses, but in the end the savages were roundly beaten by the Liberian militia. The main leader fell in the battle, while other lesser chiefs surrendered to government officials. They were declared prisoners of war and remanded for trial at the next sitting of the Supreme Court. Peace was restored, but the inhabitants continued fortifying the town.

The district is very fertile and the town offers one of the best harbors in Liberia; in former times, it had a bad reputation on account of its barracoons. Grando, from an early age, had traded in slaves, and this had brought him riches; Liberia's disruption of his business probably pushed him to commit treason, which at last ended in his death.

10. Sinon District.

This fourth district to the south of Monrovia is a centre of trade and commerce. Here there is a fine wooden chapel and a salaried clergyman of the Baptist faith, who is spreading the Word. The Presbyterians are also established in this district; they have not yet built a temple, but they have a growing number of followers. The natives are very friendly and because of their contact with Liberians, they are becoming more civilized. From the time their chiefs ceded this territory to the Liberian government they have never shown themselves to be hostile, and since the area has become part of Liberia, there has not been one recorded case of theft or robbery.

In earlier times, the chiefs used to plunder shipwrecks and kill every foreigner they encountered travelling through the country. We recall the murder of four American missionaries. These four, deeply concerned that their fellow men were doomed to die in darkness, had determined to bring them salvation and left behind all that was near and dear to them to preach peace to their unenlightened brothers and to educate them in the ways of civilization; they were to be murdered upon their arrival. Through God's Providence, the spilled blood and mortal agony of His servants served the cause of Christianity, as on the night following the murder, when the moon was high, Monokon, the chief who had slaughtered the missionaries, returned to the scene of the crime and wept at his misdeeds. The godly light that touches every man who comes into this world stirred a deep sense of guilt in his heart, and his conscience was filled with torment. He knelt down and sighed under the weight of his sins and could find no peace. The blood of the strangers he had murdered cried out for justice and their dying sighs filled his ears. Oh truly, he appeared before God like a second Cain and God said to him: The voice of your brother's blood rises from the earth and cries up to me! The next day he gathered the natives of the different tribes and through his sobs and tears he told them of his sorrow for the horrible crime they had committed.

His conscience led the proud heathen to yield remorsefully to the Throne of the Highest Grace! This so impressed the natives that they asked the missionaries in Sierra Leone to instruct them or, as they say in their own language, to teach them God's "palavra." Here again, the blood of the martyrs facilitated the planting and growth of the Christian Church in this part of Africa that was so benighted. — The venerable Mr. R.C. Murray is owed a great debt of gratitude for all his efforts on this coast.

He succeeded in establishing three schools and three preaching stations in this county. The natives are skillful at learning English and easily learn to read and write. In the Christian communities in the city of Sinon, you will find around ten natives for one Liberian. The district is rich in palm trees, coffee and rice. The inhabitants exhibit diligence and temperance and are making great progress in handcrafts and cultivation. In this city, the engineer George Harris, the same one as in "Uncle Tom's Cabin," whom German readers know, is the owner of a fine establishment where he conducts a machine-building business on a large scale. The Republic's first steam engine is being built here. We hope to see the use of steam power spread throughout West Africa as the inland waters offer no great waterfalls to power (hydraulic) machinery. In this district, there is plenty of excellent timber such as teak, rosewood, mahogany, ebony and camwood. The location of the harbor surpasses the one at Bassa as it is easier to transport merchandise to the ocean from here. A major industry is the building of small vessels for the coastal and river trades, though no large ship has yet been constructed here for want of capital. If men with the means and ability to conduct such a business were to come here, they could easily build ships up to any tonnage with the excellent and plentiful materials at hand. This coast was formerly one of the rendezvous points for the infamous slave trader Blanco and numerous Spanish ships. The number of human beings who were stolen from this area and sold into abject slavery is incalculable. Yes, for hundreds of years, they came here looking for human flesh to be turned into gold, turning humanity into brutality! Thank God in his mercy, that trade no longer exists here. The natives' city now is visited by people whose sole desire is to bring the Good News to these poor ignorant creatures, and not by gangs of robbers seeking to drag them and their children into bondage. The Gospel has come to the native and his family; the way of life and liberty lies open before them: they hope for eternal salvation, their prospects of attaining it much improved by following the Christian and moral examples set by the Liberians, so that the native and his family can now rejoice in the blessings of civilization.

11. Palmas District.

This southern border district is famed for its palm trees. The wooded areas feature an abundance of this beautiful, priceless wood and no other part of this African region produces so much oil. For many years now, the natives have found this business so profitable that they never reverted to slave trading, as other coastal tribes did. They suffered only a few problems from the fact that some envious inland tribes attacked them, seeking to drive them from the coast so as to have all the benefits of the trade themselves. As a result this tribe was much reduced in numbers; but ever since they placed themselves under the protection of the Liberian government, the disturbances have ceased.

The government now faces an opponent from a totally different quarter. As soon as the Liberians had shaken off the American yoke and asserted their own rights, the American government purchased land south of the Republic, which the Colonization Society in America still claims today. They operate a small colony of several hundred acres right on the border of this district and strive to exert their influence well beyond its boundaries. In this colony, called Cape Palmas (because it is situated in an area where palms grow), the inhabitants are growing dissatisfied. Their governor, Russworni [Russwurm], is none too happy with the American-made laws and regulations that he must apply; that is why he believes that there will come a time when the colony will be ceded to independent Liberia.

In truth, these Americans are anxious to maintain a hold on Africa in order to perpetuate the slave trade. But the time is coming when God will follow the bloody trail of his people and it will be made clear to all that America is drunk on the blood of Africa.

He will command them, as in the time of Moses He demanded of Pharaoh: Let my people go! If He so wills it, every chained son of Africa will hear His voice and the government of America will tremble! When the cup of suffering of Africa's Black children is full and God lifts the cloud of wrath hanging over His crushed people, then His Grace will shine down on them; then He will show Himself to mighty and proud America, as He did to the arrogant Nebuchadnezzar. And the man stealers and dealers in flesh will alike know the power of the God of justice.

Weeping Africa! Wipe the tear from your eye! Look up, you oppressed and downtrodden land! The chains that rob your limbs of strength, the spell that smothers your thoughts and grinds your soul in the dust; the hand that crushes your reason in its iron grip, down to the level of the brute beast—Oh you sobbing child of woe!—God will destroy them all!!

Closing remarks of the translator.

According to the latest accounts, the country consists of two states, Liberia and Maryland in Liberia (the name seems to point to an eventual union), with 300,000 inhabitants. The native states of Kru (since 1843, with a population of 40,000) and of Sanguin have joined Liberia. Among the more important centres in Liberia are Coldwell and Bassa Cove; and in Maryland, the villages of Harper and Mount Tubmann. Other reports refer to a part of the Republic of Liberia called Greenville; we must await information on this from the authorities. Also, cocoa is now an export article, and the coffee is renowned.

The author, who is now in Hamburg, was born in London and is 37 years old. He studied in Halifax, at Neadia College from 1834 to 1838. His father, a Negro born in Jamaica, was a London merchant, and his mother a quarteroon. His new wife is a pretty English lady. This work was originally published in 1853 by J. Samson at York. The author is thinking of soon returning to Monrovia and has promised to send us further information on the present state of things.

NOTES ON SOURCES

1. "WOLF!" THEY CRIED IN MAINE. Letters to the *Christian Mirror* of Portland, Me., form the basis of this chapter. None of the Maine newspapers cited here and in the next chapter was online at the time the research for this book was conducted; papers were consulted at the Maine Historical Society in Portland and the Calais Free Library. Details of Asa Cummings' career came from Joseph Griffin, ed., *History of the Press of Maine,* Brunswick, Me., The Press, 1872.

2. FORNICATION – IN BAILEYVILLE! The Revised *Statutes of the State of Maine,* 1841, c. 87, "Of Marriage, and its solemnization," Sections 3 and 5; and c. 160, "Of offences against chastity, morality and decency," Section 10, are now online at the Maine State Legislature website. Wood's wedding is recorded in Provincial Archives of New Brunswick, MC 223, S8-A-6, A1, Diocese of Fredericton Fonds, St. Stephen, Christ Church, Parish Registers, Marriages 1846–1852; and RS 148, J, 4 a 2, Charlotte County Council Records, Legal, Marriage Registers 1839–1854, Book 2, page 239. Rebecca M. Pritchard explored the career of Jeremiah Hacker of the *Pleasure Boat* in her thesis "The Life and Times of Jeremiah Hacker, 1801–1895," and his views on slavery, in *Jeremiah Hacker: Journalist, Anarchist, Abolitionist,* Philadelphia, Pa., Frayed Edge Press, 2019, pp 67–70. The accounts of jailer Abijah Crane are found in the Washington County Courthouse Archives at Machias, Me. Wood's claim for compensation is recorded in Edmund Hornby, *Report of the Proceedings of the Mixed Commission on Private Claims, Established under the Convention Between Great Britain and the United States of America of the 8th February, 1853; with the Judgments of the Commissioners and Umpire,* London, printed by Harrison and Sons, 1856, pp 57, 60 and 93.

3. UNMASKED. A list of the "Pastors of the African Meeting House Church" compiled by Boston's Museum of African American History in 2006 shows "No Pastor" in 1850. See also Table III-1 in George A. Levesque, "Inherent Reformers-Inherited Orthodoxy: Black Baptists in Boston, 1800–1873," *Journal of Negro History,* 60, no. 4 (October 1975): 491–525. The notice published by the church in the *Liberator* of 24 May 1850 and in the *Christian Watchman* of 6 Jun 1850 shows otherwise. In addition, Isaac Smith Homans, *Sketches of Boston, Past and Present, and of Some Few Places in Its Vicinity* (Boston, Phillips, Sampson and Company; Crosby and Nichols, 1851, pp III and 88) places Wood as pastor there for a brief period in 1850. On inter-racial marriage, see Stephen Kantrowitz, *More Than Freedom, Fighting for Black Citizenship in a White Republic, 1829–1889* (New York, N.Y., Penguin Press, 2012, p 64); Randall Kennedy, *Interracial Intimacies*: Sex, Marriage, Identity, and Adoption (New York, N.Y., Pantheon Books, 2003, pp 244–249, 256n); Randolph Stakeman, "Slavery in Colonial Maine," *Maine Historical Society Quarterly,* 27, no. 2 (Fall 1987): 58–81; Peter Wallenstein, *Tell the Court I love My Wife: Race, Marriage, and Law – An American History* (New York, N.Y., Palgrave Macmillan, 2004, pp 41, 43–45, 54, 136, 253–4). Details of the campaign against segregated schools are found in the *Liberator.* In Nova Scotia, a fruitless search was conducted through various collections at the Nova Scotia Archives (MG 15 Ethnic collections; RG 1 Bound volumes of Nova Scotia records for the period 1624–1867, including censuses of 1827 and 1838; RG 5 Records of the Legislative Assembly of Nova Scotia; RG 14 Education; RG 20 Lands and Forests) and Halifax newspapers of the period (*Acadian Recorder, Halifax Morning Post, Nova Scotian*).

4. LIBERIATION. The main sources were the Papers of the American Colonization Society (ACS) at the Library of Congress, especially the society's magazine the *African Repository,* containing much correspondence between Liberia and the U.S.; the *Liberia Herald,* 1842–1857 (spotty), microfilm from the Maryland Historical Society Library, now online at Archive.org; the *Maryland Colonization Journal;* the *Liberian Statutes, 1847–1857,* Book I ("Declaration of Independence," and "Constitution of the

Republic of Liberia"); and the A.T. Wood File (1850–1857) at the Southern Baptist Historical Library and Archives in Nashville, TN (SBHLA); and annual reports and other documents at the archives of the Convention's International Missions Board at Richmond, VA (IMBA). Books consulted include Tom W. Schick's *Behold the Promised Land: A History of Afro-American Settler Society in Nineteenth-Century Liberia,* and Allan Yarema's *The American Colonization Society: An Avenue to Freedom?* A handy "Table of Emigrants" printed as an appendix to the *Thirty-Fifth Annual Report of the American Colonization Society, January 20th, 1852,* pp 49–52, lists 91 ship departures from Feb. 1820 to Dec. 1851, giving the names of the ships and the month of their sailing (but not their port of departure), the number of emigrants on board and their states of origin. A longer list, covering departures Feb 1820–Dec 1866, ran in the ACS's *Memorial of the Semi-Centennial Anniversary of the American Colonization Society, Celebrated at Washington, January 15, 1867,* pp 182–190.

5. HIRED AND FIRED SIGHT UNSEEN. Much of this material is based on the ACS and IMBA papers. A copy of Wood's letter to Pinney is found in SBHLA, AR. 551-2, Box #065, A.T. Wood File (1850–1857). The hiring and firing of Wood are covered in IMBA, accession no. 2620, "Annual Report of the Foreign Mission Board," 9 May 1851; accession nos. 710 and 711, Foreign Mission Board Minutes, Richmond, Va., 9 Jul and 4 Aug 1851; accession no. 2608, Foreign Mission Board annual report, 4 Jun 1852. His departure from Liberia for England on 20 June 1851 is recorded in the arrivals and departures from the port of Monrovia listed in *Addresses Delivered in the Hall of the House of Representatives, Harrisburg, Pa., on Tuesday Evening, April 6, 1852, by William V. Pettit, Esq., and Rev. John P. Durbin, D.D.,* 45, and in the *Maryland Colonization Journal,* new series, 6, no. 7 (Dec 1851): 111. Material on Ellis is taken from *African Repository,* 25, no. 1, Jan 1849: 28, and 46, no. 7, Jul 1870: 223; *Chambers's Edinburgh Journal,* 19, no. 482, 26 Mar 1853: 202–204; *Christian Observatory,* 3, no. 3, Mar 1849: 116–128; *Emancipator,* 23 Dec 1846; *Emancipator and Free American,* 23 Mar 1843; *National Era,* 2 Jun 1853 and 22 Feb 1855. Useful sources for Hanson include the *Liberator,* 19 and 26 Jan, 21 Sep,

5 Oct, 9 Nov 1838; 3 Apr and 14 Aug 1840; 4 Feb 1842. *Colonization Herald and General Register,* 1, no. 6 (Jun 1839): 249–251. *Colored American,* 1 Sep, 8 Sep, 15 Sep 1838 and 29 Sep 1838; 9 Nov 1839; 15 May, 3 Jul, 4 and 25 Sep 1841. *Emancipator,* 29 Jul 1841 and 8 Sep 1842. *London Gazette,* no. 20603, 12 May 1846, 1727, and no. 21129, 23 Aug 1850, 2301. The *Times,* London, 22 Oct 1850. Writings by Hanson include "Communication concerning the Vei and Mendi Dialects," 135–6; "On the Grammatical Principles of the Gha (Accra) Language," 96–7; and *Matthew ke Dzhon, Sà'dzhj-kpakpáj lu; Iè Ghà Wiemà lu mli – The Gospels of St. Matthew and St. John, in the Accra Language.* Other sources include *African Repository,* 40, no. 7 (Jul 1864): 222. *Anti-Slavery Reporter,* 3rd series, 10, no. 11 (1 Nov 1862): 252–3; and 11, no. 9 (1 Sep 1863): 214–216. *Atlas,* London, 18 Jun 1861, "Diplomatic Gossip." *Evening Herald,* London, 10 Jan 1860, "Royal Geographical Society." *Evening Star and Dial,* London, 29 Jan 1861, "Royal Geographical Society," and 13 Jun 1861, "Money Market. – This Day." *Gentleman's Magazine,* new series, 40, no. 211 (Jul–Dec 1861): 156–158. *Patriot,* London, 13 Jun 1861, "Official Appointments." *Times,* London, 4 Jul 1861, "Court Circular," and 13 Oct 1862, "The Loss of the Cleopatra." Shick, *Behold the Promised Land,* 104–107.

6. THERE WILL ALWAYS BE AN ENGLAND. The *Manchester Guardian,* 4 Feb 1852, and the *Manchester Courier,* 7 Feb 1852, referred to Wood's supposed detention in Plymouth and London, as did the deposition of Rev. Christopher Newman Hall (see note to Ch. 7). Notices in London's *British Banner,* 24 Nov 1852, and the official *London Gazette,* no. 21255, 21 Oct 1851, p 2771; no. 21256, 24 Oct 1851, pp 2808–2809, also give successive addresses for him in Monrovia, London and Liverpool. Records relative to Wood's wedding are found in Cheshire Archives & Local Studies, Chester, Marriage Bonds and Allegations, 1852, p 6, no. 116, 27 Jan 1852 (online at findmypast.com), and in the Liverpool Record Office, Liverpool Registers, 283 JAM/3/9, 5 Feb 1852.

7. HELP FROM UNCLE TOM'S CABIN. The *Hull Packet* of 31 Dec 1852 and 7 Jan 1853 carried an almost complete transcript of Wood's trial. The *Hull Advertiser* devoted a full page to the trial in its issue

of 7 Jan, with follow-up remarks in the editions of 14 and 21 Jan. The *York Herald* of 18 Jan carried a comprehensive account of the case, and the *British Banner* of 5 Jan provided an informative summary. Of Hanson the *Banner* said: "The Rev. A.W. Hanson, in orders in the Church of England, and lately Her Majesty's Consul at Monrovia, a gentleman of colour, remarkably accomplished in his manners and highly educated, gave his evidence in a manner so intelligent, straightforward, and decided, as to excite the admiration of the whole Court." Other newspaper sources include the *British Banner,* 24 Nov 1852 and 5 Jan 1853. *Hull Advertiser,* 26 Nov and 31 Dec 1852, 21 Jan 1853. *Hull News,* 20 Nov 1852. *Hull Packet,* 19 and 26 Nov, and 3 Dec 1852, 21 Jan 1853. *Leicester Journal,* 21 Jan 1853. *Leicestershire Mercury,* 29 Jan 1853. *Newcastle Courant,* 17 Sep and 26 Nov, 3 Dec 1852; *Newcastle Guardian,* 4 Sep 1852. *York Herald,* 27 Nov and 11 Dec 1852, 1 Jan 1853.

Manuscript sources: Garnet's letter to John Scoble inquiring about Wood is in the Bodleian Library of Commonwealth and African Studies at Rhodes House, Oxford, Papers of the British and Foreign Anti-Slavery Society, MSS. Brit. Emp. s. 18, C17/68. Wood's petition of 25 Dec 1852 to Home Secretary Lord Palmerston is in UK National Archives, HO 18, Home Office, Criminal Petitions, Series II, 1852–1853, no. 350.

Hull History Centre, C CQB 244/494–503, Court of Quarter Sessions, Kingston-upon-Hull, December 1853 [read December 1852], depositions of Christopher Newman Hall, Joseph Hargreaves and Rev. John King, all 27 Dec 1852, and of Augustus William Hanson, 28 Dec 1852; C CQB 244/817, Court of Quarter Sessions, Kingston-upon-Hull, Calendar of Prisoners, October–December (Michaelmas) Session, pp 6–7.

8. LET THIS BE A LESSON. The main newspapers cited are the London *Patriot* of 10 and 13 Jan 1853, and the New Orleans *Picayune* of 27 Feb 1853. There is some mystery about Wood's apparent exposure in the spring of 1852. The letter in defence of the Rev. Arthur Jones, Dean of Bangor, in the *Patriot* of 13 Jan 1853, spoke of a "journal published in this neighbourhood" having exposed Wood in May 1852, but doubts about Wood's honesty had surfaced in the area press as early as February 1852 when he

was charged with fraud in Manchester. And in March that year, several newspapers in Lancashire, including the *Liverpool Standard,* had warned the public against him, though without naming him.

9. PUBLISHED IN HAMBURG. A copy of the *Geschichte der Republik Liberia* (see Appendix) was found in the New York Public Library's Schomburg Center for Research in Black Culture. It names no publisher (part of the cover page is missing), but the library's catalogue identifies the publisher as G.W. Niemeyer, as did the Jan 1855 issue of *Rudolph Garrigue's Monthly Bulletin of German Literature,* and various other sources, old and new. Wood's mention of the existence of only "two works about Liberia" in English in 1854 seems to echo Augustus William Hanson's statement at Wood's trial in Hull that he knew of two books about Liberia, "one named the 'New Republic,' and the other 'Africa Redeemed'." These were actually the U.S. and English editions of the same work by American author Sarah Josepha Hale, published in Boston in 1850 under the title *The New Republic,* and in England the following year as *Africa Redeemed: or, the Means of Her Relief Illustrated by the Growth and Prospects of Liberia.* There were, in fact, numerous books about Liberia, pro and con, available in 1854, not to mention a variety of ACS publications and journal articles. For Russwurm, co-founder and editor of *Freedom's Journal,* the first Black-owned, Black-run newspaper in the U.S., and latterly governor of Maryland in Liberia, see Winston James, *The Struggles of John Brown Russwurm,* New York, N.Y., New University Press, 2010, and Carl Patrick Burrowes, "A Child of the Atlantic: The Maine Years of John Brown Russwurm," Maine History, 47, No. 2 (July 20113): 163–169, and by the same author, "Caught in the Crosswinds of the Atlantic," *Journalism History,* 37, No. 3 (Fall 2011): 130–141.

10. PUNISHED IN MONROVIA, REDEEMED AT MONTREAL. On Woods's last doings in Liberia, the following letters were consulted: IMBA, A.T. Wood to J.B. Taylor, Corresponding Secretary, 19 Dec 1854, and A.T. Wood to Beverley Page Yates, 10 Jun 1857, No. 2 Report of the School at Farmerville. ACS, I:B6, Part 2, Doc. 291,

John Day to J.W. Lugenbeel, 22 Mar 1855. Montreal newspapers cited were consulted at the Bibliothèque et Archives nationales du Québec in Montreal (BAnQ-M), as were city directories and notarial deeds, notably those of notary J.B. Houle, CN601-205, deed 6450, 15 Feb 1859, and notary J.H. Isaacson, CN601-469, deed 6225, 7 Mar 1859; company records in TP11, S2, SS20, SSS48, Cour supérieure, Raisons sociales, Déclarations, no. 1348, Bell & Nelson, 15 Dec 1858, and no. 1397, 7 Mar 1859; and various church registers, notably those of Erskine Presbyterian, 14 Oct 1852; Notre-Dame, 16 Jul 1854 and 23 May 1867; and St. James Methodist, 5 Jun 1854, 19 Jul and 5 Oct 1858, and 15 Jan 1864.

11. ILLINOIS AND 'THE FALL OF MAN.' The sources for this chapter are all fairly identified in the text.

12. RECONSTRUCTION. None of the sources for Wood's Tennessee years identifies him by the full name of Alfred Thomas Wood. He was called variously Albert T. Woods (or Wood), A.T. Wood or Dr. Wood. He may have had his reasons to not spell out his name. For the history of Blacks in Nashville, Lyle Lovett's *The African-American History of Nashville, Tennessee, 1780–1930* was indispensable, as were the following African-American newspapers for the brief period that concerns us: The *Colored Tennessean*, Nashville, and *Freedom's Watchman*, Murfreesboro. On the history of medicine, see Robert G. Ransom, *The History of Medicine in Rutherford County*, Part I (Murfreesboro, Tenn.: Publication no. 24 of the Rutherford County Historical Society, Winter 1985); James Summerville, *Educating Black Doctors: A History of Meharry Medical College* (Tuscaloosa, Ala.: University of Alabama Press, 1983); and Thomas J. Ward Jr., *Black Physicians in the Jim Crow South* (Fayetteville, Ark.: University of Arkansas Press, 2003). Speaking in 1867 about advances in medical science, a former president of the state medical society recalled that years before, "The rule ... was to bleed, puke, purge and starve" (Ransom, op. cit., p 108). "Anybody who chooses can play doctor," the *Memphis Daily Avalanche* observed in surveying the state of the medical profession in that city in May 1867. Of its seven Black doctors, the paper said, "Several of them picked up their medical

knowledge from their former masters, who were distinguished doctors, and we believe that they will compare favorably with white political doctors," that is, White practitioners more focused on political advancement than medicine. Exeter Hall in London was, among other things, the meeting place of the Anti-Slavery Society and its successor, the British and Foreign Anti-Slavery Society. In American eyes, it was famous as the home of British abolitionism. Reporting on the Clarksville rally of 11 May 1867, a correspondent of the Nashville *Republican Banner* wrote: "Since beginning this letter, I have been informed that Dr. Wood claims to be an Englishman, a protege of Exeter Hall, after having served in the employ of that society, at one time as missionary to Honolulu, in the Sandwich Isles."

13. OBITUARY. The payment for Wood's coffin is recorded in the Rutherford County Minute Book F.F., p 83, Rutherford County Archives, Murfreesboro, Tenn. The quoted remarks about Wood's marital and clerical might-have-beens are drawn from the *Hull Advertiser* of 7 Jan 1853. Henry More Smith is the subject of *The Mysterious Stranger, or Memoirs of the Noted Henry More Smith,* first published in 1817, later updated to 1836, and often republished in Canada, Britain and the U.S., under slightly varying titles.

Printed by Imprimerie Gauvin
Gatineau, Québec